EXPLORATIONS IN SOCIOLOGY
British Sociological Association conference volume series

* *from the same publishers*

Global Futures

Migration, Environment and Globalization

Edited by

Avt
Senio
Birkb
Univ

Ma
Read
and
Univ

and

Má
Prof
Shef

pa

First published in Great Britain 1999 by

MACMILLAN PRESS LTD

Houndmills, Basingstoke, Hampshire RG21 6XS and London
Companies and representatives throughout the world

A catalogue record for this book is available from the British Library.

ISBN 0–333–71775–9 hardcover
ISBN 0–333–71776–7 paperback

First published in the United States of America 1999 by

ST. MARTIN'S PRESS, INC.,

Scholarly and Reference Division,
175 Fifth Avenue, New York, N.Y. 10010

ISBN 0–312–22135–5

Library of Congress Cataloging-in-Publication Data
Global futures : migration, environment, and globalization / edited by
Avtar Brah, Mary J. Hickman and Máirtín Mac an Ghaill.
p.   cm. — (Explorations in sociology ; 53)
"Derived from papers originally presented to the 1996 BSA annual
Conference held at the University of Reading"—Pref.
Includes bibliographical references (p.   ) and index.
ISBN 0–312–22135–5 (cloth)
1. Emigration and immigration—Congresses.   2. International
economic relations—Congresses.   3. Cultural relations—Congresses.
4. World politics—Congresses.   I. Brah, A.   II. Hickman, Mary J.
III. Mac an Ghaill, Mairtin.   IV. Series: Explorations in sociology
; v. 53.
JV6032.G56   1999
325.4—dc21
                                               98–54944
                                               CIP

This book is printed on paper suitable for recycling and made from fully managed and sustained forest sources.

Transferred to digital printing 2001

Printed & bound by Antony Rowe Ltd, Eastbourne.

Contents

Preface

This book is one of three volumes published by Macmillan which have derived from papers originally presented to the 1996 BSA annual conference held at the University of Reading. The theme was 'Worlds of the Future: Ethnicity, Nationalism and Globalization'. In organizing the conference we wanted to sharpen the political focus of the annual forum which the BSA conference represents and to widen the attendance so that it might include groups who do not always attend such events.

On both counts we estimate that we were successful. The first aim was realized in part by a series of excellent plenaries and panels. Doreen Massey gave the opening plenary: 'Imagining Globalization: Power-Geometries of Time-Space'. The other plenary speakers were Chandra Talpade Mohanty who spoke on 'Globalization, Globe-Trotting, and Other Stories of Democracy: Decolonization and the Challenges for Anti-Racist and Comparative Feminist Practice', and Robert Miles on 'Analysing the Political Economy of Migration'. The first panel discussed the relationship between Ireland, Northern Ireland and Britain, and the speakers were Ailbhe Smythe, Robin Wilson and Liam O'Dowd. The other panel was entitled 'Is There Social Justice in Social Theory for Black Women', chaired by Heidi Safia-Mirza. The conference closed with the Presidential Address which was given by Stuart Hall and was titled 'Identity and Difference in Global Times'.

The second aim was achieved in that many academics, both established and younger, drawn from a variety of ethnic minority and diasporic communities attended. The overall attendance, however, was down compared with the two previous conferences on 'The City' and 'Sexualities'. We think this partly reflects the continuing relative marginalization by mainstream sociology of the issues being addressed at the conference. We hope this and the other volumes convey something of the flavour of the conference debates and will contribute to developing understanding in this field.

AVTAR BRAH
MARY J. HICKMAN
MÁIRTÍN MAC AN GHAILL

Notes on the Contributors

Thomas A. Acton is Professor of Romani Studies at the University of Greenwich, London. Since running the first Gypsy Council Summer School in 1967 he has been involved in most areas of Romani studies, and especially the sociology of Romani and commercial-nomadic politics. He has published *Romanichal Gypsies* (1997), and has edited two volumes from the ESRC seminar series, *Gypsy Politics and Traveller Identity* (1997) and *Romani Culture and Gypsy Identity* (1997).

Avtar Brah is Senior Lecturer in Sociology at Birkbeck College, University of London. She is author of *Cartographies of Diaspora: Contesting Identities* (1996), and co-editor (with Mary J. Hickman and Máirtín Mac an Ghaill) of *Thinking Identities: Ethnicity, Racism and Culture* (1999).

Barnor Hesse is a Senior Lecturer in Sociology at the University of East London. His current research interests are political theory and the African diaspora, multiculturalisms and social theory, histories of 'race' and modernity. He is co-author of *Beneath the Surface: Racial Harassment* (1992) and editor of *Multicultural Transruptions* (forthcoming).

Mary J. Hickman is Reader in European Studies and Director of the Irish Studies Centre at the University of North London. Her main research interests are in the areas of Irish migration and diaspora studies, in particular the Irish in Britain and the USA. She also writes about multi-ethnic Britain and issues concerning the British state, the Union, Northern Ireland and British–Irish relations. Her publications include *Religion, Class and Identity: The State, the Catholic Church and the Education of the Irish in Britain* (1995), (with Bronwen Walter) *Discrimination and the Irish Community in Britain* (1997), and (with Bronwen Walter) *The Irish in Contemporary Britain* (forthcoming). She is co-editor (with Avtar Brah and Máirtín Mac an Ghaill) of *Thinking Identities: Ethnicity, Racism and Culture* (1999).

Pheobe Isard is Honorary Research Fellow in the Research Centre for Social Science, University of Edinburgh. Her main research interest is science policy in Scotland.

Máirtín Mac an Ghaill is Professor in the Faculty of Social Sciences at the University of Sheffield. His teaching and research interests include issues of contemporary social divisions and cultural differences in England. He has a specific interest in the question of the position of the Irish in Britain. He is author of *The Making of Men: Masculinities and Sexualities* (1994) and *Contemporary Racisms and Ethnicities: Social and Cultural Transformations* (1999). He is co-editor (with Avtar Brah and Mary J. Hickman) of *Thinking Identities: Ethnicity, Racism and Culture* (1999).

Doreen Massey is Professor of Geography in the Faculty of Social Science at the Open University. She is co-founder and joint editor of *Soundings: A Journal of Politics and Culture*. Her research interests range through uneven development to issues of gender and culture and the philosophy and politics of space. Her recent books include *Spatial Division of Labour* (1994) and *Space, Place and Gender* (1994).

Marie A. Mater is an Assistant Professor at Nanyang Technological University, Singapore. Her research focuses on environmental discourse, Habermasian and Foucauldian theories of discourse, and the internet as a global public sphere. She completed her PhD thesis, 'Environmental Discourse between the North and the South: a Theory of Discourse for a Global Public Sphere', at University College Cork, Ireland. She was author of a review essay in the *Asian Journal of Communication*, and she has presented papers at several regional and international conferences.

Robert Miles is Professor of Sociology at the University of Glasgow. He has been serving as Head of Department since 1993 and Associate Dean (External Relations) in the Faculty of Social Sciences since 1997. He is also Director of the Europe–Japan Social Science Research Centre at the University of Glasgow. His main research interests focus on the theories of racism, the historical development and contemporary expression of racism and nationalism, the history of international migration flows, all in the context of theories of capitalist development. His books include (with Annie Phizacklea) *Labour and Racism* (1980), *Racism and Migrant Labour* (1982), (with Annie Phizacklea) *White Man's Country: Racism in British Politics* (1984), *Capitalism and Unfree Labour* (1987), *Racism* (1989), (with Diana Kay) *Refugees or Migrant Workers?* (1992), *Racism after 'Race Relations'* (1993) and (edited with Dietrich Thranhardt) *Migration and European Integration* (1995).

Jennifer Platt is Professor of Sociology at the University of Sussex. Her current research is on the historical role of learned societies in the social sciences, and her interest in intellectual migration continues in relation to the role it has played in the history of the International Sociological Association. Her major recent publications include *A History of Sociological Research Methods in America, 1920–1960* (1996) and *A Brief History of the ISA, 1948–1997* (1998).

Roger Sibeon is Postgraduate Courses Director in the Department of Sociology at the University of Liverpool where he teaches theoretical sociology and the sociology of public policy and governance. His main recent publications are *Contemporary Sociology and Policy Analysis: The New Sociology of Public Policy* (1996) and *Sociological Theory Today* (forthcoming).

Ngai-Ling Sum is Simon Research Fellow at the International Centre for Labour Studies, University of Manchester. She has research interests in globalization/regionalization, cross-border growth regions, newly industrializing countries, and the relationship between political economy and cultural/identity politics in the Asia-Pacific. She has published in *Economy and Society, New Political Economy, Millennium Journal* and *Journal of International Development*. Two forthcoming books are *New Regionalisms and Identity Politics in East Asia*, and *Globalization and Cross-Border Regions* (edited with Markus Perkmann).

Claire Wallace is researcher at the Institute of Advanced Studies, Vienna, and Professor of Social Research at the University of Derby. Her current research interests include xenophobia in Austria and Eastern Europe, household economic changes in East Europe, a comparative study of youth in Europe, and migration in East and Central Europe. Her recent publications include *Migration Potential in East Central Europe* (1998), (with S. Kovatchera) *Youth in Society: The Construction and Deconstruction of Youth in East and West Europe* (1998) and *Central Europe: New Migration Space* (forthcoming).

Ian Welsh lectures in sociology in the School of Social Sciences at Cardiff University where he is a member of the Socio-Environmental Research Group (SERG). His primary research interest lies in the science, society and environment area. He is author of numerous articles on nuclear power, the globalization of environmental politics and environmental social movements. His books include *Environment and*

Society in East and Central Europe (co-edited with Andrew Tickle; 1998). His forthcoming work *Mobilising Modernity: The Nuclear Moment* is on the relationship between modernity and the scientific assemblage originating within the nuclear nexus of the 1950s.

Part I
Imagining the Global

1 Introduction: Whither 'the Global'?

AVTAR BRAH, MARY J. HICKMAN and MAIRTIN MAC an GHAILL

The proliferation of globalization-speak in the last decade of the twentieth century raises some critical questions about the current configurations of this discourse on the 'global'. What does the idea of 'globalization' at present signify? What meanings are attached to this term within differing enunciations of the discourse? What economic, political, and cultural shifts is this discursive formation marked by? What is the relationship between the contemporary discussions around 'globalization' and the historical processes of globalization? These are some of the main questions with which this book is concerned.

The literature on globalization is vast and diverse. The globalization thesis finds support on both the right and the left of the political spectrum. Its advocates come from different subject disciplines, ranging from sociology, economics, through politics to cultural studies. The issue of globalization is as likely to be the subject of discussion in the lofty citadels of 'global' institutions such as the International Monetary Fund, the World Bank, and the World Trade Organizations, as it is in governmental circles of 'nation-states', or indeed, amongst 'pan*ic*' collectivities such as ethnic groups, migrants, immigrants, refugees, asylum-seekers, and other contemporary diasporic formations whose terms of the debate always problematize a notion of the nation-state. Our purpose here is not to rehearse this debate through a survey or summary of the reams of literature on the subject. Rather, we aim to explore some of the main issues through the various themes addressed by our contributors.

In a very broad sense, 'globalization' may be understood as referring to the processes, procedures and technologies – economic, cultural and political – underpinning the current 'time-space' compression which *produces a sense of immediacy and simultaneity* about the world. The question of globalization is inextricably linked with the movement of capital, commodities, people and cultural imaginations and practices.

The idea of 'the global village' introduced in the book *Explorations in Communications* (Carpenter and McLuhan, 1960) is sometimes taken as a watershed moment in the iconography of globalization. The more recent discourse of globalization surfaced during the 1980s, as a way of understanding the socio-economic changes that befell advanced capitalist societies in the decades since the Second World War. Commentators emphasize the development of new information technologies, massive expansion of global networks of communication, and the emergence of complex global systems of production and exchange. These developments, according to one strand of the argument, have the effect of dramatically weakening the role of the nation-state. Correspondingly, supranational cartels, organizations and agencies of governance – e.g., transnational companies, the EU, NAFTA, the IMF, the World Bank – are likely to assume an increasingly central position in relation to the running of the world economy. All this, it is suggested, is making a profound impact on social and cultural relations. At the same time, a degree of scepticism is expressed in some circles of academic and political opinion as to whether what we are facing is much more a 'conjunctural change toward greater international trade and investment within an existing set of economic relations' as opposed to 'the development of a new economic structure' (Hirst and Thomson, 1996, p. 7).

Overall, the processes subsumed under 'globalization' seem to elicit somewhat contradictory responses. On the one hand, there is serious concern that these processes may serve to reinforce global inequalities of wealth and quality of life, accelerate changes which lead to the degradation of eco-systems, and strengthen non-democratic forms of governance. On the other hand, the intensification worldwide of economic, financial, ecological and cultural interdependence is heralded by some as an opportunity for creating new forms of political solidarity which could lead to the elimination of scarcity, demilitarisation, care of the planet, and multi-layered democratic participation. Globalization, within the latter scenario, is viewed as transforming the existing world order and generating a new consciousness about the need for transnational co-operation so as to secure better futures for humanity as a whole (cf. Harvey, 1989; Giddens, 1990; Nazir, 1991; Hall et al., 1992; Robertson, 1992).

The allusion to 'humanity' does not mean, however, that discourses of globalization invariably embody a critique of asymmetrical global social relations. Indeed, some discourses of globalization may serve to reinscribe and further entrench global inequities of class, gender, racism and other social divisions. Similarly, despite a great deal of talk about the 'global', certain debates remain firmly centred upon 'the West' (cf. Chomsky, 1993; Said, 1993; Spivak, 1995; Brah, 1996, and chapters in this volume). Yet, the point about globality is precisely that the historical, contemporary or future life worlds of diverse peoples cannot be reduced simply to an aspect of the Western project of 'modernity' or 'enlightenment'. Rather, contestations of and challenges to power-relations underlying particular discourses and practices of modernity form a key constitutive element within the various formations of the global. Here we would include struggles against slavery, colonization, racism and 'ethnic cleansing'; liberation movements for economic and political self-determination; ecology movements; feminist contestations; campaigns against economic exploitation; activism concerning inequities of social divisions associated with gender, racism, class and sexuality. At the same time, globalization may also take the form of all manner of cultural creativity in music, art, literature, science, as well as in bringing people together – actually or 'virtually' – in moments of collective affirmation.

As noted above, migration is a key dimension of 'globalization'. In one sense, globalization as a long-term historical process of the movement of people is as old as humankind itself. But migrations dating from the period of the trans-Atlantic slave trade through different phases of the development of capitalism have tended to acquire a dynamic of their own. The history of these 'modern' population movements is peppered with 'voluntary' and 'involuntary' immigration, ranging from enslavement of African peoples, indenture of peoples from Asia, Ireland and so on, the 'mass migration' after 1815, especially of Europeans to the Americas, Oceania, and South and East Africa; through the displacement of peoples during the two World Wars, the labour migrations following the Second World War; to the refugees, 'asylum seekers', and the wealthy business, professional and cultural entrepreneurs traversing the globe during the 1980s and the 1990s. What has become increasingly clear is that, all the rhetoric of globality notwithstanding, a world market in labour does not exist the same way as it does for goods and services. Labour markets are predominantly regulated at the national level, and multiple barriers are experienced by both 'legal' and 'illegal' migrants. As a growing literature argues, labour or 'economic' migrants are likely to find their movement increasingly restricted owing to the political imperatives of receiving countries. Ironically, the situation between 1815 and 1914 was evidently much more open than is the case today

(Potts, 1990; Castles and Miller, 1993; Segal, 1993). As Hirst and Thomson suggest:

> The supposed era of 'globalization' has not seen the rise of a new unregulated and internationalized market in labour migration. In many ways, for the world's underprivileged and poor there are fewer international migratory options nowadays than there were in the past. At least in the period of mass migration there was the option to uproot the whole family and move in the quest for better conditions, something that now seems to be rapidly closing off for present-day equivalent sections of the world's population. They have little option but to remain in poverty and stick it out. (Hirst and Thomson, 1996, p. 31)

There is, however, one general feature of contemporary migrations that proves the exception to the above trend. That is to say, that migratory prospects are better for two categories of employment at opposite ends of the scale. First, there is the 'club-class' migrant – predominantly male and most likely to be white – with high-level professional or managerial qualifications and technical skills, employed within the 'core' sectors of the world economy. Secondly there is growing demand for women willing to travel in response to an increasing demand for domestic labour in middle-class or wealthy homes, or, in other low-paid sectors of the labour market. As Mitter (1986, 1994), Sassen (1988) and Pettman (1996), among others, have shown, there is a global phenomenon of disposable labour, especially women's labour as firms and enterprises increasingly seek a flexible, often casualized workforce.

Hence, globalization at the end of the second millennium of the Christian calendar is marked by a major contradiction – the continuing need of the capitalist world economy for cheap labour in 'secondary' sectors is combined with political demands in overdeveloped countries for curtailing the migration of so-called 'economic migrants' (read poor, the underprivileged, or the racialized). This contradiction is not entirely new in itself but rather has new late capitalist dynamics as noted above. It has constituted a significant condition in the formation of a wide variety of contemporary diasporas, as we shall explore later.

IMAGINING GLOBALIZATION

It is clear that both the discourse of 'globalization' and the processes of globalizaton are marked by power. But what kinds of power dynamics are constituted and played out in different discursive constructions of globalization? What are the effects of different interpretations and conceptualizations of 'globalization'? These questions form the focus for the discussion by Doreen Massey. Her chapter is concerned with the interlinks between two main themes: power-relations and space-time. As she argues, it is important always to be aware of power-relations both as they are played out in the social sphere and as they are embedded within the power-knowledge system which our ways of imagining, conceptualizing and theorizing construct. One of the most productive mobilizations of the term 'globalization', according to Massey, has been in its use in the 're-telling of the classic story of modernity' so that modernity can no longer be understood in terms of 'the unfolding, internal story of Europe alone'. This 'post-colonial' discourse of globalization addresses colonialism as a major world-historical moment and emphasizes its centrality in the formation of the identity of 'the West' itself. This spatialization/globalization of the history of modernity reveals as culturally distinctive what the Euro centric world-view tried to pass off as globally 'universal'. A case in point is how a historically specific European way of conceptualizing the relation between polity, state, and territory through the idea of the 'nation-state' was legitimized as the norm for the division of the earth into bounded political entities, with little or no attention paid to local socio-economic and political institutions. Thus, the 'post-colonial' discourse of spatialisation has served to expose 'modernity's preconditions in and effects of violence, racism and oppression' (Massey, Chapter 2, p. 30).

The classic story of modernity as a narrative of European progress, Massey argues, ushers a discursive victory of time over space. This linear narrative could not easily accommodate the possibility of other stories, of the existence of alternative representations. But spatiality, Massey insists, can and must be imagined differently. Here a central feature of the spatial would be precisely its potential as the realm of the temporal co-existence of distinctive, even disparate and dissonant, narratives. If understood in this way, the 'spatial', she says, 'itself becomes generative of narrative. ... This way of "doing globalization" then – of spatializing the story of modernity – begins to specify the potential contribution of the spatial to social theory. It is an approach which brings together space and time, spatiality and temporality, and forces both of them into the plural. It tells a genuinely *spatial* story of globalization' (Massey, Chapter 2, p. 33).

But this is not always how the spatial tends to figure within discussions of globalization. As likely as not, it calls up a vision of unfettered mobility, unbounded space, and of a glorious complex mixity. Massey registers uneasiness about this view on four counts. In its move towards a closer engagement with the social and the cultural, and in its concern not to fall into the messy terrain of economic reductionism, it is as if it can no longer look seriously at the economy. The economy still features in the discourse but as a pre-given backdrop to the 'social' and the 'cultural'. That is to say that economic globalization is accepted as an always already present fact so that, ironically, economism persists without any close analysis of economic change actually being undertaken. As a consequence, economic globalization comes to be represented as inevitable, and it is assumed that countries currently outside its net are just lagging behind, and will eventually catch up. Akin to modernization theories of development, this discourse of globalization ends up unfolding as if it were yet another grand narrative.

Secondly, this vision of unfettered movement can so easily be conflated with the idea of 'free trade', a conflation which then becomes a powerful alibi for countries of the North to impose – via institutions such as the IMF, the World Bank, and the World Trade Organization – programmes of structural adjustment on countries of the South, with hardship for the poor, the excluded and especially for women. In other words, the powerful countries of the North are able to exercise their power by pleading powerlessness in the face of the supposed globalizing market forces! Whilst representing itself as a description of the world as it is, this vision of neo-liberal globalization is in actual fact "an image in which the world is being made'. The third reason for Massey's unease is that empirical data raise some serious questions about the nature, degree, and extent of 'globalization' as a worldwide phenomenon. If anything, these data seem to underscore the point that forms and direction of economic flow which are generally assumed to characterize globalization are spectacularly concentrated in the North. Fourthly, far from generating practices informed by visions of the common good of the whole of humanity, this 'non-spatialized globalization' marshals the imagination of exclusion, xenophobia, nationalism and racism. In contrast, as we have already noted above, Massey endorses an approach which views space/society as a product of power-filled social relations, a sphere of encounters between and amongst diverse narratives, and one which fully recognizes the ruptures, inequalities and structural divides that mark contemporary processes of globalization. That is, globalization must be understood in terms of what Massey calls the 'power-geometries of space–time'.

THE RISK SOCIETY AND GOVERNANCE

It is interesting that over the recent decades, especially during the 1990s, sociology has been re/discovering the concept of 'risk society' when, like the idea of globalization, risk itself is as old as, if not older than, the human organism itself. What are the characteristic features of this particular discourse of the 'global'? What kind of power dynamics are embedded in its constitution and operations?

One of the arenas in which the concept of risk society finds considerable purchase is that of the debate on the environment. The 1990s is widely regarded as the decade when the environmental and ecological issues moved centre stage of the global agenda of countries in the North and South alike. The United Nations Conference on Environment and Development (UNCED) held in Rio de Janeiro in 1992 was a watershed which was welcomed as a cause for optimism. It had been preceded by long preparatory processes involving the world's highest diplomats and political leaders as well as thousands of non-governmental organizations. These interactions precipitated a general recognition not only about the environmental crisis itself but also about the ways in which this crisis is embedded in economic and social processes of the local and global political order. There were high hopes that here was an occasion when it would be possible to craft strategies based on the understanding that realistic and long-term solutions lay in dealing with the environment as part of the global inequalities within and between nations. The chapters by Ian Welsh and Marie Mater deconstruct the Rio Summit in order to highlight why the initial euphoria was somewhat misplaced.

Ian Welsh explores what propelled environmental issues to the centre of international debate when the same issues were all but excluded from serious consideration during the 1970s by governments and international agencies. The main catalysts in this process are summarized as the continually growing systematic research evidence on issues like global warming, which even the most recalcitrant governments could by now ill afford to ignore; the cumulative momentum of the United Nations environment and development conferences held since the 1970s which led to the 1992 Rio Summit and formalized an agenda for environmental governance; and the growing awareness of the negative impact of humans on the environment, especially those living in the advanced countries of the North. Welsh uses the concept of a 'Green regime of accumulation' in order to address the 'power-geometries' of environmental and ecological politics on a global scale. Defining the environment as a site of social contestation and struggles over meaning, Welsh argues that the 'Green regime' is marked by a commitment to production strategies and regulatory mechanisms aimed at minimizing environmental risks while simultaneously legitimizing advantage for the advanced economies of the North through claims of superior knowledge. It is argued that this assertion of superior knowledge claims by the North constitutes a form of racism which finds expression in both the distribution of environmental risks and the appropriation of indigenous peoples and their resources.

The liberal discourses are identified as a key to the emergence of the 'Green regime', purporting to advance inclusionary practices and address common concerns but with rather stark exclusionary consequences. The agenda of the 'official' Rio conference, for instance, was strongly influenced by the interests, aesthetics and cultural preferences of the most powerful nation-states together with those of a small number of Northern non-governmental organizations. The notion of sustainability, according to Welsh, plays a crucial role in environmental governance. A key aspect of the debate on sustainability has been the extent to which human products in the form of – including minerals, food stuffs, and fibres used in manufacturing fabrics – can be substituted for organically created resources. Welsh questions the kind of relations of production such major transformations in the forces of production are likely to produce. Unlike the early periods of accumulation which pre-figured mature capitalism, when state assistance was mobilized through armed force and other technologies of coercion, currently brokerage and regulation play a similar role in installing global inequities around 'raw materials of the next post-industrial revolution'. Liberal environmental discourses mobilize powerful symbolic registers through the language of 'technological leading edges', and 'the frontiers of knowledge' presented to the public as necessary for the 'immeasurable rewards' of being able to ensure 'the future of civilisation' through 'risk taking'. One serious consequence of this has been that the public has been excluded from the development phase by protocols of political and commercial secrecy.

Using as a case in point the analysis of the regulatory regime under-pinning the attempts to control nuclear weapons and nuclear power, Welsh shows how the latitude made available to governments by the agreements reached at the Rio Summit produced very variable degrees of commitment to action by different countries, and, indeed, enabled powerful countries to exploit regulatory gaps in the 'less developed' countries. Moreover, the close links between state and industry have meant that bio-tech/gen-tech interests have been able to circumvent the intellectual property-rights implications of the Rio Summit by arguing that they are incompatible with the commercial exploitation of technology, with the result that companies in the North have been able to patent plants developed through traditional selec-tive breeding by farmers of the South over long periods of time. Even the genetic codes of 'minority peoples' have been appropriated by companies as part of 'preserving human diversity'.

Marie Mater's analysis of the global environmental discourse fore-grounds allied but somewhat different concerns. The two authors share some considerable common ground but Mater places a particu-larly strong focus on the voices from the South. Noting that an over-whelming majority of studies tend to focus almost exclusively on the Northern views of the situation, she seeks to address the alternative Southern constructions of the discourse of 'global environmental change' as they are articulated by Southern critics. Mater does this by examining the shifts in discourse before, during, and after the 1992 Rio Summit.

Southern scientists and researchers have long taken issue with the conclusions of the various reports which preceded the Summit. One such critique emerged, in part, as a response to the publications of the Washington-based private research group the World Resource Institute (WRI), which produced reports on tropical and global warming. Vandana Shiva, of the Research Foundation for Science, Technology and Natural Resource Policy in India, mounted a tren-chant criticism of the claims by the WRI report that the 'developing world' is the major culprit in environmental degradation. Shiva char-acterized this report as 'a contemporary example of Orwellian double-speak in which ecological destruction is called environmental protection' (Shiva, 1987, p. 145). Similarly, Anil Agarwal and Sunita Narain challenged the methodological drawbacks of the the 1991–2 annual report by WRI, which resulted in calculations of greenhouse emissions that favoured the biggest polluters such as the USA and Japan. It was not surprising, then, that the world congress in Rio developed into a major site of conflict and polarization. The Northern discourse of saving humanity, Mater notes, was received by delegates from the South as a 'new colonialism', designed to preserve the privileges of the rich nations of the North.

By transforming biodiversity from a local resource to a 'global resource' under the protection of the World Bank through its 'Global Environmental Facility', the convention on biodiversity generated a major controversy at Rio. Far from being seen as a collective global resource which, inter alia, would entail changing patterns of production and consumption in the North, biodiversity became an issue of protected property rights. When the USA placed the responsibility for the protection of tropical forests on countries of the South, Southern governments and non-government organisations responded by demanding payment from the North for such a service. The post-UNCED emphasis has suffered a similar fate, the critics from the South claiming that, as Soto (1992) has argued, the Northern conception of 'sustainable development' is concerned predominantly with the physical environment whilst, in contrast, the South perceives sustainability in terms of social and economic issues, such as disparities in wealth and opportunities. In conclusion, Mater highlights moves in the South to construct alternatives which are informed by traditional knowledges but which do not necessarily idealize these knowledge complexes; nor, indeed, do they condemn everything new as negative without dispassionate assessment.

A special issue of the journal *Third World Resurgence* (May/June 1997) entitled 'Globalization and Sustainable Development since Rio' would seem to endorse a number of the points made above. Five years after the World Earth Summit global ecology seems to have deteriorated with carbon dioxide continuing its build-up in the atmosphere, forests are cut down just as relentlessly as before the Summit, and water shortage and pollution have emerged as a new global crisis. On 2–3 April 1997, a Roundtable Seminar bringing together Third World network experts, diplomats and policy makers, as well as United Nations staff, met to discuss the environmental and social effects of economic globalization. The conference concluded that the two major political agreements of Rio 1992 – provision of economic aid (read loans), and environmentally friendly technology transfer to 'developing countries' to enable their transition to sustainable development – had been broken. Instead of an increase in the flow of financial resources, there has been a drop in aid. The start in aid decline followed the ending of the Cold War and has continued ever since.

Transfer of technology has been impeded by the intellectual property rules, which in fact may also facilitate 'bio-piracy', or a reverse unpaid flow from South to North of biological materials and knowledge.

The World Trade Organization (WTO) Agreement of 1994 at Marrakesh further institutionalized the narrow-commercial form of globalization which seems to have become the order of the day. This Agreement has over-ridden many of the UNCED Agreements of Rio 1992. The economic and social structures underlying the environmental crisis have been strengthened, and countries are under pressure to further liberalize and deregulate following the rules of Bretton Woods and WTO institutions. Social and environmental priorities would seem to have been sidelined as global competition, the impetus to increase profit margins, and the needs of big business assume growing ascendancy. In most Southern countries too, environmental concerns have not featured high on the agenda as these countries have remained entangled in problems of external debt, low commodity prices, low rates of foreign investment flows, the effects of structural adjustment programmes based on market liberalization, and a decline in aid. The spirit of international co-operation is undermined by the more legally binding and enforceable rules of the global trade system. A major drawback of the Rio Summit of 1992 had been its failure to propose any measures for regulating big corporations. Evidently the regulatory situation relating to transnational companies and business in general had worsened over the last five years. The efforts to finalize a Code of Conduct on TNCs were seriously eroded in 1993, and the agency in charge of the Code, The UN Centre on Transnational Corporations, was closed down. Similarly, initiatives in other institutions, such as the Code of Conduct on Technology Transfer and the Set of Principles and Rules on Restrictive Business Practices, both at UNCTAD (the United Nations Commission for Trade and Development) have been marginalized owing to lack of support from the powerful interests.

On the other hand, the last few years have also seen strengthened activities of citizen groups, increasing networking and collaboration among groups in the North and the South, and a cross-fertilisation of ideas and interests in issues including the environment, programmes towards economic and social equality, human rights, and women's rights. And all this, we would suggest, should make anyone concerned about these social problems more rather than less determined to keep the hopes for better world futures alive. One way of keeping such hopes alive would be not to regard globalization as an inexorable, unified and irreversible process; to leave room for political action. This point is pursued by Roger Sibeon who emphasizes a view of globalization as a differentiated, open-ended and processual phenomenon. He argues for anti-reductionist analysis of contemporary governance, and foregrounds four policy-related themes associated with such analysis. First, there is the need not to regard either the nation-states, world-regional blocks, or the global 'systems' as monolithic entities. Secondly, it is inappropriate to accord 'globalization', or any other single substantive principle, primacy as the most significant mode of explanation. Thirdly, the whole question of globalization is, in part, an issue of empirical investigation that cannot be settled on *a priori* theoretical grounds. Fourthly, the role of the state needs re-thinking in so far as the state itself is not a policy actor; rather, the institutions and networks of relations that constitute the state are aspects of the conditions for action.

Sibeon advances a 'policy network "model"' as a useful tool for analysing public policy and governance. Within this framework, it is important to recognize the increasing significance of transnational organizations such as the Organization for Economic Co-operation and Development (OECD), national policy dimensions such as the deregulation of the institutions of the City of London under the Thatcher government, as well as subnational governance in terms of the variation from one local authority to another in the development of and implementation of policies in response to transnational socio-economic processes associated with de-industrialization, unemployment and deprivation. These levels of policy do not represent a unified integrated totality but are relatively autonomous, with some considerable element of contingency built in. Drawing upon a wide range of theoretical currents within sociology, Sibeon situates his discussion of postnational governance within an account of what he calls 'anti-reductionist sociology' in which he rejects reductionism, essentialism, reification and functional teleology. It is argued that agency, structure (the 'conditions of action') and social chance 'interact' and that the social world is indeterminate until segments of it are contingently institutionalized. Following Hindess, Sibeon conceptualizes the actor – whether individual human actor or social ('organizational') actor – as an entity that has the means of formulating and acting upon decisions. Such logocentric conceptions of agency have had many critics. But others may argue that perhaps a logocentric conception is understandable in discussions of policy where formulation of political strategies is largely dependent upon conscious action.

SYNERGETIC OR DISCREPANT DIFFERENCES?

So far we have discussed the effects of different ways of 'imagining globalization', the consequences of 'green regimes of accumulation', the contestation of global environmental discourse by voices from the South, and the possible purchase of an anti-reductionist sociology of 'postnational governance'. But how does the idea of difference feature in discourses and practices of 'globalization'? How do processes of 'othering' mark the space of contemporary forms of late capitalism? We have used terms such as North and South as if they, and other allied notions such as the First-, Second- and Third-World, are unproblematic constructions. Yet we know that all of these are constituted in and through power-filled discourse. Each term inscribes, as well as contests, historically specific power dynamics within the global social and political order. The idea of North/South is not an always already constituted dichotomy but is a shorthand for 'power-geometries' at a broad macro level between geographically and spatially dispersed nations. But this binary, as indeed any other binary, needs to be contextually understood; its meanings need continual interrogation. Neither the Northern nor the Southern spheres of the globe are internally homogeneous in terms of their position on indices generally subsumed under the discourse of 'development', such as the level of industrialization. Japan, for example, is a Northern country on this particular index but its position shifts to the South when one addresses the issue, for instance, of racialized discourses, through which 'non-Europeans' are represented as Europe's Other. Ngai-Ling Sum probes some of the complexities surrounding the inside/outside of Self and Other in discourses and practices of trade and commerce.

By addressing internal/external heterogeneity and differentiation within and across discursive fields, with due attention to the micrologies of power that sustain hegemonic perspectives via continual re-articulation of insider/outsider distinctions, Ngai-Ling blurs and erodes simple notions of the bi-polarity Orient/Occident. This chapter is concerned with analysis of three 'new kinds of orientalism' evident in the discursive constructions of trade relations between the USA, Japan and the East Asian Newly Industrialized Countries (NICs). It examines the role of discourses and practices about trade, competitiveness and development in the remaking of global capitalism and demonstrates the extent to which these are not purely techno-economic in nature but are also shaped by political and ideological considerations. It provides both a general perspective on these issues and three case studies on the Asian-Pacific. The theoretical framework draws on critical discourse analysis to show the importance of binary categories (East–West; friend–enemy; security–threat) in re-ordering international relations, and reveals the complexity that surfaces once one takes account of the different types of 'others' and the capacities of global and regional hegemons to turn processes of 'othering' to their own advantage.

The three 'new' post-World War II orientalisms discussed are shown to re-combine binary categories, re-define identities and geo-economic interests, and connect them to defensive and/or offensive strategies in the struggle for competitive advantage in a globalizing–regionalizing world. These 'new orientalisms' are often hybrids: for example, Japan has adapted notions of 'developmental state' to its own time-space: and the USA combines its neo-liberal mercantilism with a strategy of 'factory-level Japanization'. These orientalisms also have extra-discursive dimensions evident in their role in shaping institution-building and guiding geo-economic and geo-political strategies, often in ways that point beyond the dominant 'neo-liberal' paradigm of Anglo-American capitalism. In this way the chapter foregrounds the culturally embedded politics of international trade and explores the relationship between and across power relations underpinning discourses of hybridity/difference/synergy and the operations of late capitalism.

It will be clear from the above that racialized forms of 'othering' feature at the heart of local, regional, as well as global configurations of power. Academic discourses are no exception as they, too, are productive of power-relations. Are academic discourses of globalization implicitly or explicitly implicated in processes of 'othering'? What kinds of exclusions may be set in train by the 'othering' processes embedded within certain theories of globalization? What alternative theoretical and conceptual formulations of globalization might provide more critical insights into the variety of global inequities which continue unabated? These are some of the questions which form the basis of the chapter by Barnor Hesse. This chapter highlights a number of ways in which dominant ideas about globalization have tended to *repress* discussion of the formative influence exercised by colonialism in the constitution of European modernity. Hesse demonstrates how some highly influential 'mainstream' theories of globalization continue to operate within a eurocentric 'planetary consciousness' (Pratt 1991); and argues, instead, for an approach which takes the hierarchical distinction between 'European' and 'non European' as a constitutive *inside* of European identity. Systematic critique of what he describes as 'racialized forms of globalization' is essential to the disruption of a Eurocentric hegemony of the *'Western spectacle'*.

A central feature of Hesse's analysis is his deconstruction of formulations drawn from the influential book *Globalization* (1992) by Roland Robertson. Such theories, Hesse argues, are marked by 'a racialized logic of disavowal'. According to psychoanalytic theory, disavowal points to deep-seated processes of repression that are not easily accessible to conscious thought. Disavowal, therefore, is not about whether or not the author did or did not have a particular conscious intention. Indeed, a text on globalization may well give some general recognition to the existence of racialized processes, but this will be descriptively acknowledged without taking account of its significance at the theoretical level. Hesse posits the concept of 'reflexive globalization' as a way out of the problematic of intellectual/academic *repression*. Reflexive globalisation, he suggests, describes the logic of post-colonial discourses framed in terms of critique of, and alternatives to, the assymetry of global socio-economic and cultural relations. Drawing upon recent theories of diaspora, Hesse emphasizes the 'significance of diaspora as a recurrent transnational and cross-cultural formation [which] emerges as a conduit of relexive globalization'. The various forms of 'reflexive globalization' embedded in the Black diaspora are analysed as constituting modes of astute theoretical insight that serve to seriously undo the hegemony of the racialized gaze. The work of Aimé Césaire is offered as an 'almost paradigmatic exposition of reflexive globalization'. The networks of Black aesthetic practices, cultural exchanges, and political communicativity produced within a context of the history of slavery and imperialism, are understood as embodying reflexive globalization. Hesse also foregrounds 'environmental racism' as a major element of what sociological accounts speak of as the 'risk society'. The prevalence of 'risk' across the Black diaspora, he argues, exposes the logic of its time-space compression.

The use of psychoanalytic concepts by Hesse is useful because this overcomes some of the difficulties associated with logocentric forms of analysis. As the book *The Wages of Whiteness* by David R. Roediger demonstrates for example, sociological analysis could be immeasurably enriched by non-logocentric conceptual repertoires. Drawing upon W. E. B. DuBios's argument that low-paid white workers in the USA were in part compensated by a psychological wage which served as a 'bonus' in their struggles with American capital, Roediger analyses the ways in which the formative years of working-class racism were marked by articulation between psychological mechanisms and material dynamics in producing certain forms of white working class identity as antagonistic towards black people. Roediger deconstructs the history of ideas such as 'white free labour'; the blackening of white faces as well as the dressing-up of men as women in minstrel music; and the struggle of the Irish workers to shed their contradictory positionality within the discourse of blackness and to be accepted as 'white'. Such complex phenomena, as Hesse's chapter on the Black diaspora and British identity shows, cannot be adequately addressed by a sociology that relies exclusively upon voluntaristic notions of agency.

The question of 'difference' and agency is also explored by Thomas Acton. He is concerned to underline the ways in which European thought continues, on the whole, to remain oblivious to the endemic persecution, discrimination, racism and even genocide experienced by the Gypsy and other traveller communities in Europe. He draws attention to the processes whereby the development of the nation-state was fully implicated in the racialized exclusionary practices against the Gypsy. The specificity of the Gypsy, as a nation without a state, which crossed the emergent arbitrary boundaries of nation-states remains outside the frame of conceptualizations which conflate 'nation' with nation-state. Rather, the history of diasporas such as the Gypsy challenges the concept of the nation-state to be a recent political and territorial unit, an aberration almost, within the much longer human history. The idea of the nation-state as *the* primary political and cultural icon of modernity achieves hegemony precisely through silences about the Romani people. In contrast with other categories of 'insiders' within Europe who are similarly constructed as 'outside the nation', such as the Jewish people, the Gypsy are generally forgotten even within histories of the racialized subaltern. This amnesia is nowhere more evident than in the fact that there is no general European apology to the Gypsies, as there is to the Jewish victims of the Holocaust. This is not to pit one racialized subaltern group against the other. Rather, it is to lay bare the 'differential racialization' (Brah, 1996) of different groups in the bid to secure hegemony.

Given this background, the discourse of globalization, Acton suggests, provides the Gypsy with the means to carve out a new political space for themselves. Romani political activists are able to appropriate this discourse in order to affirm a collective identity. Acton examines these issues in the context of the relationship between Gypsy groups and organized religion by exploring the strategies used in a specific case involving the Catholic Church. For some considerable time there had been concern in Catholic circles at the high rate of conversion from Catholicism to Pentecostalism amongst the Gypsy. In order partly to stem this tide of conversions there were attempts by prominent Catholic figures such as the scholar-priest Bruno Niccolini and the Romanian Gypsy sociologist and activist Nicolae Gheorghe to develop a programme that would gain the support of Gypsy organizations as well as elicit the formal support of the Roman Catholic Church at the highest level for the political strategies of the Romani Union. A conference was called in Rome for this purpose, and it achieved a major success when, on 26 May 1991, the Pope delivered a speech to a largely Gypsy audience.

The Pope's speech, according to Acton, marks a definitive break with previous paternalistic stances of the Catholic Church towards the Gypsy peoples with ramifications that go beyond this specific constituency; that is, the Pope's intervention constitutes a discourse 'with theoretical, spiritual and sociological implications of greater complexity and depth than any previous Papal statement'. The Pope characterizes the Gypsy as a group which is paradigmatic in its transnational dimensions in that this diaspora includes people dispersed around the world, who are diverse in ethnicity, language and religion. The Papal statement condemns 'marginalization and violent discrimination' as well as policies of assimilation, and it calls for an appreciation of diversity and pluralism. Furthermore, it calls for a democratic system of organisation. Acton sees the statement as embodying the possibility of imagining the Catholic Church itself along more democratic lines, with a critique of the centralized and authoritarian arrangement of its present structure and organization: 'As much as any text issued from the Vatican, this text shows the ineluctable movement of the Roman Catholic Church, through its endorsement of political democracy, away from its own authoritarian tradition to a far more congregational understanding of the governance of the church' (Chapter 8, p. 150). Moreover, the definition of the Gypsy as a transnational community repudiates the Hobbesian insistence of Renaissance Europe that the nation-state constitutes the seat of all sovereignty. Acton regards the event as a reminder of the historical forces of sixteenth-century Reformism when transnational Christianity itself fell victim to the ideology of the nation-state, as did the Gypsies and the Jews, who were viewed as people without territory. The nation-state fortified itself through 'othering' the colonized abroad, whilst doing the same to the

Jews and the Gypsy as the 'aliens within'. In other words, diasporic transnationalism contradicts the main tenet of those sociological theories that represent the nation-state as the quintessential emblem of modernity, even if the nation-state might well be accepted as one of its dominant forms.

MIGRATION AND GLOBALIZATION

We have already noted the centrality of the migration of people, alongside that of capital and commodities in processes of globalization. What is the nature of the relationship between these three forms of global mobility? The last three chapters of this book are devoted to a discussion specifically of this aspect. Robert Miles analyses the political economy of migration with a focus on the airport as a sign for the social relations of travel. Airports are understood as the site for the institutionalization of immigration control, the reproduction of class differentiation, and the arena where discourses of who does or does not belong to 'the nation' are embedded within the routine structures, organization and everyday practices of the immigration service. The airport as a 'national frontier' is a reminder not only of national identity but also about the passengers' juridical status in the international order.

Previous academic research in Britain spanning nearly four decades has demonstrated the racist and sexist effects of immigration legislation. Both the Conservative and Labour governments are shown to have been equally implicated in the introduction and maintenance of immigration legislation from the Commonwealth Immigration Acts of 1962, 1968 and 1971, and the Prevention of Terrorism Act of 1974; through the Nationality Act of 1981; to the Carriers' Liability Act of 1987 and the Asylum and Immigration Act of 1996. The exercise of controls on the movement of Irish people, and their inclusion in deportation regulation under the 1962 Act, is rarely noted, as Miles emphasizes, in the academic discourse on immigration (see also Hickman 1998). Despite the introduction of increasingly stricter immigration control, especially in the receiving countries of the North, the scale and velocity of the migration of people across international borders has increased dramatically in the last thirty years (Castles and Miller 1993), with women migrants as a very significant proportion of these late twentieth-century population movements.

Robert Miles's main focus of analysis here is the National Audit Office Report (1995) which monitored the efficiency and effectiveness of controls on entry into the UK between November 1993 and April 1994. The report reveals that more than 57 million persons arrived at UK airports in 1993/4. Approximately 83 per cent of these were EU nationals so that they were subject to a very brief check lasting on average six seconds. Of those who need 'leave to enter' the majority in possession of a visa will be questioned for a slightly longer period – about one to two minutes. Only those whose answers are not deemed to be satisfactory are delayed further, with the length of delay taking anything from thirty minutes to several days. During 1993/94 some 10 million were processed through this system, of whom approximately 63,000 were subject to further examination. From the figures reported it is arguable that in practice the Immigration Service is employed primarily to decide whether or not to grant entry to non-EU nationals. The Audit Office acknowledges that the pressure of delivering quick decisions about entry without detailed or necessarily reliable information means that such decisions are 'largely instinctive and based on experience' (National Audit Office Report, 1995).

Miles uses the concept of a 'socially organized moment' to analyse this 'instinctive' exercise of power which permits racialized, sexualized, class-based cultural discourses to come into play through the professional common sense of the immigration officer implementing control. Power is exercised through the agency of subjective evaluations performed in the guise of professional competence. As a result of this exercise of power, suspected persons may end up staying overnight or for months in poor conditions at detention centres provided by the Immigration Service and/or the Prison Service.

Noting the understandable reluctance on the part of academics to be drawn into the racist logic of the 'numbers game' and hence their avoiding involvement in studying the process of illegal and clandestine migration, Miles argues that there are, nevertheless, at least two reasons – which have little to do with numbers – for studying this problematic. First, it is important that research is undertaken so as to expose the global effects of unequal development, which results in providing impetus to migrations from the less well-off areas to more prosperous places, as well as to highlight the ways in which the legal status of the 'illegal immigrants' makes them vulnerable to the unscrupulous practices of those who transport them together with those who employ them. Secondly, the process by which this category of person becomes clandestine is itself 'commodified and is therefore an integral feature of the world capitalist system, a moment in the ongoing globalization process' (Chapter 9, p. 171). Evidently, a clandestine journey from China to Germany can cost up to $30,000 with massive profits to international 'smuggling rings'. Some women migrants may be offered 'free' passage only to find themselves forced into sex-work. In December 1996, a ferry full of 'illegal' migrants sank off the shores of Italy, with only a handful of those on board surviving to tell the tale. Miles reminds us that immigration offenders form a tiny proportion (10,300 out of 57 million in 1993) of all entrants at UK ports. Thus it is arguable that the supposed threat posed by the 'illegal immigrant' tells us more about collective disavowal of the 'hidden' economy which clandestine labour globally lubricates than about the actual numbers of migrants involved.

If Miles wishes to emphasize the political economy of migration, Claire Wallace wishes us to understand investment, trade and migration rather in terms of cultural, historical and social factors. Her primary concern is the complex ways in which ethnic and linguistic ties are an integral part of the patterning of economic relations. That is, economic imperatives do not exist outside culture; they are always socially embedded. To this end, Wallace explores what happened to the Central European region (Germany and Austria to the west, Poland, the Czech and Slovak Republics in the middle, and Ukraine, Belaruse and Russia to the east) when borders were closed, opened, selectively restricted or moved. Beginnining with a historical overview of border-change in this region the chapter converges upon the post-1989 period and examines the implications of the opening of this area towards liberal capitalist market relations along with political democracy and greater access to global capitalism. With the fall of communism, previously illegal activities such as trading, currency speculation, business ventures, and profit-making came to be vested with new meaning. They were now seen as indicators of enterprise and initiative. Uninhibited by regulations which had not yet been set in place, a great deal of spontaneous movement and activity ensued.

One key aspect of these processes, and especially as a consequence of European Union policies, there has emerged what Wallace et al. have elsewhere called the 'buffer zone' encompassing countries which border the European Union, namely Poland, the Czech and Slovak Republics and Hungary. The integration of these buffer-zone countries into Western Europe has involved a range of agreements to regulate migration. Drawing upon a variety of data, surveys and official statistics the chapter looks at the circulation of people from the former Soviet Union into the buffer zone, and from there into the European Union. This movement is backward and forward between countries and, according to Wallace, is best described as mobility rather than migration as the latter holds for her the connotations of permanent movement from one place to another. The research by Wallace and her colleagues seems to suggest that parts of the buffer zone are significant for different kinds of mobility: people are likely to go to Poland to trade, to the Czech Republic to work, whilst refugees go mainly to Hungary. This reflects the different situation of each Central European country with respect to East and West Europe. Wallace gives the example of building workers in Germany and Austria who are mainly from the buffer zone, whereas in the buffer zone itself, the building workers are drawn from Eastern Europe. The flow of goods at the moment operates mainly in the opposite direction.

Evidently, the opening of the borders in Central Europe has resulted not so much in globalization as in regionalization, with investment and trade moving mainly across the next border. Historical, cultural and social ties play a key role in this process, acting as conduits for economic activities. The limits of migration seem to be determined largely by the resources of the migrants in terms of language, family, ethnicity and social networks. This has encouraged a certain degree of ethnic revivalism which has helped a number of the peoples of the region to re-define themselves. But this has also been encouraged by new economic and trading relations. The transnational features of ethnicity have been mobilized for cross-border trading, shopping and working. Cross-marriages in some instances may also serve similar purposes for economic advantage. In addition new groups such as the Chinese or Vietnamese, as well as the new strata of Western experts and professionals, or employees of multinational companies or business people, have moved in from beyond the regional borders. The point about borders, Wallace concludes, is that they: 'are not fixed. They can be more or less permeable and more or less fluid. They can allow no-one to pass or only selected people to pass. They can allow people to pass in one direction but not another. They can be constructed in different ways and extend in different directions' (Chapter 10, p. 207). For some of Wallace's respondents the best strategy was not so much to cross the borders as to wait for the borders to change, as when the buffer-zone countries join the European Union.

It is clear that migrations take many forms. Whilst the general literature on migration has been largely concerned with mass movements, the chapter by Jennifer Platt and Phoebe Isard is concerned to explore the specificity of migration of the intelligentsia. Platt and Isard report research into the flight of Hungarian intellectuals to Britain after the 1956 Uprising, with a view to evaluate the impact of their ideas on British intellectual life. They argue that the migration of intellectuals may result in the creation of local enclaves of different ideas which enter into some relationship with the intellectual life of the receiving country even if they do not find a place in the 'mainstream' or become dominant. Evidently, a major factor affecting the decision to leave Hungary – whether or not the individual concerned had been active in the Revolt – would seem to be the communist policy of denying educational and occupational opportunities to those of bourgeois or aristocratic class origin. Personal career chances were limited for such young people, even if they might have supported the regime's general aims. Known Catholics or orthodox Jews were also similarly disadvantaged. Others left because they feared that this might be their last chance to avail themselves of better intellectual and economic opportunities abroad. For some the need for the preservation of Hungary's traditional and national(ist) literature was paramount. Platt and Isard emhasize the point that the 1956 Revolt was for, and not against, indigenous concerns, so that emigration by those involved in it did not imply the rejection of their 'national values'. Many of those who left did not initially regard their stay to be long-term, and chance played a major role in who ended up where.

The global context of Cold War politics, combined with sympathy for the victims of the extensively reported brutal repression of the revolt, meant that the emigrants were viewed as deserving. Indeed, an extremely warm and cordial welcome was accorded to the Hungarians collectively. This would seem to contrast with the experience of other categories of immigrants to Britain in the period after the Second World War, especially those from Britain's former colonies. Though economically indispensable, they were not constructed as particularly deserving. The demonization of communism combined with a sense that the Hungarians were European 'kith and kin' paved the way for a friendlier reception for these exiles. Britain's formal admission procedure at this time was much more sympathetic to those with a background in scientific and technical fields rather than in the humanities, and this had some impact on the nature of Hungarian migration into Britain. Platt and Isard are cautious about making wide generalizations about the intellectual effects of this migration. But they suggest that, inter alia, the distinctly Hungarian training and experience in research led to industrially valuable innovation in Britain. The exile in Britain led some Hungarian writers writing in the Hungarian language to experiment. Hence, literary production informed by the British experience resulted in the creation of new critical styles in work in Hungarian. The case of the Hungarian exiles places into relief the positionality of diasporic intellectual production as an emergent transnational formation continually interrogating the relationship between the 'local' and the 'global'.

This book, then, is a testament to the complexity of all that passes as globalization. It eschews those perspectives on globalization which regard it as an inexorable, unified and irreversible process that leaves little room for political action. It critiques linear narratives of history that are unable to countenance the existence of alternative stories. Instead, it foregrounds a power-embedded relational notion of time and space figuring a form of spatiality performed within and through the temporal co-existence of distinctive, even dissonant narratives. The text instantiates this claim across a variety of academic, economic, political and cultural discourses and practices as it: explores the consequences of 'green' regimes of accumulation; analyses the challenges posed by voices from the South to the hegemony of environmentalist discourses of the North; deconstructs both theoretically and empirically the very binary of North/South and prises open the repressed trajectory of each pole as a constitutive inside of the other; addresses the political economy of contemporary migrations as well as highlighting investment, trade and migration rather in terms of cultural, historical and social factors; and it emphasizes diasporic communities and diasporic forms of knowledge production as paradigmatic cases of contemporary transnationalism. The chapters that follow represent a sustained analysis of the discourses as much as the processes of globalization.

REFERENCES

Brah, A. (1996), *Cartographies of Diaspora: Contesting Identities* (London and New York: Routledge).

Carpenter, E., and McLuhan, M. (eds) (1960), *Explorations in Communication: An Anthology* (Boston, Mass.: Beacon Press).

Castles, S., and Miller, M. J. (1993), *The Age of Migration: International Population Movements* (London: Macmillan).

Chomsky, N. (1993), *Year 501: The Conquest Continues* (London: Verso).

Giddens, A. (1990), *The Consequences of Modernity* (Cambridge: Polity).

Hall, S., and Gieben, B. (eds) (1992), *Formations of Modernity* (Cambridge: Polity Press).

Harvey, D. (1989), *The Condition of Postmodernity: An Inquiry into the Origins of Cultural Change* (Oxford: Blackwell).

Hickman, M. J. (1998), 'Reconstructing/Deconstructing "Race": British Political Discourses about the Irish', *Ethnic and Racial Studies*, 21, no. 2 (March 1998).

Hirst, P., and Thomson, G. (1996), *Globalization in Question: The International Economy and the Possibilities of Governance* (Cambridge: Polity).

HMSO (1995), *National Audit Office report*.

Mitter, S. (1986), *Common Fate, Common Bond: Women in the Global Economy* (London: Pluto Press).

Mitter, S. (1994), 'On Organising Women in Casualised Work: A Global View', in Rowbotham, S., and Mitter, S. (eds) *Dignity and Daily Bread: New Forms of Economic Organising among Poor Women in the Third World and the First* (New York: Routledge).

Nazir, P. (1991), *Local Development in the Global Economy: The Case of Pakistan* (Aldershot: Avebury Press).

Pettman, J. J. (1996), *Worlding Women* (London and New York: Routledge).

Potts, L. (1990), *The World Labour Market: A History of Migration* (London: Zed).

Pratt, M. L. (1991), *Imperial Eyes: Travel Writing and Transculturation* (London and New York: Routledge).

Robertson, R. (1992), *Globalization* (London: Sage).

Roediger, D. R., The *Wages of Whiteness* (London: Verso).

Said, E. (1993), *Culture and Imperialism* (New York: Alfred A. Knopf).

Sassen, S. (1988), *The Mobility of Labour and Capital: A Study in International Investment and Labour Flow* (Cambridge: Cambridge University Press).

Segal, A. (1993), *Atlas of International Migration* (London: Hans Zell).

Shiva, V. (1987), 'Forests, Myths and the World Bank: A Critical Review of *Tropical Forests: A Call for Action*', *Ecologist*, 17 (4/5), pp. 142–9.

Soto, A. (1992), 'The Global Environment: A Southern Perspective', *International Journal*, 47 (4), pp. 679–705.

Spivak, G. C. (1995), *Whither Marxism? Global Crisis in International Perspective* (New York and London: Routledge).

Third World Resurgence, May/June 1997.

2 Imagining Globalization: Power-Geometries of Time-Space

DOREEN MASSEY

There are, as we know, many ways of imagining globalization. They vary in terms of their empirical content, in terms of the structures of their conceptualization, in terms of the implicit or explicit periodizations which they envisage, and so forth. It is impossible, and probably undesirable, to legislate on one interpretation over others.

There are, however, certain aspects of this debate over meaning and interpretation which it does seem worth arguing about, and the purpose of this chapter is to take up one of them. For, it seems to me, there are certain ways of conceptualizing globalization, ways which are in very general currency in both academic and popular discourses, which are in need of critique on both intellectual and political grounds. They are conceptualizations which are careless about things that in other circumstances we would be scrupulous about, they have an unwitting innocence about positionality, and they lend credence to a particular kind of politics (in this case in the form of a particular kind of globalization) not by being explicit about it but by accepting it as an inevitability.

I want, then, to examine some ways of 'imagining globalization' and to explore their effects. This exploration, moreover, will weave itself around two core themes. The first is the importance always of being aware of power-relations. And this is meant both in the sense of the power-relations in the social spheres we are examining and in the sense of the power-relations embedded in the power-knowledge system which our conceptualizations are constructing. The second theme revolves about space-time (or time-space) and how we conceptualize it. One of the most constructive of interdisciplinary meetings in recent years has been between sociology/cultural studies and geography around the project, in a variety of ways, of spatializing social theory. My own view is that this project has already been enormously productive, that it could be even more so, and that its implications concern the nature as well as the content of our theorizing. The different imaginings of globalization presented below give some hint of the issues involved. 'Globalization' would seem to be an intrinsically spatial subject. Surely anyone exploring globalization is thinking spatially? In fact this is not so, as I argue in what follows. And the difference between thinking globalization spatially and thinking it *a*-spatially is considerable – and significant. Finally, these two themes (power-relations and space-time) are linked in what I have called power-geometries of time-space.[1]

GLOBALIZATION AS THE SPATIALIZATION OF THE STORY OF MODERNITY

One of the most provocative and productive mobilizations of the term 'globalization' has been in its use, in particular by 'post-colonial' theorists, in the re-telling of the classic story of modernity. Globalization in this guise has had dramatic effects, effectively dislocating and *dis*-locating (in any number of senses of those words) the story of modernity as it used so often to be told. Hall (1996) indeed argues that this is one of the main contributions of the post-colonial critique:

> It is the retrospective re-phrasing of Modernity within the framework of 'globalization' which is the really distinctive element in a 'post-colonial' periodisation. In this way, the 'post-colonial' marks a critical interruption into that whole grand historiographical narrative which, in liberal historiography and Weberian historical sociology, as much as in the dominant traditions of Western Marxism, gave this global dimension a subordinate presence in a story which could essentially be told from within its European parameters. (p. 250)

The effects of this globalization of the story of modernity are profound. The first effect, which has indeed been the main intent, is to re-work modernity away from being the unfolding, internal story of Europe alone. The aim has been precisely to decentre Europe. Thus:

> This re-narrativisation displaces the 'story' of capitalist modernity from its European centring to its dispersed global 'peripheries'. ... Colonisation, understood or re-read in this sense, was only intelligible as an event of global significance. (p. 250)

'Colonization' becomes more than a kind of secondary by-product of events in Europe. Rather 'it assumes the place and significance of a major, extended and ruptural world-historical event'. Moreover not only is it more important – more central – as a phenomenon, it also changes its meaning and its effects. 'Colonization', here, in this globalization story is also a crucial moment in the formation of the identity of 'the West' itself.

The second effect of globalizing in this way the story of modernity is that, once the history of modernity has been understood as more than the history of Europe's own adventures, it is possible to appreciate how the previous way of telling the story (with Europe at its centre) was in fact generated and powered by the way in which the process was experienced *within Europe*. It was a history told through the experience of exploration outward from Europe and of the discovery of lands and people other than Europe. It was a story told from the point of view of Europe as the protagonist. Globalizing that story enables an understanding of its positionality, its geographical embeddedness.

Thirdly, really globalizing/spatializing the history of modernity brings to light just how the standard discourse of that history was used to legitimize so much. It is through that Eurocentric discourse of the history of modernity that the (in fact particular and highly political) project of the generalization across the globe of the nation-state form could be legitimated as progress, as 'natural'. Moreover, that project – of the division of the earth into bounded political entities – was just one aspect, though a particularly powerful one, of the development of a way of imagining 'cultures' and 'societies' more generally and in particular of conceptualizing them as having a specific relation to space. Both cultures and societies were imagined as having an integral relation to relatively bounded spaces. And this in turn – a point we shall reflect more upon later – was to be reflected in a characteristic approach to space in general. 'Places' came to be seen as bounded, with their own internally-generated authenticities, as defined by their difference from other places which lay outside, beyond their borders. It is an approach which remains dominant today. As Gupta and Ferguson (1992) argue,

Representations of space in the social sciences [and, one might add, not only in the social sciences but in popular and political discourses as well] are remarkably dependent on images of break, rupture, and disjunction. The premise of discontinuity forms the starting point from which to theorize contact, conflict, and contradiction. (p. 6)

Our starting point, in other words, is very often an imagination of spaces which are already divided up, of places which are already separated and bounded. What is at issue here, then, is both a way of organizing space and of controlling it and a manner of conceptualizing it. As Walker (1993) has argued of the particular case of the nation-state,

> Theories of international relations are more interesting as aspects of contemporary world politics that need to be explained than as explanations of contemporary world politics. As such, they may be read as a characteristic discourse of the modern state and as a constitutive practice whose effects can be traced in the remotest interstices of everyday life.   (p. 6)

In other words, that previous way of understanding modernity enabled the establishment and universalization of particular theoretical/conceptual frames, which in turn underpinned the material enforcement of certain ways of organizing both society and space.

Fourthly – and again part of what the post-colonial project of spatialization is all about – re-telling the story of modernity through globalization exposed modernity's preconditions in and effects of violence, racism and oppression. It is here that the oft-told story of the question posed to modernity by Toussaint l'Ouverture is relevant. In his critique of the ethnocentricity of Foucault's account of modernity, Bhabha writes:

> The ethnocentric limitations of Foucault's spatial sign of modernity become immediately apparent if we take our stand, in the immediate post-revolutionary period, in San Domingo with the Black Jacobins, rather than Paris.   (1994, p. 244)

Toussaint l'Ouverture, leader of rebel slaves, had the principles of the French Revolution (modernity) always in his mind. C. L. R. James writes:

> What revolutionary France signified was perpetually on his lips, in public statements, in his correspondence. If he was convinced that San Domingo would decay without the benefits of the French connection, he was equally certain that slavery could never be restored.   (1938, p. 290)

He was, of course, 'wrong'. As Bhabha puts it, he had to grasp 'the tragic lesson that the moral, *modern* disposition of mankind, enshrined in the sign of the Revolution, only fuels the archaic racial factor in the society of slavery', and Bhabha asks 'what do we learn from that split consciousness, that "colonial" disjunction of modern times and colonial and slave histories?' (p. 244). In other words, the (some of the) material preconditions and effects of the project of modernity, when brought to light by this spatial opening-out, undermine the very story which it tells about itself:

> This re-narrativisation displaces the 'story' of capitalist modernity from its European centring to its dispersed global 'peripheries'; from peaceful evolution to imposed violence.   (Hall, 1996, p. 250)

Fifthly, finally, and following directly on from this, the exposure of those preconditions and effects reveals that story of modernity as precisely being also about the establishment of an 'enunciative position' which (i) although particular, made a claim for universality, but which (ii) was not to be (could not be) in fact universalized or generalized. In other words, one of the effects of modernity was the establishment of a particular power/knowledge relation which was mirrored in a geography, which was also a geography of power (the colonial powers/the colonized spaces). And in the post-colonial moment it is that which has come home to roost. For exposing that geography – by the raising of voices located outside of the accepted speaking-space of modernity – has helped also to expose and undermine the power/ knowledge relation.

In all these ways, then, the globalization/spatialization of the story of modernity has provided a commentary upon, and thereby challenged, *both* a system of rule *and* a system of knowledge and representation.

Now, this reveals a lot about ways of thinking about (including not thinking about) space itself. Most evidently, the standard version of the story of modernity – as a narrative of progress emanating from Europe – represents a discursive victory of time over space. That is to say that differences which are truly spatial are interpreted as being differences in temporal development – differences in the stage of progress reached. Spatial differences are reconvened as temporal sequence. Thus, Western Europe is understood as being 'advanced', other parts of the world as 'some way behind' and yet others as 'backward'. Euphemistically to re-label 'backward' as 'developing' does nothing to alter this process of thinking of spatial variation in terms of a temporal series.

However, the impact is more complex than a simple annihilation altogether of the spatial. Certainly, this ordering of co-existing (that is to say: spatial) differences into temporal sequence has important effects. Most significantly, it obliterates, or at least reduces, the real import and the full measure of the real differences which are at issue. And this observation in itself begins to indicate what might be meant by 'the spatial'. After all, as indicated already, the 'old' version of the story of modernity did have some concept of space – as carved-up and bounded, for instance politically, into nation-states. What is at issue is that it convened the spatial differences which it did recognize into a temporal sequence. It is this act which deprives these spatial differences of their 'real import', deprives them of 'the full measure of the real differences which are at issue'. The implication must be that recognizing true spatiality necessitates recognizing a greater degree of difference and a different kind of difference – one that involves the existence of trajectories which have at least some degree of autonomy from each other (which are not simply alignable into one linear story). A connection between real spatialization and the possibility of different stories, and of the existence of alterity, begins to emerge.

Ironically, then, not only is this temporal structuring of the geography of modernity a repression of the spatial, it is also the repression of the possibility of other temporalities (other, that is, than the stately progress towards modernity/modernization/development on the Euro-Western model). Indeed, it is in these terms – that is, about the existence of other temporalities and stories – that the argument against modernity's dominant formulation is usually posed. In other words, for different temporalities to co-exist there must be space.

This act of globalization, then, has told us something about the potential of spatiality itself. What it most clearly underlines as a characteristic inherent in the spatial is the temporal co-existence of distinct narratives. In spatial figurations, previously unrelated temporalities may come into contact, or previously related ones be torn apart. On this reading, the spatial, crucially, is the realm of the juxtaposition of dissonant narratives. Places and spaces, rather than being locations of distinct coherence, become precisely the foci of the meeting of the unrelated. Moreover, if this is so, then the spatial itself becomes generative of narrative. The spatial in its role of bringing into contact distinct temporalities generates a provocation to interaction, which sets off new social processes. (And in turn, this emphasizes the nature of narratives as being not about the unfolding of some internalized story [some already-established identities] – the self-producing story of Europe – but about interaction and *the process of the constitution of* identities – the reformulated notion of colonization.) This way of 'doing globalization' then – of spatializing the story of modernity – begins to specify the potential contribution of the spatial to social theory. It is an approach which brings together space and time, spatiality and temporality, and forces both of them into the plural. It tells a genuinely *spatial* story of globalization.

NON-SPATIALIZED GLOBALIZATION

However, although it has certainly been used, as just described, in a sophisticated fashion genuinely to spatialize the narrative of modernity, the term 'globalization' is in fact more often used – by academics, politicians and in popular currency – in a much slacker way. The difference between these two ways of using the concept is important because (at least in my view) while the first approach achieves a genuine spatialization, with all the productive-disruptive effects which have just been discussed, the second does not. Moreover, because of that – and this is the point – this slacker notion of globalization is subject to many of the same criticisms as was the non-spatialized story of modernity.

'Globalization' is currently one of the most frequently-used and most powerful terms in our geographical and social imaginations. At its extreme (and though 'extreme', this version is none the less highly popular) what it calls up is a vision of total unfettered mobility; of free unbounded space. In academic work, perhaps particularly in sociology and cultural studies, its most characteristic presence is as a summary of economic globalization in the opening paragraphs to a treatise on something 'more social'. At its worst, it has become something of a mantra. Characteristic words and phrases make an obligatory appearance: instantaneous; Internet; financial trading; the margins invading the centre; the annihilation of space by time. In these texts, the emerging world economy will be captured by an iconic economics: reference to CNN, McDonald's, Sony. And judicious alliterations will strive to convey the maziness of it all: Beijing – Bombay – Bamako – Burnley. (What is at issue in all of this is our geographical imaginations. And in this regard the alliterations are of particular interest: how often they reveal, in their expectations of the effects they will produce, an imaginative geography that still knows which is 'the exotic' and which 'the banal' and when it is bringing them into unexpected [though in fact now so common a trope] juxtaposition.)

Anyway, this mantra, run through so often as a preliminary to the study itself, is also an evocation of a powerful vision. It is a vision of an immense, unstructured, free unbounded space and of a glorious, complex mixity. It is also a vision which, although apparently in some sense glorying in its recognition of the spatial (while at the same time speaking of its annihilation), makes me very uneasy. And it does so for four, intertwined, reasons.

First of all, in this era of the understanding of the significance of discursive constructions, it exhibits a curious acceptance of the material 'factness' of the stories (some) economists tell. There is a strange and troubling anomaly here. It is as if, in the move towards a greater engagement with the social and the cultural which itself was part of a wider and positive rejection of a previous economism, we have moved away from looking seriously at the economy ourselves at all. But the ironic result of this has been that 'the economic' still gets put in, but now as the essential but usually unquestioned background to our stories of the social and the cultural. There '*is*', we assume, before we go on to recount the complex and nuanced results of our own researches, economic globalization. It is the reintroduction, by omission and therefore unnoticed, of a kind of persistent economism.

Now, that acceptance-as-background of a particular version of economic globalization brings other effects in its train. Precisely because of its lack of specification, and especially because of a lack of analysis of its causes – except for an unthinking technological determinism – this version of economic globalization comes to have almost the inevitability of a grand narrative. (With 'history' – read: with technological change – these things just happen, don't they?) Globalization, then, is inevitable. It is like modernity's story of progress. And with that in turn comes an imagining, yet again and just as in modernity's discourse, of spatial differences as temporal. Once again, spatial differences are convened under the sign of temporal sequence. Mali and Chad are not 'yet' drawn into the global community of instantaneous communication? Don't worry; they soon will be. Soon they will, in this regard, be like us.

This is an *aspatial* view of globalization. The potential differences of Mali's and Chad's trajectories are occluded. They are assumed to be following the same ('our') path of globalization. Because space has been marshalled under the sign of time these countries have no space – precisely – to tell different stories, to follow another path.

What has been forgotten in this iconic economics with its implicit inevitabilities is that economic globalization can take a variety of different forms and, yet more fundamentally, that 'economics' is a discourse too. It is time we carried our deconstructive abilities into that field as well. For, crucially, the material and the discursive interlock: the way we imagine globalization will affect the form that it takes.

Which leads directly to the second source of my unease with the unfettered-movement view of globalization. For the imagination of globalization in terms of unbounded free space chimes all too well with that powerful rhetoric of neo-liberalism around 'free trade'. It is a pivotal element in a powerful, political, fully-fledged discourse. It is a discourse which is predominantly produced in the countries of the world's North. It is a discourse which has its institutions and its professionals – the IMF, the World Bank, the World Trade Organization, Western governments. It is a discourse which is normative; and it is a discourse which has effects.

In the world's 'South' it is this understanding of the world of the future (as unbounded global trading space) which enables the imposition of programmes of structural adjustment, with all their horrendous and well-documented effects of polarization, of yet-increasing hardship for the already-poor and especially for women. It is this understanding of the inevitability (unavoidability) of this form of globalization which legitimizes the enforcement of export orientation on the economy of country after country, the prioritization of exports over production for local consumption. It is this discourse of, this particular form of, globalization in other words which is an important component in the continuing legitimization of the view that there is one particular model of 'development', one path to one form of 'modernization'.

In the 'North' (the 'First World') too, this discourse of globalization has effects: the constant talking about it, the endless describing it in a particular form, is part of the active project of its production. The discourse becomes the basis for decisions precisely to implement it. The signing of the Uruguay round of GATT pushed it a step further, the World Trade Organization is committed to producing it, Mrs Thatcher in one of her first acts on becoming Prime Minister in 1979 abolished financial/currency controls. It is an extraordinary demonstration of the utter intermingling of 'representation' and 'action' in the (project of) production of a particular spatiality. On the one hand globalization (in this, particular, unquestioned, neo-liberal form) is represented as an utter inevitability – a force in the face of which we must adapt or be cast into oblivion. On the other hand some of the most powerful agencies in the world are utterly intent on its production – against all the rioting and recalcitrance being demonstrated by the 'less dynamic' (read: those who have a different imagination of the world) sectors of the world's population and economy. The duplicity of the powerful in this is deep. World economic leaders gather (in Washington, Paris or Davos) to congratulate themselves upon, and to flaunt and reinforce, their powerfulness, a powerfulness which consists in insisting that they (we) are powerless – in the face of globalizing market forces there is absolutely nothing that can be done. Except, of course, to push the process further.

This vision of neo-liberal globalization, then, is not so much a description of how the world is, as an image in which the world is being made. But this vision once having been raised, and installed as hegemonic, it provides the context for the actions of others. In particular it provides the excuse for *in*action. John Gray (1996), having assumed this version of globalization, proceeds to argue that – therefore – the possibilities of social democracy are at an end. Conservative governments preside over the decline of a goodly part of manufacturing industry and explain to us that growth must now mainly come through inward investment. Tony Blair throws up his hands at suggestions of more progressive policies on tax and social welfare ('couldn't possibly do that – we've got globalization you know'). Just as in the case of modernity, here we have a powerful imaginative geography. It is a very different imagination: in the place of space divided-up and bounded here is a vision of space as barrier-less and open. But both of them function as images in which the world is made. Both of them are imaginative geographies which *legitimize*, and which legitimize in the name of (though of course without saying so) the powerful and those whose imaginations they are.

And yet – and this is the third reason for my unease with this notion of globalization – it is anyway inaccurate. Clearly, the world is not yet totally globalized (whatever that might mean); the very fact that some are striving so hard to make it so is evidence of the project's incompletion. But this is more than a question of incompletion – it is more than a question of waiting for the laggards (much of the Third World and those immobilized in the First) to catch up. Once again, as in the case of modernity, this is a geographical imagination which ignores the structured divides, the necessary ruptures and inequalities, on which the successful projection of the vision itself depends. It is – I would argue – a geographical imagination which ignores its own real spatiality.

Just consider for a moment some *alternative* iconic economics. First, Hirst and Thompson (1996a; 1996b) argue that the major world national economies are no more open in terms of trade or capital flows than they were in the period of the Gold Standard. Moreover, they point to the fact that, over the medium term (say the last century), there has been no monotonic linear direction of change. Instead, the degrees of openness have fluctuated over time with the nature of economic development. Secondly, Hirst and Thompson also do some calculations about the forms of flow which are generally said to characterize globalization at the moment. What they demonstrate is its quite spectacular geographical concentration. 91.5 per cent of foreign direct investment is invested in parts of the world where only 28 per cent of the world's population lives. The figure for trade is nearly as high – at 80 per cent. The immediate point here, then, is the startlingly unequal nature of the incorporation of the world's people into globalization-as-it-is-usually-described. Moreover, – third alternative iconic fact – this is a *produced* inequality. One of the most notable, yet least noticed, characteristics of the inequality within the current type of globalization is that between capital and labour. There is no world market for labour as there is for capital. While capital – in the form of financial transactions, investment, and traded goods – has indeed in the most recent period moved ever more freely around the world, and has been encouraged to do so under the sign of 'free trade', the world's people are by no means encouraged to move. Capital can move around in search of the best opportunities to invest, and is marvelled at for its flexibility and responsiveness when it does so. But labour, people wishing to roam the world in search of work, are castigated as 'only' economic migrants. Barriers are thrown up against them and, between major areas of the world, they are held in place. International migration does of course continue, but it is reduced and hedged about; controlled. Quite different from the exuberance with which capital's free movement is cheered-on. Moreover, what international migration remains is clearly segregated, between the rich, those with skills and/or money to invest, on the one hand, and who can move with relative ease, and the poor and the unskilled on the other, against whom the barriers are increasingly raised (King, 1995).

None of this is to argue that 'globalization' isn't happening. Rather, the argument is that this is globalization of a particular form, one which is the product of, and which is embedded in, that discourse of free movement and unboundedness which neo-liberalism shares with too much of social and cultural studies. And, of course, one of the characteristics of this form of globalization (quite contrary to the built-in assumptions of equilibria of the neo-liberal theory on which it is based) is that it exacerbates inequality both within countries and between them.

Moreover, those few alternative iconic economic facts about the current form of globalization highlight something else: that the sudden consciousness of globalization in the First World cannot be as a result of a new 'openness' in general. As we have seen, in some ways openness is not new. What have more likely brought about the flurry of concern are the changing terms, and geography, of that openness. It is now the First World which is subject to inward investment. (And of course 72 per cent of the world's population lies beyond the reach of the vast bulk of it.) It is First World cities which have, in the medium term, been experiencing the arrival of people from other parts of the world. As has often been remarked, much of the work on diasporas and hybridity has been stimulated by the famous 'arrival of the margins at the centre'. (This was the provocation to re-tell the history of modernity.) In that sense it is already acknowledged to be a story told from the First World.

Except that this is more of a First World story even than that account indicates. For the margins have *not* arrived at the centre. This is the view of those who were already 'in the centre' and of those from the periphery who have managed over the years to get in. Most of 'the margins' have been very strictly excluded. And the current shifts in migration policy mean that very few of them are likely to arrive in the near future. Their arrival is being actively prevented.

All of which raises my fourth and final source of concern about this formulation of globalization. It returns us again to the discursive form of the neo-liberal view of globalization: that is, how it imagines the world. Think, to begin with, of some of the strongest proponents of free trade on the right-wing of the political spectrum. They argue for free trade in terms which suggest that there is some self-evident right to global mobility. The very term 'free' immediately implies something good, something to be aimed at. Yet, come a debate on immigration, and they immediately have recourse to another geographical imagination altogether. It is a vision of the world which is equally powerful, equally – apparently – incontrovertible. Yet it is in total contradiction to the vision of globalization. This second imagination is the imagination of defensible places, of the rights of 'local people' to their own 'local places', of a world divided by difference and the smack of firm boundaries, a geographical imagination of nationalisms. In one breath such spokespeople assume that 'free trade' is akin to some moral virtue, and in the next they pour out venom against asylum-seekers (generally assumed to be bogus) and 'economic migrants' ('economics', it seems, is not a good enough reason to want to migrate – *what* was that they were saying about capital?!).

So here we have two apparently self-evident truths, two completely different geographical imaginations, which are called upon in turn. No matter that they contradict each other; because it works. And so in this era of globalization we have sniffer dogs to detect people hiding in the holds of boats, people die trying to cross the Rio Grande, and boatloads of people precisely trying to 'seek out the best opportunities' go down in the Mediterranean. That double imaginary, *in the very fact of its doubleness*, of the freedom of space on the one hand and the 'right to one's own place' on the other, works in favour of the already-powerful. They can have it both ways.

Once again there are echoes here of how the story of modernity was told, and this way of envisioning globalization must be subject to the same critique. Just as was Toussaint l'Ouverture's claim to participate in the principles of modernity's legitimating discourse, so too today the claim to free mobility (the discourse of globalization) by the world's poor is rejected out of hand. The new world order of capital's (anyway highly unequal) globalization is as predicated upon holding labour in place as was early modernity upon slavery. If, in Bhabha's words, the discourse of modernity fuelled 'the archaic racial factor in the society of slavery' (1994, p. 244) (although of course it was anything but archaic), then too the discourse of globalization as free movement about the world is fuelling the 'archaic' (but not) sentiments of parochialism, nationalism, and the exclusion of those who are different.

Today's hegemonic story of globalization, then, relates a globalization of a very particular form. This is not the globalization of early modernity nor that of High Imperialism. But integral to its achievement (as in theirs) is the mobilization of powerful (inconsistent, falsely self-evident, never universalizable – but powerful) geographical imaginations of the world.

However, they are imaginations of a geography which is not thoroughly geographical. This, I would argue, is a story of globalization which is not truly spatialized. In this it is of precisely the same form as that story of modernity – as a story of Europe's internal history –

which has been so heavily criticized by post-colonial theorists. Indeed, this version of the story of globalization, in spite of being about a 'spatial' phenomenon (as indeed was the exploration and colonization recounted in the story of modernity), is potentially subject to all the same criticisms to which the classic narrative of modernity was subject. This is a story of globalization which has been (as was the story of modernity) precisely provoked by what is happening to 'the West', by the experiences of that West; it is in some measure (just as was colonial discourse) founded upon a Western (First World) anxiety. Moreover, just as was modernity, this discourse of globalization provides a legitimation of things. It is not merely a description but a discourse, an imaginative geography, which justifies the actions of those who promulgate it, including a particular attitude towards space and place. Again too, just as in the case of modernity's story, this is a discourse which is not simply generalized, nor generalizable. Capital's current globalization is, at least for the moment, predicated upon holding others in place. That 'other' discourse of closed borders and fearful defensive parochialisms is not some ancient hangover. Nor are the two discourses, in fact, simply contradictory. Both are part and parcel of constructing the particular form of economic globalization which we face at the moment. And finally, this version of globalization is once again about the construction of privileged speaking positions which install a framework of thought as (though it were) a universal. This is, once again, a highly particular geography of power/knowledge.

  My argument is that this narrative of globalization is not truly spatialized. It is a story told as a universal from one geographical speaking position. It is an imagination which ignores the structuring inequalities, breaks and divides on which it is constructed. It convenes, yet again, real spatial difference into the homogeny of temporal sequence (we'll all be globalized in this way eventually) and thereby occludes the possibility of real difference. It is a story of globalization which remains in need of spatializing. And just as the post-colonial re-working of the former story of modernity productively disrupted so much about it, so too would a genuine spatialization of how we think about globalization enable us to tell a very different story altogether.

POWER-GEOMETRIES OF TIME-SPACE

Three different ways of imagining the relation between space and society have emerged in the previous sections. First, there is modernity's story: of space divided up into parcels, of an assumed isomorphism between spaces/places and cultures/societies. Secondly, there is the currently hegemonic notion of the space of flows: the space of the story of unfettered globalization. Both of these views of space, I have argued, are deficient. In both cases they have been mobilized in stories which in fact annihilate their spatiality, where spatial differences lose any possibility of autonomy by their discursive arrangement into temporal sequence. In both cases, too, they (to put it at its mildest) overstate their cases. There was no simple isomorphism of place and culture under modernity, in spite of efforts (including through the mobilization of this discourse of space) to produce it. Similarly today, in the midst of the so-called space of flows of globalization, new barriers are being erected, new fortresses being built.

But a third approach to the understanding of space/society has also emerged. This would imagine the spatial as the sphere of the juxtaposition, or co-existence, of distinct narratives, as the product of power-filled social relations; it would be a view of space which tries to emphasize both its social construction and its necessarily power-filled nature (see note 1). Within that context, 'places' may be imagined as particular articulations of these social relations, including local relations 'within' the place and those many connections which stretch way beyond it. And all of these embedded in complex, layered, histories. This is place as open, porous, hybrid – this is *place as meeting place* (again, the importance of recognizing in 'the spatial' the juxtaposition of different narratives). This is a notion of place where specificity (local uniqueness, a sense of place) derives not from some mythical internal roots nor from a history of relative isolation – now to be disrupted by globalization – but precisely from the absolute particularity of the mixture of influences found together there.

But 'cultures' and 'societies', too, may be imagined in this way (Hall, 1995). As constellations of social relations configured as forming a time-space. Again they are open, porous, invented and particularized as a product of interaction. It might indeed be a 'local community' (an indigenous group, say), or a nation-state, where the hybridity within is none the less related to a particular space. But it might just as easily be Paul Gilroy's Black Atlantic, more geographically diffuse and complex; intermingled with other cultural traditions yet also forming its own time-space. The shapes and characteristics of these constellations may (will) change over time. They cohere; and they may dissolve. They are not necessarily spatially closed or excluding (though there may be attempts to make them so).

Now, boundaries may be drawn around either places or cultures: geographical boundaries or institutional ones. Sometimes there may be attempts to force their coincidence. Whether or not such boundaries are drawn will be a result of, and an expression of, social power (which may, in turn, be either offensive or defensive). But when drawn, such boundaries will enclose, will constitute, *envelopes of space-time*. So we have, for instance, been witness to a (modern) period in which envelopes of space-time called 'nation-states' were typical. And, with the assumption that isomorphism between culture and place was 'natural', a nostalgia developed for 'local communities'. Bounded entities were (still are, in part, as we have seen) that period's way of domesticating space-time, of fixing and stabilizing, or trying to fix and stabilize – for the task is an impossible one – meanings and identities in relation to time-space.

And I do mean *time*-space. Usually, perhaps, we think of 'countries' (for example), in relation to space-time, as areas on a flat map. Yet think of Hungary, or Montenegro, or the USA. They are not areas on maps. They are socially-constructed and labelled envelopes of space-time, which once did not exist (there was no such bounding and labelling), which have changed in spatial shape along the time dimension, which have always existed *in relation to* elsewhere (there are no pure identities, no internal histories of uniqueness; those boundaries have always been holding-operations), and which maybe one day will cease to exist. The nation-state (like any society or culture) is a *spatio-temporal event*.

We are constantly making and re-making the time-spaces through which we live our lives. And globalization, imagined through the lens of this conceptualization of space-time, the globalization which we are facing now, is a thoroughgoing, world wide, restructuring of those time-spaces, along particular lines. It is a re-making of those, inherited but always temporary and provisional, spaces, places and cultures which are all themselves the hybrid products of previous restructurings.

Such an alternative imagining of globalization, then, would be most unlikely to subscribe to the notion of some massive and absolute shift from a 'space of places' to a 'space of flows'. That big story makes incorrect assumptions about the past (there was never a simple space of places – at its extreme, of cultural isolates); it fails to recognize the 'places' (the enclosures, the fortresses of the powerful) which continue to be built in the midst of today's globalization; it fails to recognize both the divided-spaces of modernity and the globalization-as-free-space as *projects* in which particular discourses of the relation between space and society are important and effective components; and, in consequence and most of all, it misses out a lot about the construction of time-spaces through relations of social power.

Such an alternative imagining of today's globalization, relatedly, would also recognize the ruptures and inequalities, and the structural divides, within it. Today's global world is not just some glorious hybrid, complex, mixity; it is also systematically riven. Moreover, these 'geographical differences' are not just a question of some places' need to 'catch up'. Rather they are differences – deep inequalities – produced within the very process of (this current form of) globalization itself.

And finally, therefore, this different imagining of globalization – in my terms, a truly spatialized understanding of globalization – would refuse to convene spatial differences under the sign of temporality. It would reject the tales of inevitability that necessarily accompany such singular narratives. It would in consequence recognize more clearly the agents and agencies, and the relations of power, which lie behind the very particular form of globalization we are experiencing at the moment. It would in other words hold open the possibility of the existence of alternative narratives. Imagining today's globalization in its real power-geometries of space-time would be the beginnings of its fully spatial understanding.

NOTE

1. Questions of the spatialization of social theory are explored in a forthcoming book. The notion of power-geometry was first introduced in Massey (1993, 1994).

REFERENCES

Bhabha, H. (1994), *The Location of Culture* (London: Routledge).
Gray, J. (1996), *After Social Democracy* (London: Demos).
Gupta, A., and Ferguson, J. (1992), 'Beyond "Culture": Space, Identity, and the Politics of Difference', *Cultural Anthropology*, vol. 7, pp. 6–23.
Hall, S. (1996), 'When was the "post-colonial"? Thinking at the limit', in I. Chambers and L. Curti (eds), *The Post-Colonial Question* (London: Routledge), pp. 242–60.

Hall, S. (1995), 'New Cultures for Old', in D. Massey and P. Jess (eds), *A Place in the World? Places, Cultures and Globalization* (The Open University with Oxford University Press), pp. 175–213.

Hirst, P., and Thompson, G. (1996a), *Globalization in Question* (Oxford: Polity).

Hirst, P., and Thompson, G. (1996b), 'Globalization: Ten Frequently Asked Questions and Some Surprising Answers', *Soundings*, number 4, pp. 47–66.

James, C. L. R. (1938), *The Black Jacobins* (London: Allison and Busby).

King, R. (1995), 'Migrations, Globalization and Place', in D. Massey and P. Jess (eds), *A Place in the World? Places, Cultures and Globalization* (The Open University with Oxford University Press), pp. 5–44.

Massey, D. (1993), 'Power-geometry and a Progressive Sense of Place', in J. Bird, B. Curtis, T. Putnam, G. Robertson and L. Tickner (eds), *Mapping the Futures* (London: Routledge), pp. 59–69.

Massey, D. (1994), 'A Global Sense of Place', in D. Massey, *Space, Place and Gender* (Oxford: Polity), pp. 146–56.

Walker, R. B. J. (1993), *Inside/Outside: International Relations as Political Theory* (Cambridge: Cambridge University Press).

Part II
Risk, Society and
Governance

3 Risk, 'Race' and Global Environmental Regulation
IAN WELSH

Ecology is like universal suffrage or the 40-hour week: at first, the ruling elite and the guardians of social order regard it as subversive, and proclaim that it will lead to the triumph of anarchy and irrationality. Then, when factual evidence and popular pressure can no longer be denied, the establishment suddenly gives way –
... and fundamentally nothing changes.

(Gorz, 1987, p. 3)

The 1990s are widely regarded as the decade when the environment and ecological issues moved centre stage in terms of the social, political and economic agendas of developed and developing nations alike. Despite this, Gorz's words remain as relevant today as when they were written. In the 1970s many environmental issues, such as global warming, were simply excluded from serious political consideration by reference to inconclusive or conflicting scientific evidence. Other claims, more amenable to measurement, like the impact of pesticides on birds and humans produced more rapid action (Carson, 1962). In short, the 1970s response to the environment was shaped by the prevailing regulatory climate, which accepted as legitimate only those issues within its technical, economic and political reach.

The prevailing view of the environment was one dominated by the natural sciences, and subject to a reductivist means of investigation generated by male-dominated scientific institutions and practices (Merchant, 1980). Technical discourses of environmental management apart, the environmental problematic was also translated into familiar neo-Malthusian population debates (see Erlich, 1968). The emphasis placed on population growth in developing countries implicitly raised racial discourses, especially where these resulted in a linkage between development aid and repressive population-control measures. In the, then corporatist, developed world there was a cross-class consensus subordinating the environment to the twin goals of capital accumulation and upward social mobility. In Crosland's view

47

environmentalism represented the middle classes pulling 'the ladder' to the good life up behind them.

What then has precipitated the environment to the forefront of political agendas and how does this mean that nothing fundamentally changes? First, it has become increasingly difficult to ignore incomplete or conflicting scientific evidence over issues like global warming. Factual evidence accumulated alongside popular opinion to produce a political commitment to regulation and control. Secondly, the cumulative momentum of United Nations (UN) environment and development conferences, held since the 1970s, resulted in the 1992 Rio Summit and formalized an agenda for global environmental governance. Thirdly, the impact of humans on the natural environment, particularly those in advanced societies, began to be identified as the source of systemic and potentially uncontrollable impacts affecting everyone in the world (Beck, 1987, 1992). Here I will argue that whilst risk has become an axial principle of global regulation the outcome is a 'Green regime of accumulation' based on social categories which have traditionally distributed inequalities and risks. The notion of regime is derived from the increase in direct linkages between nation-states and their capacity to exercise effective power-influence within a diversity of supra-national and global negotiating fora. The 'Green regime' pursues *new production strategies and regulatory regimes to minimize environmental risks whilst simultaneously ensuring Northern economic advantage via the assertion of superior knowledge claims.* I will show how these superior knowledge claims become mobilized through categories of 'race' to introduce forms of environmental racism and exclusion. Before doing so it is necessary to qualify my use of the notion of a 'Green regime'.

A GREEN REGIME?

The work of the regulation school introduced the idea of regimes of accumulation in the context of the postulated transition from Fordism to post-Fordism (Aglietta, 1987). Similar approaches have been applied to the relationship between post-Fordism and post-modernism (see Harvey, 1989, 1996). These earlier debates established that gendered and 'racially' ascribed differences became crucial as part of the associated labour processes. This suggests that any 'Green regime of accumulation' must be scrutinized for similar processes. I approach the 'Green regime' as emergent or prefigurative and it would be premature to argue that a distinctive regime of Green accumulation has yet been consolidated, let alone achieved ascendancy. There are, however, some clearly identifiable elements and historical precursors which direct attention towards considerations of central importance for sociology and sociologists whether they are directly interested in the environment or not.

Expressed concisely, these elements comprise the development of new scientific advances in the North which, through a combination of scientific hubris and political expediency, become presented as the foundation for a 'new age'. I argue here that the institutional structures developed to usher in the nuclear age are being paralleled by the emergent institutional structures surrounding the genetic or bio-tech age (see Bauer, 1995). The presentation of technological breakthroughs as the harbingers of a new dawn, and the subsequent pursuit of related goals are central to the exercise of Northern power-knowledge. Expressed simply, Northern knowledge forms subordinate all other knowledges as inferior. Relations of superiority/inferiority are primary relations necessary for the expression and mobilization of racism. Whilst Barker (1981) has argued that discourses of superiority have been replaced by discourses of cultural difference the emergence of 'new' scientific abilities and technological capacities seems set to resurrect notions of absolute genetic difference in relation to issues of 'race', ethnicity and sexuality.

The attempted hegemony built around such new scientific practices by coalitions of Northern states and multinational interests within global decision-making fora, distant from direct democratic influences, thus represents an important new arena of institutional racism where the superiority of both Northern technology and Northern culture can be asserted over the South. Science and technology thus become central to institutional racism in an analogous manner to arguments advanced by feminist scholars in relation to gender (e.g., Haraway, 1994, 1995; Bleier, 1988). The practice of environmental racism is not confined to developing nations but also operates at home in developed countries.

Wieviorka convincingly argues that inferiority is bolstered by exclusion and that racism must be understood in terms of the interaction between both factors (Wieviorka, 1995, p. 119). I will argue that exclusion has led to processes of direct environmental racism within particular Northern countries, exposing people of colour to negative environmental consequences. The emergence of environmental activism amongst people of colour enables me to extend Wieviorka's typology of processes particularly prone to racism, and to further elaborate the distinction drawn between community activism and social-movement formation (Wieviorka, 1995, pp. 108–14). Before I can embark upon this work it becomes vital to rescue the 'environment' from its close association with the natural sciences.

THE ENVIRONMENT IN QUESTION

The environment is closely associated with 'nature' and 'the natural' and as such is a sphere from which the social, and particularly the social scientific, has historically been distanced. The successful strategy of separation from the 'natural sciences' owes much to Durkheim's assertion of 'social facts'. The depth of the divorce between the social and the natural has left the social sciences ill-equipped to reconceptualize the relationship.

The idea of an environmental crisis in effect displaces the significance of a series of crises in societies onto nature. What is at stake is the socially and culturally prioritized material practices of societies in the late twentieth century. Without a vigorous global civil society to constrain the most pre-eminent of globalizations – the economic – the established tendency for national civil societies to reproduce inequalities in relation to categories such as 'race' and gender are reproduced at a global level. In America environmental activism amongst people of colour emphasizes the inseparability of social and environmental justice (Bryant and Mohai, 1992) in a manner echoed at the margins of UK environmental activism (Welsh and McLeish, 1996) and replicated by black activists in the UK. The linkages being built here are a material reminder that the social and the environmental are so intimately entwined as to be inseparable in late modernity. In this sense there are interlinked crises of nature and society.

By defining the environment as a site of intense social contestation and definitional struggle I can engage with the global in a way that avoids the over-inclusive 'sociology of one world' perspective which dominated early work on globalization (Featherstone, 1990; Albrow, 1990).

It is in this connection that the natural, the global and the social assume positions of prime importance as a context within which a new form of civil society is emerging. If the environment is regarded as a site within which a number of social, cultural, economic and political

forces intersect, compete and co-operate (Welsh, 1996) then it represents the only basis upon which all expressions of civil society can be
formed. The material practices which have created the environment as
a global site in the late twentieth century make the active creation of a
global civil society almost inescapable. A notion of a global civil
society is vital to redress the widely held, though mistaken, view that
there is a crisis of the environment *qua* nature. The idea of common
problems facing a world population convincingly criticized by Smart
(1994) has, however, permeated global environmental discourse.

The rhetorical force of this discourse is clearly revealed in the titles
of central contributions to this debate. Key here has been the World
Commission on Environment and Development (WCED) report *Our
Common Future*. This report originated the most widely adopted
definition of sustainable development, 'to ensure that it [development]
meets the needs of the present without compromising the ability of
future generations to meet their own needs', taking into account limits
derived from the prevailing technical and social resources available
(WCED 1987, p. 8). The Bruntland report was a more or less self-
conscious attempt to garner a consensus amongst world leaders in
support of a regime of global environmental governance.

A follow-up report described *Our Common Future* as 'a hard won
consensus of policy principles forming the basis for sound and
responsible management of the Earth's resources and the common
future of all its creatures' (Starke, 1990, p. xiii). Had the report
appeared under its working title, *A Threatened Future*, the whole tenor
and impact of the document would have been altered. The promotion
of commonality and an orientation towards problem solving played a
key role in the creation of a climate of political optimism emphasizing
the potential for common cause over environmental protection. The
International Panel on Climate Change (IPCC), responsible for
offering scientific advice on global warming, is one product of this
early phase of regime formation. Global climate-change protocols,
translating science into policies and practices, quickly revealed that
the idea that there could be an easily won political consensus over
protecting the environment was a chimera. Despite this, the UK
government's primary environmental legislation followed the trend of
consensus naming with the title *This Common Inheritance*.

The UN Conference on Environment and Development (UNCED)
at Rio created an influential environmental agenda shaped primarily
by Northern interests, concerns and culturally determined preferences. It is important to recognize that this process of prioritization

embodied a range of registers based in forms of rationality, aesthetic appreciation, as well as economic interests. Biodiversity campaigning by groups such as the World Wildlife Fund (WWF, now the World Wide fund for Nature), for example, relies heavily upon images of the 'mega fauna' aesthetically valued by Northern publics (Ross, 1994). The biologically vital lower orders such as insects and bats, crucial to rainforest regeneration as seed carriers, lack this ready appeal and are neglected.

The transformation of the discourse of dark, threatening jungle into one of emerald green rainforest revalorized Southern forest as the 'lungs of the world' and a potential source of plant based cures for AIDs (McKechnie and Welsh, 1994). These taken-for-granted, axiomatic elements of environmental protection did not, however, meet with any easy consensus as they neglected the views of the South in general and more importantly the groups most affected within the South.

The proposed schedule for phasing out CFCs in refrigerators and freezers was resisted by China and India as the substitute gases were prohibitively expensive and a threat to GDP. Tropical rainforest preservation was denounced as the application of a Northern double standard on Southern countries long after the North had clear-felled its own forests. A coalition of low-lying states, mostly Pacific Island states, challenged the proposed time scale of remedial greenhouse measures on the grounds that they would be completely inundated unless more stringent targets were set.

The structure of the Rio conference granted full delegate status to a small number of Northern environmental non-governmental organizations (ENGOs), granting them parity with nation-states at the conference table. The agenda that was struck at Rio thus emerged from both nation-states and prioritized elements of the Northern environmental movement. Social-movement and development activists were carefully segregated in a parallel conference spatially distant from the 'real' conference. There was an effective attempt at a top-down agenda capture over the environmental domain at Rio.

The extent to which Agenda 21 and Local Agenda 21 have subsequently dominated the public environmental arena diverts attention away from a number of much more significant 'closures' within the wider discursive domain of international summitry. The notion of sustainability plays a crucial role in environmental governance.

One of the key debates which has raged around Bruntland's definition of sustainability relates to the use of prevailing technical and social relations. A key debate here has been the extent to which human products in the form of technologies can be substituted for organically created resources. Substitution could be made for a wide range of raw materials including minerals, food stuffs, and fibres used in fabric manufacture. The idea of technical substitution assumes a position of central importance to my arguments about superiority and 'race'. Significant transformations in the forces of production require new relations of production. An important purpose of the primitive accumulation which pre-figured mature capitalism was to secure supplies of raw materials and labour power through physical enclosure. Whilst, in the past, the state assisted this process through armed force, now brokerage and regulation are playing essentially similar roles in relation to the raw materials of the next post-industrial revolution.

The language used to discuss such technological leading edges mobilizes a powerful range of symbolic registers frequently invoking imagery of 'the frontiers of knowledge' needed to deliver 'immeasurable rewards', which 'ensure the future of civilization' and reward necessary 'risk taking'. These examples all come from the 1950s discourses around nuclear energy. I invoke them here because the language and the associated institutional structures resemble closely elements of the biotechnology and genetic-engineering enterprise. The view that the bio-tech sector is purely the product of entrepeneurial zeal and unfettered market forces is in effect a modern myth.

Bud, for example, argues that both biotechnology and nuclear power have to be seen as the product of state regulatory bodies identifying technologically strategic priorities. One consequence is that public resistance is shaped by a range of factors including political and commercial secrecy, which excludes publics during the development phase (Bud, 1993, 1995). During the 1980s biotechnology and information technology were identified as strategically important technologies by the USSR (Kusin, 1986, p. 43), the USA (Krimsky, 1991), Japan and other Pacific rim players. Whilst the state played a direct role in the development of nuclear energy throughout the world, the new 'commanding heights' have been served by a more distant, though no less important, role as we shall see.

NUCLEAR ENERGY AND GLOBAL REACH

Vandana Shiva has promoted the notion of global reach as a means of describing the capacity of Northern interests to exercise dominance throughout the world. Global reach is necessary for the development of a 'Green regime' but such a regime requires quite specific institutional structures and agreements. One of the first regulatory regimes operating on a global level was created to regulate and control nuclear weapons and nuclear power. The global fora created played a crucial role in legitimating the practices of nation-states by conducting and then policing global risk assessments.

The threat of nuclear proliferation made the exportation of nuclear power problematic and led to the creation of the International Atomic Energy Authority (IAEA) under the auspices of the United Nations. The regulatory regime established sought to define what had to be achieved in order to secure nuclear safety and prevent proliferation. This was accomplished through the promulgation of Northern knowledge via common educational and training initiatives. A scientific cadre of American and British scientists established the syllabi, generalizing, amongst other things, a model of radiological protection derived from the atomic bombings used on Japan and the data gained in their own 'national sacrifice zones' (Davis, 1993). The International Commission on Radiological Protection (ICRP) set global guidelines subject to nationally derived action levels.

In certain senses there was a global risk determination here, but when subjected to closer scrutiny the setting of international protection standards was gender blind. This risk determination ignored sex, age and important cultural differences such as dietary preference. The scientific acronym Roentgen Equivalent Man (REM) *meant* literally man, as the differing radiosensitivities of women and children were not taken into account.

The inability of such universal concepts to deal with real-world consequences of nuclear adventurism was quickly revealed. After the Windscale fire in 1957, health physicists attempting to determine the actual dose to the affected population found themselves 'short both of philosophical and quantitative information' as 'with indecent haste we had to conceive our own model child … our assessment was personal and arbitrary' (PRO file no. AB86/25). The reassuring language of global scientific risk assessment was thus found to be meaningless when confronted by the complexity of lived relations requiring action levels for children and pregnant women amongst others. The model used for setting 'acceptable' human doses was based on the adult male. Institutions such as the IAEA, ICRP, NRPB and MRC formulated global protection standards which first excluded, then denied the somatic and genetic effects of radiation on women as discrete social categories. Dr Alice Stewart, one of the first epidemiological experts to suggest enhanced in-utero radiosensitivity, was met with dismissal and rebuttal, as were other experts who deviated from the official line.

Behind this regulatory regime a deeper cultural appropriation and subordination of indigenous peoples occurred. Uranium, the raw material for weapons and reactors, was mined, sometimes illegally, in the 'homelands' of peoples in Australia, America, Canada (Robinson 1992), and South Africa. Native lands also became the sites for the testing of nuclear weapons in a further appropriation. In Australia the Aboriginal practice of walkabout was appropriated through cash payments which neither compensated for what was lost nor stopped the practice. Atomic bomb tests by the British, American and French have all been conducted in 'native lands'. America and Britain both conducted secret radiation experiments on their citizens (often members of disadvantaged, powerless groups) and fallout from bomb tests affected both people of colour and whites (Davis, 1993). Conducting bomb tests on sacred native lands represented a transgression based on the inferiority of native people and their cultural practices. The presence of visible difference such as skin pigmentation combined with a view of these peoples as primitives made the choice of bomb-test locations simple for 'imperial' races. The examples above are all clear infringements of any conception of universal human rights but for the purposes of my argument they are less important than the global regulatory regime which was constructed around nuclear energy.

The desire to promulgate the 'peaceful' atom reflected a wide range of factors. Not least of these was the prospect of massive industrial regeneration in the countries supplying nuclear technology (Welsh, 1994). In America and the UK, scientists seriously discussed the prospects for greening the Sahara using water desalinated by cheap nuclear power. The US also envisaged using nuclear explosions to create a new Panama canal and for the creation of a deep water port in Northern Australia to facilitate mineral exports, including uranium.

Having appropriated the uranium for nuclear power from the developing nations the North attempted to sell them nuclear reactors as part of a modernization project. The energy needs of developing nations became focused through the lens of export markets for Northern nuclear vendors. Reactor sales to the South required the transformation of the entire social, economic and cultural infrastructure as the typical electricity demand of these countries was insufficient to warrant even one nuclear power station. Technical-development packages became accompanied by attractively priced loans to secure nuclear orders. The ability to underwrite preferential loans became one of the key factors in securing sales and lent the Americans a strategic advantage in this area. The development of the nuclear enterprise thus impacted directly upon the preferred practices of 'native' peoples by assuming them to be, or actively depicting them as, primitive and thus inferior in relation to Northern scientific knowledge and technical prowess.

Like the nuclear age before it, the biotechnology age has been presented as the solution to the most pressing world problems. A 1984 US Office of Technology assessment summarized the technology in the following manner:

> Biotechnology has the technical breadth and depth to change the industrial community of the 21st century because of its potential to produce substantially unlimited quantities of:
>
> - products never before available
> - products currently in short supply
> - products that cost substantially less than products made by existing methods of production
> - products that are safer than those that are available, and
> - products made with new material that may be more plentiful and less expensive than those now used.
>
> By virtue of its wide-reaching potential applications, biotechnology lies close to the centre of many of the world's major problems – malnutrition, disease, energy availability and cost, and pollution.   (Cited in Krimsky, 1991, p. 25)

The combination of biotechnology and genetics was seen as having even more profound implications for human society. Commenting on American progress in this area by 1971, the *New Scientist* opined that this 'heralded the dawn of an age which many have forecast – some with hope some with fear: an era when the spectacular research achievements of molecular biology begin to be applied to the correction of genetic abnormalities in man' (cited in Bud, 1993, p. 174).

At the global level biotechnology rapidly became axiomatic in relation to development issues.

> Biotechnology is a global issue. It cannot be assigned such attributes as positive, negative, or neutral. Like any other technology, it is

inextricably linked to the society in which it is created and used, and will be as socially just or unjust as its milieu ... rational biotechnology policy must be geared to meet the real needs of the majority of the world's people and the creation of more equitable self-reliant societies while in harmony with the environment.

(The Bogeve Declaration on Biotechnology in the Developing World, 1987; cited in Krimsky, 1991, p. 205)

This quote contains many examples of the kind of commonality discussed earlier, further underlining the extent to which the discourse of environmental harmony had pervaded development issues by the late 1980s. The tension between the ascribed social and cultural attributes of any technology derived from its place of development, and the pursuit of self-reliance, equity and environmental harmony, form the basis for subsequent discussion. A central question must be: How can the embedded social attributes of America, Britain and Japan contribute to increased equity if those technologies are used in India, Pakistan, Bangladesh and so on? This brings into focus the relationship between developments in the forces of production and the qualitative consequences of such developments in both vendor and client countries.

Technological developments become one important feature in the formulation of a Green regime through a direct linkage with sustainability via technical substitution. Sustainability and the UNCED become key discursive nodes in the forging of new regulatory practices. Unlike nuclear weapons there is, as yet, no equivalent to the IAEA in these spheres. However, through the translation of the Rio sustainability agenda into national programmes and agendas, global environmental risks and the adequacy of environmental risk assessments become areas of key concern.

The UK government's response to the Rio initiative has included publications on sustainable development (HMSO, 1994) and risk assessment (DOE, 1995) as well as establishing new national fora such as the Roundtable on Sustainable Development. Rio, and other global fora, thus represent a top-down approach to environmental regulation with considerable latitude in terms of the implementation strategies in particular countries. Such latitude mirrors the approach of earlier nuclear regimes which specified 'what had to be achieved' and 'not how' this should be accomplished. This variability allows considerable difference in regulatory emphasis. The former Conservative government, for example, took a much weaker interpretation of the precautionary principle than the rest of the EU.

Differences in regulatory emphases are crucial to my argument in two senses. First, they produce different consequences in different vendor countries, and secondly they enable powerful vendor countries to exploit regulatory gaps in 'less developed' countries. This is particularly problematic given the difficulty in distinguishing between global environmental regulation and more traditional forms of health and safety regulation in industry. It is part of my argument here that the nascent 'Green regime' is implicitly and explictly exploiting such elisions. The accident in the Union Carbide plant at Bhopal in India is one such example where weak health and safety regulation contributed to an appalling human and environmental disaster. In the UK the BSE scare revealed an analogous weakness. Bovine products used in medicines were subject to pharmaceutical regulatory practices whilst bovine derivatives in food products were subject to a much more lax set of regulatory procedures. This essentially replicates one of the key divisions in the initial regulatory practices for genetically modified organisms (GMOs) in the USA. Similarly the US decision to concentrate on environmental rather than work-place regulation was taken at the expense of workers (Krimsky, 1991, p. 91).

It is perhaps in America that the combination of scientific hubris aligned with elements of dominant discourse, notably those of free-market individualism, has been at its clearest. Krimsky's account of this is particularly lucid and useful, revealing a direct relationship between Federal funding of basic research and the development of commercial biotechnology companies throughout the 1980s.

The long association between state and industry in the area of biotechnology and genetic engineering was one reason why President Bush refused to sign up to the Rio Earth Summit protocols in 1992[1]. As Purdue (1995) argues, significant elements of the US bio-tech/gen-tech networks regarded the intellectual property-rights implications of the Rio Summit as incompatible with the commercial exploitation of leading-edge science and technology. Purdue details how the pursuit of a more restrictive definition of intellectual property rights via the GATT and WTO enabled bio/gen-tech companies in the North to patent plants which were the product of generations of traditional selective breeding by farmers in the South. Ownership was extended to those who had carried out certain types of laboratory-based labour, enabling them to patent plants and rendering the indigenous producers liable to a licensing fee.

The rosy periwinkle of Madagascar was identified as an effective anti-leukaemia agent but under existing patent laws Madagascar receives no share of the profit accruing to the patent-holder. This is a trend set to accelerate rapidly – as Jon Tinker expresses it, 'If it takes 50 Amazonian peoples at least 10,000 years to identify 50 psychotropic plant-based drugs, how long would it take 50 transnational companies to rediscover them by checking through one million Amazonian plant species?' (Tinker, cited in Alston and Brown, 1993, p. 191).

Claiming ownership over carefully husbanded plant species is the assertion of the absolute superiority of Northern knowledge and practices over those of the South for commercial gain. Completely subordinating indigenous people's practices and any rights arising from those practices constitutes a form of racism by superior knowledge.

The World Bank technical report *Agricultural Biotechnology: The Next 'Green Revolution'* (World Bank, 1991) discusses elements of an appropriate regulatory regime. The document reproduces ascendant Northern environmental arguments and advocates an international regime of knowledge power in relation to biotechnology. The definition of biotechnology adopted in the document is drawn so widely that it includes the manipulation of both plant and animal genes.

Food shortages are identified as a problem for the South, requiring the introduction of new biotechnologies which, like the hybrids of the first Green revolution, will require further consolidation of land holdings, displacing more small farmers from the land (ibid., p. 6). The document identified 134 US companies involved in the development of biotechnology noting the American, European and Japanese dominance in the area. The annual research investment of some US firms was in the region of 5 million dollars. Owing to such high costs and the risk of failure, 'research operations need to be flexible enough to capture the profit from product or licence sales' (ibid., p. 9). The assertion that biotechnology will provide solutions pre-empts consideration of other possible technical and/or social measures capable of optimizing food production in line with existing social and cultural practices (for one account of the potential here, see Norberg-Hodge, 1991).

Despite this it is envisaged that the primary areas where biotechnology products will be used will be in relation to the 'crops of primary interest to industrialised countries' (Ibid., p. 21). As these crops are predominantly cash crops grown for export they play no role in meeting direct food needs of the countries of origin. Again Northern interests predominate. There is also, in protean form, the outline of a regulatory system which emphasizes similar relations of knowledge-based subordination embodied in the IAEA model.

The World Bank promoted the establishment of International Agricultural Research Centres (IARCs) (Goodman and Redclift, 1991, p. 152), whose clients are seen as the countries of the developing world. Such countries are advised to consider establishing one national centre of research which can shape the wider national effort through 'collaborative links' (ibid., p. 10). The discourse of collaboration and co-operation sounds open-ended and pluralistic but the concentration of expertise and knowledge in a few countries enables them to shape regulatory practices. In one section the report repeats almost word for word the section of the IAEA regulation which defines its task as to establish 'what needs to be done' (ibid., p. 21) rather than 'how it is to be done'.

The World Bank report argued that an 'appropriate' intellectual property-rights regime was vital to the future of biotechnology, depicting this as a dependency structured around the vital need to enable positive benefits to flow to the developing world. 'Strong patent laws are important to technology sellers' (ibid., p. 24). The absent articulation is that huge government and private investments have created an industry with pretensions to a global market. These companies require a dominant global intellectual property-rights regime, part of 'what is to be done', and uneven regulatory regimes at the national level, part of 'how it is to be done'.

GLOBAL DOMINANCE ENSURES PROFIT FLOWS AND NATIONAL VARIANCE ENABLES MARKETING OF PRODUCTS WHICH MEET RESISTANCE IN HOME MARKETS

The raw materials for this revolution are appropriated from the plants of the developing countries, and in some instances the genetic codes of minority peoples are appropriated by companies as part of 'preserving human biodiversity'. Products synthesized from genetic material derived from individual caucasians have been appropriated through patents, but the appropriation of a people's entire genetic code is enabled through a combination of perceived racial inferiority and threatened species status.[2]

Having selectively appropriated peoples from the 'third' world via slavery (Fryer, 1988), subordinated their economies to the tastes of Northern markets through colonialism, appropriated their cultures through a range of tourisms including eco-tourism (Munt, 1994), the North seems set to embark on a variety of forms of further colonization.

The distant application of heavily mediated 'environmental' regimes discussed above reveals how the application of categories of environmental concern and action generated in the North extend previous articulation of superiority necessary to racisms. These processes also have implications at 'home'. Here I will substantially discuss an American literature on environmental racism. It is, however, important to acknowledge that far less clearly articulated, though similar, concerns do find expression within the UK. Stuart Hall reminds us how the aesthetic registers of white English environmentalism are so easily disrupted by the insertion of a black subject into any of the iconic 'chocolate box' images used to depict nature in the photographic work of Ingrid Pollard.

ENVIRONMENTAL RACISM AND RESISTANCE

Despite the efforts of the 'Black Environment Network',[3] environmental organizations like Friends of the Earth and Greenpeace have predominantly white memberships. It is, however, possible to present a range of evidence suggesting that the operation of environmental racism at a global level has more local consequences and implications for environmental politics though these are mediated by prevailing national and local circumstances.

In America, for example, church involvement proved influential in highlighting the relationship between the location of toxic waste disposal facilities of all kinds and local populations dominated by people of colour (Bryant and Mohai, 1992, p. 2). This is a finding advanced further by Bullard in a book appropriately entitled *Dumping in Dixie* (Bullard, 1990).

Sociologically there is a particularly striking reliance on arguments about community within this literature. Community activism, community action and communal mobilization are recurrent themes (Lichterman, 1995). Another significant regenerative force in community studies can be seen arising from the increasing attention given to social and actor networks as important constitutive social and political processes. Given the linkage between networks, social movements and democracy advanced by Melucci (1989, 1992, 1993), then, the relationship between community movements and social movements assumes considerable importance.

The UK communes movement continues to report the activities of MOVE a radical American movement drawing on Rastafarian roots to mount a critique of the 'world systems' on the ground of universal respect for all life. In 1985 a MOVE, commune in Philadelphia was destroyed in a police action which burned 62 neighbouring homes, killing 5 children and 6 adults. MOVE activists are supported in speaking tours throughout the UK in their pursuit of environmental justice.[4]

Wieviorka's work in relation to 'race' (Wieviorka, 1995) addresses these concerns via an interpretation of Alan Touraine's work on social movements. Amongst the important arguments advanced here is the idea that the opportunity structure for racism within any society depends upon the presence or absence of a major conflictual divide. In societies where there is a well organized class struggle or social-movement contestation over common cultural and social goals, then the freedom for racist expression is constrained.

In the case of the US he thus argues that in the earlier part of the twentieth century the existence of labour-movement organizations for people of colour, irrespective of their success, exercised a constraining factor on overtly racist mobilizations. The steady weakening of the American labour movement, which accelerated rapidly in the 1980s, thus coincides with the emergence of environmental community action by people of colour. The example serves to remind us that the contingent circumstances of particular nations mediate the range of racism articulated within a society. The American experience of slavery, immigration and segregation are all relevant factors here.

The biotechnology and genetic-engineering industries discussed in this chapter do not just lead to distantiated racist practices. The abstract levels of subordination exercised by superior scientific knowledge have lived relations of production, consumption and pollution in the vendor countries and elsewhere. The production of toxic waste residues from this complex of technologies leads to major disposal problems. There is an almost reflexive tendency to locate 'dirt' amongst groups that can be seen as 'other'. In this sense the economically and socially excluded become 'natural' targets for dumping by dominant groups. In America the association between 'dirt' and 'other' has been central in locating disposal practices in social margins defined by visible markers of ethnic difference. Driving new roads through poor communities is another area where research may reveal a similar imposition in the UK. Dumping is not just a practice exercised within nation-states however, and the same powerful global forces responsible for the development of the latest technological revolutions also play a central role in disposal strategies.

A widely leaked and much cited World Bank internal memo written by Lawrence Summers, the bank's chief economist, was particularly revealing in this sense. Rather than abridge the memo to the two most cited sentences it is reproduced more extensively here. Having underlined the confidentiality of the memo and it's status as something for consumption within an 'in' group, Summers offers the following key arguments:

> shouldn't the World bank be encouraging MORE migration of the dirty industries to the Less Developed Countries? I can think of three reasons:
>
> (1) The measurement of cost of health impairing pollution depends on the foregone earnings from increased morbidity and mortality. From this point of view a given amount of health impairing pollution should be done in the country with the lowest cost, which will be the country with the lowest wages. I think the economic logic behind dumping a load of toxic waste in the lowest wage country is impeccable and we should face up to that.
>
> (2) The costs of pollution are likely to be non-linear as the initial increments of pollution probably have very low cost. I've always thought that the under-polluted areas in Africa are vastly UNDER-polluted; their quality is probably vastly inefficiently low compared to Los Angeles or Mexico City. Only the lamentable facts that so much pollution is generated by non-tradable industries (transport, electrical generation) and that the unit transport costs of solid waste are so high prevent the world welfare-enhancing trade in air pollution and waste.
>
> (3) The demand for a clean environment for aesthetic and health reasons is likely to have very high income elasticity... . Clearly trade in goods that embody aesthetic pollution concerns could be welfare enhancing. While production is mobile the consumption of pretty air is a non-tradable.
>
> (Cited in Bullard and Chavis, 1993, p. 20)

Following this logic, world trade in toxic waste grew by a factor of five in the three years up to 1994, with a proportion of it being classified as foreign aid on the grounds that the wastes were recyclable (Puckett, 1994). Recyclable in this context is a weasel word in that the product may be recyclable provided the necessary technical facilities are present at the point of destination. Where no such facilities exist then it remains toxic waste. This trade was eventually banned by international convention following the concerted action of one hundred developing countries. Such exports are part of accumulation and regulation regimes. To the extent they are regulated for 'risk' this is done at a distantiated level which neglects the prevailing national and local implications of such practices. It is common practice to export toxic waste to Eastern European countries where local conditions, including civil wars, make global risk determinations meaningless. The logic revealed by Summers, which values pollution impact in relation to the lost earnings of affected peoples, is reflected within other global regulatory regimes. A draft UN report on the environment and global warming thus valued a US human life at 1.5 million US dollars and an Indian life at 100,000 US dollars (BBC Radio Four, Today, 9 December 1995).

The American literature discussed here reveals a persistent linkage between discourses of social and of environmental justice. Appropriating the environment as a site for race-sensitive activism produces a significant shift towards a social definition of environmental praxis. The emphasis of established white environmentalism on 'nature preservation' is broadened to address central concerns about social inequality and environmental deprivation. This is a linkage made in various key reports on the environment in relation to 'third' world environmental degradation but one which has not been readily applied in developed nations.

In making this connection people of colour are enunciating an environmental agenda which does not allow the environment to be rendered as a substantially organic site to do with 'nature', natural resources, pollution sinks and 'natural' cycles (air, water, carbon, etc.). By foregrounding some of the ways in which domination of the organic environment is dependent upon domination of human subjects the pursuit of environmental justice becomes predicated on the pursuit of social justice.

This is a profoundly uncomfortable message for the global institutions, which in 1992 captured the environmental agenda of white critics developed over the past thirty years. It is also a profoundly challenging position for existing environmental movements in the developed countries. Amongst these even the most 'radical' (i.e. eco-centric/deep green) groups have been denounced for their racist positions. Most famously the American deep greens have been attacked for their statements that HIV/AIDs represents a form of life, entitling it to rights, with the loss of human life in Africa being seen in a Gaian perspective as the planet protecting itself from over-population.

Other deep green sensibilities are reproduced within the American movements of people of colour. The pre-amble to a seventeen-point programme for action by people of colour over environmental issues sought to 're-establish our spiritual interdependence to the sacredness of our Mother Earth' (Bryant and Mohai, 1992, p. 215). The need to reassert such associations after centuries of appropriation, exclusion and destruction of 'native' lands is clearly strong. Whether it forms the basis for moving towards a tolerance of cultural difference and a hybrid respect for different knowledge forms, or a temporary position-ing device necessary for movement unity, remains to be seen.

CONCLUSIONS

The connection between social and environmental justice made so powerfully by people of colour has the potential to provide an en-vironmental version of the more class-based black vanguardism so famously advanced by the late C. L. R. James. As the most economi-cally, socially and environmentally disadvantaged groups, there is a radicalism to their position which can be easily obscured in less oppressed locations.

This raises a range of issues to do with the variability of racially defined margins in late modernity. In countries like the UK where active segregation has played a more minor role, racism has been mobilized through other, no less virulent, channels. In the eyes of the establishment British environmental extremism is identified not so much through skin colour as through adopted identities of difference, though the attempts of groups like the National Front to recruit en-vironmentalists are usually ignored.[5] The self-styled Donga Tribe, central in the obstruction of many road-construction initiatives, were particularly scathing of environmentalists' campaigns to save forest Indians whilst ignoring the Dongas' self-claimed plight as 'threatened indigenous people' (Fairlie, 1993, p. 4).

In the UK it is precisely amongst the most marginalized elements of the environmental movement that the association between environ-mental and social justice as inseparable campaigning objects is made (Welsh and McLeish, 1996). This whole area becomes one where the campaigning effectiveness of First World environmental movements and organizations could be immeasurably strengthened by embracing this message. Already, the moral acceptability of World Bank programmes is the subject of considerable campaigns.

The promotion by the World Bank, alliances of nation-states, and powerful commercial interests of biotechnologies has resurrected fears over positive eugenic programmes. At precisely the same juncture as governments are urging citizens to take out private insurance against ill health as part of economic restructuring, the new genetic technologies seem set to create a growing pool of the uninsurable. The pre-identification of genetically transmitted diseases will lead to the creation of an uninsurable under-class. Alliance-building within the environmental movements seems set to provide another forum within which 'black and white unite and fight' strategies can be attempted.

Wieviorka identified five processes historically significant for the expression of racism. These were defence of community; war and conquest; crises of the state and rise of community; transformation of community politics and the transition from communal movement to social movement (Wieviorka, 1995, pp. 108–14). To these significant processes I think it is now reasonable to add environmental appropriation. In terms of the bridge between community mobilization and social-movement mobilization I think that there are grounds for cautious optimism.

The developing significant social movements in Europe, including anti-nuclear and environmental movements, have had their origins in community-based politics aimed at immediate welfare and quality-of-life issues (Offe, 1985). It is clear that environmentalism cannot continue to be confined to the preservation, conservation or management of nature. A social environmental agenda beyond the idea of inalienable rights to clean air, water and soil is urgently needed.

In terms of sociological considerations of risk, then the idea that there are global risks which are 'somehow universal and unspecific', recognizing none of the social categories which have stratified societies (Beck, 1992, pp. 22 and 53), is only true at the level of rational abstraction used in global risk assessments. As I have argued throughout this chapter, environmental risks like radioactive releases do not distinguish between the social categories touched. The regulatory frameworks built on the self-same science, however, neglect the importance of gender and 'race' as mediating categories determining the severity of exposure. When economic considerations are added into this amalgam of concerns then, as Summers argued, there is an impeccable logic in ensuring that environmental hazards are endured by the poorest nations and people.

NOTES

1. Other more obvious lobbies here included the US coal industry nervous about carbon taxes and the impact of greenhouse regulation on coal burning.
2. I am grateful to Sarah Franklin for the example of Unilever's appropriation of Aboriginal genetic material, as discussed at the BSA Theory Conference, University of Wales, Cardiff, 2–3 March 1996.
3. UK Office, 9 Llainwen Uchaf, Llanberis, Wales, LL55 4LL.
4. I am grateful to Derek Wall, of the University of the West of England, Bristol, for his account of MOVE activities and UK linkages.
5. The work of Ian Coates, Dept. of Sociology, University of Bristol, provides a rare examination of the links between extreme right-wing politics and environmentalism in the UK.

REFERENCES

Aglietta, M. (1987), *A Theory of Capitalist Regulation* (London: Verso).

Albrecht, G. (1994), 'Ethics, Anarchy and Sustainable Development', *Anarchist Studies*, 2 (2), pp. 95–117.

Albrow, M. (ed.) (1990), *Globalization, Knowledge and Society* (London: Sage).

Alston, D., and Brown, N. (1993), 'Global Threats to People of Color', in Bullard, D., and Chavis, B. Jr (eds), *Confronting Environmental Racism: Voices from the Grassroots* (Boston: Southend), pp. 179–94.

Barker, M. (1981) *The New Racism* (London: Junction Books).

Bauer, M. (ed.) (1995) *Resistance to New Technology: Nuclear Power, Information Technology and Biotechnology* (Cambridge: Cambridge University Press).

Beck, U. (1987), 'The Anthropological Shock: Chernobyl and the Contours of the Risk Society', *Berkeley Journal of Sociology*, pp. 153–65.

Beck, U. (1992), *Risk Society* (London: Sage).

Bleier, R. (ed.) (1988), *Feminist Approaches to Science* (Oxford: Pergamon).

Bryant, B., and Mohai, P. (1992), *Race and the Incidence of Environmental Hazards: A Time for Discourse* (Boulder: Westview).

Bud, R. (1993), *The Uses of Life: A History of Biotechnology* (Cambridge: Cambridge University Press).

Bud, R. (1995), 'In the Engine of Industry: Regulators of Biotechnology, 1970–86', in Bauer, M. (ed.), *Resistance to New Technology: Nuclear Power,*

Information Technology and Biotechnology (Cambridge: Cambridge University Press).

Bullard, R. D. (1990), *Dumping in Dixie: Race, Class and Environmental Quality* (Boulder: West View).

Bullard, R. D., and Chavis, B. Jr (eds) (1993), *Confronting Environmental Racism: Voices from the Grassroots* (Boston: Southend).

Carson, R. (1962), *Silent Spring* (Boston: Houghton Mifflin).

Davis, M. (1993), 'Dead West: Ecocide in Marlboro Country', *New Left Review*, 200, pp. 49–73.

Deutch Lynch, B. (1995), 'The Garden and the Sea: US Latino Environmental Discourses and Mainstream Environmentalism', *Social Problems*, 40 (1), pp. 108–24.

DOE (1995), *A Guide to Risk Assessment and Risk Management for Environmental Protection* (London: HMSO).

Douglas, M., and Wildavsky, A. (1982), *Risk and Culture* (London: University of California Press).

Erlich, P. R. (1968), *The Population Bomb* (London: Pan).

Fairlie, S. (1993), 'Tunnel Vision: Lessons from Twyford Down', *The Ecologist*, 23 (1), pp. 2–4.

Featherstone, M. (ed.) (1990), *Global Culture* (London: Sage).

Fryer, P. (1988), *Staying Power* (London: Verso).

Goodman, D., and Redclift, M. (1991), *Refashioning Nature: Food, Ecology, Culture* (London: Routledge).

Gorz, A. (1987), *Ecology as Politics* (London: Pluto; original Paris, 1975).

Haraway, D. (1994), *Primate Visions* (London: Verso).

Haraway, D. (1995), 'Situated Knowledges: The Science Question in Feminism and the Privilege of Partial Perspective', in Feenberg, A., and Hannay, A. (eds) *Technology and the Politics of Knowledge* (Indiana: Indiana University Press), pp. 175–94.

Harvey, D. (1989) *The Condition of Post-Modernity* (Oxford: Blackwell).

Harvey, D. (1996), *Justice, Nature and the Geography of Difference* (Cambridge: Blackwell).

HMSO (1990) *This Common Inheritance: Britain's Environmental Strategy*, Cm 1200 (London: HMSO).

HMSO (1994), *Sustainable Development: The UK Strategy*, Cm 2426 (London: HMSO).

Krimsky, S. (1991), *Biotechnics and Society: The Rise of Industrial Genetics* (New York: Praeger).

Kusin, V. K. (1986), 'Gorbachev and Eastern Europe', *Problems of Communism*, XXXV, pp. 39–53.

Larsen, E. (1958), *Atomic Energy: A Layman's Guide to the Nuclear Age* (London: Hennel Lock).

Lichterman, P. (1995), 'Piecing Together Multicultural Community: Cultural Differences in Community Building Among Grass-roots Environmentalists', *Social Problems*, 42 (4), pp. 513–34.

McKechnie, R., and Welsh, I. (1994), 'Between the Devil and the Deep Green Sea: Defining Risk Societies and Global Threats', in Jeffrey Weeks (ed.), *The Lesser Evil and the Greater Good* (London: Rivers Oram) pp. 57–78.

Marien, M. (1992), 'Environmental Problems and Sustainable Futures: Major Literature from WCED to UNCED', *Futures*, 24 (8), pp. 731–57.

Melucci, A. (1989), *Nomads of the Present* (London: Radius Hutchinson).

Melucci, A. (1992), 'Liberation or Meaning? Social Movements, Culture and Democracy', *Development and Change*, 23 (3), pp. 43–77.

Melucci, A. (1993), 'Paradoxes of Post-industrial Democracy: Everyday Life and Social Movements', *Berkeley Journal of Sociology*, XXXVIII, pp. 185–92.

Melucci, A. (1996), *Challenging Codes: Collective Action in the Information Age* (Cambridge: Cambridge Umiversity Press).

Merchant, C. (1980), *The Death of Nature* (London: Harper and Row).

Munt, I. (1994), 'Eco-Tourism or Ego-Tourism?', *Race and Class*, 36 (1), pp. 49–60.

Norberg-Hodge, H. (1991), *Ancient Futures: Learning from Ladakh* (London: Rider).

Offe, C. (1985) 'New Social Movements: Challenging the Boundaries of Institutional Politics', *Social Research*, 52 (4), pp. 817–68.

Puckett, J. (1994), 'Disposing of the Waste Trade', *The Ecologist*, 24 (2), pp. 53–8.

Purdue, D. (1995), 'Hegemonic TRIPS: World Trade, Intellectual Property and Biodiversity', *Environmental Politics*, 4 (1, 8), pp. 8–107.

Robinson, Wm P. (1992), 'Uranium Production and its Effects on Navajo Communities Along the Rio Puerco in Western New Mexico', in Bryant and Mohai (eds) (1992), *Race and the Incidence of Environmental Hazards: A Time for Discourse* (Boulder: Westview), pp. 153–63.

Ross, A. (1994), *The Chicago Gangster Theory of Life* (London: Verso).

Smart, B. (1994), 'Sociology, Globalisation and Postmodernity: Comments on the "Sociology for One World" Thesis', *International Sociology*, 9 (2), pp. 149–59.

Starke, L. (1990), *Signs of Hope: Working towards our Common Future* (Oxford: Oxford University Press).

WCED (World Commission on Environment and Development) (1987), *Our Common Future* (Oxford: Oxford University Press).

Welsh, I. (1994), 'Letting the Research Tail Wag the End-user's Dog: The Powell Committee and UK Reactor Choice', *Science and Public Policy*, vol. 21, no. 1 (February), pp. 43–53.

Welsh, I. (1996), 'Risk, Global Governance and Environmental Politics', *Innovation*, 9 (4), pp. 407–20.

Welsh, I. and McLeish, P. (1996), 'The European Road to Nowhere: Anarchism and Direct Action against the UK Roads Programme', *Anarchist Studies*, 4 (1), (Spring), pp. 27–44.

Wieviorka, M. (1995), *The Arena of Racism* (London: Sage).

World Bank (1991), *Agricultural Biotechnology: The Next 'Green Revolution'*, Technical Paper no. 33.

Yanarella, E. J., and Levine, R. S. (1992), 'Does Sustainable Development Lead to Sustainability', *Futures*, 24 (8), pp. 759–74.

4 Global Environmental-Change Discourse: the Southern Critique

MARIE A. MATER

Increasingly, the environment has gained prominence as a contentious social and political issue. Originally debated at the local and national levels, environmental issues have now become a routine theme of international discussions. Perhaps the most important global discussion to date about environmental issues was the United Nations Conference on Environment and Development (UNCED) in Rio de Janeiro in June 1992. This meeting was significant because of the sheer number and diversity of the participants. Heads of state of more than 100 countries, delegations from 178 countries, and representatives of more than 1000 non-governmental organizations gathered to consider environmental problems and development issues (CIESIN 1996, paragraph 1). The UNCED will also be remembered as the site at which the increasing conflict between the 'developed' nations of the North and the 'developing' nations of the South became most pronounced.[1] The growing rift between the South and North was the result of a discursive conflict over the construction of 'global environmental change' within the international environmental debate.

In order to understand what happened at Rio, we must examine the different constructions of 'global environmental change' that emerged before, during and after the UNCED. Unfortunately, most studies of 'global environmental change' either focus exclusively on the Northern constructions of this discourse (Dunlap, 1992; Dunlap and Catton, 1992–3, 1994; Martell, 1994; Miller, 1991; Stern, Young and Druckman, 1992; Thacher, 1991; Turner et al., 1990), or they acknowledge that Southern constructions exist, but do not examine them as they are presented by Southern authors (Buttel, Hawkins and Power, 1990; Redclift, 1992; Redclift and Benton, 1994; Yearly, 1992). There are only a few studies (Buttel and Taylor, 1992, 1994; Taylor and Buttel, 1992; Yearly, 1996) which actually cite several

Southern critics of Northern constructions of 'global environmental change'.

This situation has occurred for several reasons. Slater (1992, p. 314) explains that there is an absence of Southern voices in the discussion of contemporary issues [like the environment] and theoretical strategies because in the representation of what is presumed to be the main arguments, the key authors cited are from the North. Furthermore, there is no awareness '... that the intellectual in the West can *learn* from the Third World other' (Slater, 1992, pp. 322–3). Soto (1992, p. 681) argues that this is a result of a stereotypical, unilateral, Northern perception of the South and its problems with the underlying assumption that Southern scholars produce few worthwhile studies and solutions. Unfortunately, this has been the case with 'global environmental change'. Although Southern intellectuals have been critiquing the North's construction of 'global environmental change' and examining the alternative constructions produced in the South, this has rarely been acknowledged.

In order to facilitate future international debate and discussion on 'global environmental change', the observations and opinions of the South must be taken into account. Soto (1992) concludes by calling for a transnational exchange of ideas, culture and knowledge between the South and North. Furthermore, Garaudy (1992/1987, p. xii) explains that because of the problems that are a direct result of the Northern path to modernity, there is an urgent necessity for this dialogue:

> The dialogue of civilizations has become a necessity, urgent and unexceptionable. A question of survival .... The central and valid debate of our times is the one outlined by Nandy: that between an 'alternative perspective' and 'modern oppression'. That alternative can only emerge from a free 'dialogue of civilizations' which would show how the non- Western cultures conceived and lived with other kinds of relationships with nature, with people and with the direction of their life, not for 'returning to the past', but for distilling a future out of the experience of all civilizations and not that of simply one.

As a contribution to this 'free dialogue of civilizations' and following the lead of the Commission on Developing Countries and Global Change's *For Earth's Sake* (1992) and Wolfgang Sachs's *Global Ecology* (1993a), this chapter examines the alternative Southern constructions of 'global environmental change' as they are articulated by

Southern critics.[2] First, it presents the 'environmental colonialism' critique of the pre-UNCED World Resources Institute's reports on 'global environmental change'. Next, the 'globalism' discourse prevalent at the UNCED is examined. Finally, the chapter concludes with a call for a multidisciplinary, bipolar study of the construction of 'sustainable development' as it is emerging in the global environmental debate in the aftermath of the UNCED.

THE ENVIRONMENTAL-COLONIALISM CRITIQUE OF THE WORLD RESOURCES INSTITUTE REPORTS

The Northern view of 'global environmental change' is generally constructed from arguments by Northern scientists and researchers. Southern scientists and researchers have taken issue with the conclusions of many of these reports. The basic Southern critique of the North's construction of 'global environmental change' is that it justifies the North's continued colonialism of the South under the guise of solving global environmental problems. The catalyst for this critique was the Washington-based private research group the World Resources Institute (WRI), which published two different studies on tropical forests and global warming.

In 1985, WRI, along with the World Bank and the United Nations Development Programme (UNDP), published the report *Tropical Forests: A Call for Action*. The basic arguments of the report are that (1) the rural poor destroy tropical forests for fuelwood; (2) destructive land use on upland watersheds is taking place on a vast scale throughout the developing world; (3) scientific management of forests for industrial uses is needed; and (4) institutions for research, training and extension need to be strengthened (WRI, World Bank and UNDP, 1985).

Vandana Shiva (1987a, 1987b) of the Research Foundation for Science, Technology and Natural Resource Policy in India harshly criticizes the WRI report's major arguments, identifying them as 'pervasive myths'. According to Shiva (1987b, p. 142), the four myths prevalent in the report are:

1) That people, not profits, are the primary cause of tropical deforestation;
2) That the 'developed' world has protected its forests and must teach conservation to the Third World;

3) That commercial forestry, based on private ownership, can solve the fuelwood crisis for the poor; and
4) That commercial afforestation can guarantee ecological recovery.

These four myths are similar to the British colonial power's justification for the Indian Forest Department, which felled trees in large numbers to support the building of the Indian Railway in the 1800s. Today, however, these myths are being used to justify the commercial afforestation of Southern tropical forests by Northern companies. This substitution of fast-growing tree species in place of naturally occurring tree species is motivated by the global demand for paper. Consequently, she characterizes these myths as a continuation of the colonial 'conservation' discourse:

> We in the Third World in general, and India in particular, are familiar with these myths. They were the political tools used for the colonisation of common forest resources by the British. The centres of exploitation and planned destruction might have shifted from the East India Company and the Crown in London a century ago to the World Bank in Washington in contemporary times, but the logic of colonisation has not changed. ... The World Bank... is talking of conservation of tropical ecosystems while financing projects that will destroy tropical ecosystems. (Shiva, 1987a, p. 20)

Hypocritically, the World Bank funds environmentally damaging projects in the South like commercial afforestation, while at the same time implying that the people in the South do not have the ability to preserve their own natural resources. On the whole, she perceives the report to be 'a contemporary example of Orwellian double-speak in which ecological destruction is called environmental protection' (Shiva, 1987b, p. 145).

In addition to this special report on tropical forests, the WRI annually produces a general report on the state of the world's environment. In a special section on climate change in its 1990–1 report, *World Resources 1990–1*, WRI, along with the United Nations Environment Programme (UNEP) and the United Nations Development Program (UNDP), lists the countries with the highest greenhouse emissions. Besides the United States and the former Soviet Union, the report argues that the developing countries of Brazil, China and India are also responsible for the accumulation of gases that contribute to global warming. In fact, it claims that 'When all countries are considered, Asia (excluding the [former] Soviet Union) is the largest contributor among the major regions of the world, followed by North and Central America, and by Europe' (WRI, UNEP and UNDP, 1990, p. 15).

Anil Agarwal and Sunita Narain (1991) of the Centre for Science and Environment (CSE) in India cite this report as another example of the 'global environmental change' discourse which justifies environmental colonialism. They dispute the WRI's method of calculating the emissions for India and maintain that:

What WRI has done ... is to calculate the percentage of India's total emissions of carbon dioxide and methane before they are absorbed and then hold India responsible for the same quantitative share of the gases actually accumulating in the Earth's atmosphere. This manner of calculating each nation's responsibility is extremely unfair and amounts to a scientific sleight of hand.   (Agarwal and Narain, 1991, p. 39)

They believe that this method of calculating emissions is inequitable because it favours the biggest polluters like the United States. At issue is each country's share of the natural cleansing ability of the Earth's ocean 'sinks'. The WRI report distributes these sinks at the same rate for each nation. Agarwal and Narain argue for distributing these 'sinks' on the basis on population. As a result, each country would get its own share of the sinks in proportion to its share of the world population. When this is done, they say, 'the production of carbon dioxide and methane produced by countries like the US and Japan [is] totally out of proportion to their populations and that of the world's absorptive capacity' (Agarwal and Narain, 1991, p. 40). In this case, the North is attempting to claim the South's share of the Earth's regenerative capability.

As these critiques of the WRI reports illustrate, environmental issues have begun to be defined in terms of 'global' effects. By communicating about 'global environment change', instead of the local environmental condition, the global debate justifies the environmental regulation of the Southern countries by the nations of the North. 'The global managers thus threaten to unleash a new wave of colonialism, in which the management of people – even whole societies – for the benefit of commercial interests is now justified in the name of environmental protection' (Hildyard, 1993, p. 33). Nowhere was this trend more discernible than the UNCED.

'GLOBALISM' DISCOURSE AT THE UNCED

At the UNCED, the Northern nations wanted an environmental regulatory presence in the South, while maintaining their own economic *status quo*. This environmental regulation of the South by the North was cloaked in the discourse of 'globalism' at the UNCED. Tariq Banuri (1993, p. 49) argues that most Northerners saw the UNCED as a way to save humanity, while most Southerners feared the emergence of a new colonialism designed to preserve the lifestyle of the rich. This manifested itself in two ways: through the Northern control of Southern resources and through the sharing of environmental costs between the South and the North. Like the original discourse of colonialism, the 'globalism' discourse privileges a small wealthy minority in the North and excludes the poor majority in the South. According to Shiva (1993a, pp. 154–5),

> The 'global' in the dominant discourse is the political space in which a particular dominant local seeks global control, and frees itself of local, national and international restraints. The global does not represent the universal human interest, it represents a particular local and parochial interest which has been globalised through the scope of its reach. The seven most powerful countries, the G-7, dictate global affairs, but the interests that guide them remain narrow, local and parochial.

The interests of this wealthy group (like those of the original colonialists) include continued (or in some cases expanded) exclusive access to natural resources. The best example of this at the UNCED was the controversy surrounding the convention on biodiversity. In this convention, biodiversity is transformed from a local resource to a 'global resource':

> by treating biodiversity as a global resource, the World Bank emerges as its protector through the GEF (Global Environmental Facility), and the North demands free access to the South's biodiversity through the proposed Biodiversity Convention. ... Globalisation becomes a political means to erode these sovereign rights, and to shift control over and access to biological resources from the gene-rich South to the gene-poor North. (Shiva, 1993a, p. 152)

Basically, the North is arguing that the South should preserve its forests so that the plants and animals in them are protected for future biotechnological research in the North. Moreover, the North sees the issue, not as one of national sovereignty, but as one of intellectual property rights. The South feels that they should have monetary compensation, but the North does not agree. Consequently, 'globalism' becomes the means by which the North can argue for access to the South's resources without fair monetary compensation.

At the UNCED, however, a new interest emerged – the 'global' sharing of the environmental costs of modern development. Shiva (1993a, p. 151) explains:

> 'Global environmental problems' have been so constructed as to conceal the fact that globalisation of the local is responsible for destroying the environment which supports the subjugated local peoples. The construction becomes a political tool not only to free the dominant destructive forces operating world-wide from all responsibility but also to shift the blame and responsibility for all destruction on to the communities that have no global reach.

The United States' push for a Tropical Forest Convention at the UNCED is a good example of the Northern attempt to shift environmental responsibility from the North to the South. This issue is also about tropical-forest preservation, but this time the concern is for 'carbon sinks'. The North argues that tropical forests are the Earth's 'lungs' and cleanse global-warming gases from the atmosphere. The conservation of these forests would allow Northern societies like the United States to continue their lifestyles, which contribute significantly to global warming. Southern governments and non-governmental organizations maintain that 'protection of tropical forests was being used, by the US in particular, as a substitute for changing consumption and production patterns in the North' (Shiva, 1993b, p. 81). While the United States strongly insisted on the protection of tropical forests because of their 'carbon sink' capabilities, Southern governments countered this position by stating that the North must pay for this just like they would for any other service.

POST-UNCED: CONSTRUCTING 'SUSTAINABLE DEVELOPMENT'

In the aftermath of Rio, the construction of 'sustainable development' (SD) has become the focus of the global environmental debate.

Because of its elasticity, 'sustainable development' can accommodate and incorporate the communication of competing corporate, political and social actors in both the North and the South. For example, Lele (1991, pp. 611–12) contends that it has the potential to be a tool for consensus:

> The strength of the concept of SD stems from the choice of an apparently simple definition of fundamental objectives – meeting current needs and sustainability requirements – from which can be derived a range of operational objectives that cut across most previous intellectual and political boundaries.

To promote consensus-building, however, 'sustainable development' must be able to embody the perceptions of both the South and the North. To do this, all constructions must be heard, acknowledged and incorporated into the global environmental debate. On the other hand, Redclift (1992, p. 34) explains how the ambiguity of 'sustainable development' can be a weakness in actual policy formation:

> Sustainable development ... has frequently been used in a highly normative way, to express desirable forms of action, and confusion has followed from the juxtaposition of both 'sustainable' and 'development'. ... Although 'sustainable development' is a goal that everybody considers desirable, the absence of agreement about what 'sustainable development' means, has led to contradictory expectations from policy.

Although development implies increased economic activity, sustainability conveys awareness of the impact of economic activity on the environment. The seemingly conflicting interests of increased economic development and environmental protection can both be justified with the concept of sustainable development. This contradictory construction is typically the Northern view of 'sustainable development'.

Within the South, the construction of 'sustainable development' is subject to controversy. For example, Soto (1992, p. 680) argues that 'sustainability' or 'sustainable development' requires a focus on development:

> An agenda which addresses the development–environment impasse from the Southern perspective will require a redefinition of some of the terms currently being used in international discussions. For

example, at present, the primary focus in Northern definitions of the concept of 'sustainability' is on the physical environment. The South, in contrast, believes that 'sustainability' should be concerned more with social and economic issues, such as disparities in wealth and opportunities.

Sachs has an opposing view and believes that the discourse of development places the South at a political disadvantage. He maintains that:

> In using the language of development, the South continues to subscribe to the notion that the North shows the way for the rest of the world. As a consequence, however, the South is incapable of escaping the North's cultural hegemony; for development without hegemony is like a race without a direction. Apart from all the economic pressures, adherence to 'development' puts the South, culturally and politically, in a position of structural weakness, leading to the absurd situation in which the North can present itself as the benevolent provider of solutions to the ecological crisis. (Sachs, 1993b, p. 7)

By 'buying into' the development rhetoric of the North, Sachs sees the South as justifying the continuation of the North's wasteful ways while at the same time preserving the environmental resources of the South for its own use.

There has also been a move in the South to construct an alternative to 'sustainable development' which is informed by traditional knowledges. Shanmugaratnam (1989, p. 29) argues that this construction of alternatives:

> Rather than simply idealising the traditional systems and condemning more recent ones ... need[s] to think in terms of possible new options. ... Such a point of departure together with a detailed critique of the past policies should offer new vistas of sustainable development.

By incorporating traditional knowledges, there is a shift in emphasis from the 'global' to the 'local'. These new 'local' constructions will have important implications for 'global' discourse:

> the organizing strategies of these groups ... revolve more and more around two principles: the defense of cultural difference, not as static

UWE Library Services

Frenchay Campus
Tel 0117 32 82277

Item Title	Due Date
Key issues in childhood and youth studies	
7?0?1?804	?9/04/2012 23:59:00
? ? ? and media in ?ociety	
?1?1?4??	?19/04/2012 23:59:00
?ros?s?gihtennmael to risk : social theory and ?	
70?036?806 *	?19/04/2012 23:59:00
M?dern social theory ? ? introduction	
70?034?842	?19/04/2012 23:59:00
* Beyond c?im?n?logy : taking harm seriously	
7?004?? ??	?9/04/2012 23:59:00
* Terro?? ?? ?isk and the response to ? the liberal state	
7?00?4????	?9/05/2012 23:59:00
* ?nders?and?n? ?err?r?sm : challenges, perspe	
70?0496???	?9/04/2012 23:59:00
* Global t??e??s : migration, environment and g	
7?0?0????	?1?/04/2012 23:59:00

but as a transformed and transformative force; and the valorization of economic needs and opportunities in terms that are not strictly those of profit and the market. The defense of the local as a prerequisite to engaging with the global ... [is a principal element] for the collective construction of alternatives.   (Escobar, 1995, p. 226)

By calling for an alternative to Northern notions of 'development', these Southern scholars may be able to provide a solution for global environmental change.

CONCLUSIONS

Conflicts such as the one at the UNCED between the South and the North are likely to increase as environmental problems transcend national boundaries and developing economies continue to grow. The possibility of international agreements on the environment are remote unless there is a mutual understanding of 'global environmental change' between the North and the South. Because the South and the North construct these discourses in different ways, the possibility for international agreements between them is remote unless both sides can communicate their interests in a political arena which encourages mutual understanding of the issues. As the Committee on the Human Dimensions of Global Change for the National Research Council has noted:

Sustained international cooperation is one essential element in the overall response to global environmental changes. It is essential because efforts to cope with some large-scale environmental changes such as ozone depletion and global warming seem doomed to fail if some of the major national actors do not cooperate.   (Stern, Young and Druckman, 1992, pp. 152–3)

Any attempt to promote international co-operation must begin with an understanding of how actors from both the North and the South construct their discourses in the global context of conferences like the UNCED. This understanding is crucial if solutions to the current global environmental crisis are to be found. Smith (1992, p. 390) concludes:

we must learn to communicate about the environment across and through cultural, social and political barriers. Ecosystems do not recognize our cultural and political boundaries, so just as many environmental problems are cross-cutting, so must solution efforts be.

The first step to achieving this understanding is to study the 'global environmental change' debate from a multidisciplinary perspective which incorporates the work of scholars from both the North and the South. Consequently, studies on these constructions must examine the specific role language and arguments play when actors from both the South and the North meet at global forums such as the UNCED. Perhaps by understanding the way each group communicates its interests and concerns, there can be hope for real consensus on 'global environmental change' at the next UNCED.

NOTES

1.   I have chosen to use the geographical terminology 'North/South' when referring to the division of nations in the world. Although I recognize the limitations of these terms, I agree with the Commission on Developing Countries and Global Change (1992, p. 12) that most countries in the South share the same perspectives on the causes and consequences of global change and that the environmental and developmental conditions of these countries are clearly distinct from those of the North. For a thorough discussion of the different terms used to describe the division of nations, see the Commission on Developing Countries and Global Change (1992).

2.   Most of the literature presented here is from the well-known group of Southern 'deprofessionalized intellectuals' whose works are available in English (Escobar, 1992). I have also included some work by Northern scholars who collaborate frequently with them. I regret that I have been unable to access a great deal of other important material because of my language constraints.

REFERENCES

Agarwal, A., and Narain, S. (1991), 'Global Warming in an Unequal World: A Case of Environmental Colonialism', *Earth Island Journal,* pp. 39–40.
Banuri, T. (1993), 'The Landscape of Diplomatic Conflicts', in W. Sachs (ed.), *Global Ecology: A New Arena of Political Conflict* (London: Zed Books), pp. 49–67.

Buttel, F. H., Hawkins, A. P., and Power, A. G. (1990), 'From Limits to Growth to Global Change: Contrasts and Contradictions in the Evolution of Environmental Science and Ideology', *Global Environmental Change*, 1, pp. 57–66.

Buttel, F. H., and Taylor, P. J. (1992), 'Environmental Sociology and Global Environmental Change: A Critical Assessment', *Society and Natural Resources*, 5, pp. 211–30.

Buttel, F. H., and Tayler, P. J. (1994), 'Environmental Sociology and Global Environmental Change: A Critical Assessment', in M. Redclift and T. Benton (eds), *Social Theory and the Global Environment* (London: Routledge), pp. 228–55.

CIESIN (Consortium for International Earth Science Information Network) Dataset Guide (1996), Abstract/summary. In *United Nations Conference on Environment and Development Collection* (WWW): available: http://www.ciesin.org/datasets/unced/unced.html

Commission on Developing Countries and Global Change (1992), *For Earth's Sake* (Ottawa, Canada: International Development Research Centre).

Dunlap, R. E. (1992), 'From Environmental to Ecological Problems', in C. Calhoun and G. Ritzer (eds), *Social Problems* (New York: McGraw-Hill), pp. 1–32.

Dunlap, R. E., and Catton, W. R., Jr (1992–3), 'Toward an Ecological Sociology: The Development, Current Status and Probable Future of Environmental Sociology', *Annals of the International Institute of Sociology*, 3, pp. 263–84.

Dunlap, R. E., and Catton, W. R., Jr (1994), 'Struggling with Human Exemptionalism', *American Sociologist*, 25, pp. 5–30.

Escobar, A. (1992), 'Reflections on 'Development': Grassroots Approaches and Alternative Policies in the Third World', *Futures*, 24 (5), pp. 411–36.

Escobar, A. (1995), *Encountering Development: The Making and Unmaking of the Third World* (Princeton, NJ: Princeton University Press).

Garaudy, R. (1992), Foreword, in A. Nandy, *Traditions, Tyranny and Utopias: Essays in the Politics of Awareness* (Delhi, India: Oxford University Press; original work published 1987), pp. ix–xiii.

Hildyard, N. (1993), 'Foxes in Charge of the Chickens', in W. Sachs (ed.), *Global Ecology: A New Arena of Political Conflict* (London: Zed Books), pp. 22–35.

Lele, S. M. (1991), 'Sustainable Development: A Critical Review', *World Development*, 19, (6), pp. 607–21.

Martell, L. (1994), *Ecology and Society: An Introduction* (Cambridge, UK: Polity Press).

Miller, R. B. (1991), 'Social Science and the Challenge of Global Environmental Change', *International Social Science Journal*, 130, pp. 609–17.

Redclift, M. R. (1992), 'Sustainable Development and Global Environmental Change: Implications of a Changing Agenda', *Global Environmental Change*, 2 (1), pp. 32–42.

Redclift, M., and Benton, T. (eds) (1994), *Social Theory and the Global Environment* (London: Routledge).

Sachs, W. (ed.) (1993a), *Global Ecology: A New Arena of Political Conflict* (London: Zed Books).

Sachs, W. (1993b), 'Global Ecology and the Shadow of "Development"', in W. Sachs (ed.), *Global Ecology: A New Arena of Political Conflict* (London: Zed Books), pp. 3–21.

Shanmugaratnam, N. (1989), 'Development and Environment: A View from the South', *Race and Class*, 30 (3), pp. 13–30.

Shiva, V. (1987a), *Forestry Crisis and Forestry Myths: A Critical Review of 'Tropical Forests: A Call for Action'* (Penang, Malaysia: World Rainforest Movement).

Shiva, V. (1987b), 'Forests, Myths and the World Bank: A Critical Review of *Tropical Forests: A Call for Action*', *Ecologist*, 17, (4/5), pp. 142–9.

Shiva, V. (1993a), 'The Greening of the Global Reach', in W. Sachs (ed.), *Global Ecology: A New Arena of Political Conflict* (London: Zed Books), pp. 149–56.

Shiva, V. (1993b), 'International Controversy over Sustainable Forestry', in H. O. Bergesen and G. Parman (eds), *Green Globe Yearbook, 1993* (Oxford, UK: Oxford University Press), pp. 75–86.

Slater, D. (1992), 'On the Borders of Social Theory: Learning from Other Regions', *Environment and Planning D: Society and Space*, 10, pp. 307–27.

Smith, L. R. (1992), 'The Creation of Life Consciousness: Mediated Discourse and the Globalisation of the Environment', in C. Oravec and J. G. Cantrill (eds), *The Conference on the Discourse of Environmental Advocacy* (Salt Lake City, UT: University of Utah Humanities Centre), pp. 387–99.

Soto, A. (1992), 'The Global Environment: A Southern Perspective', *International Journal*, 47 (4), pp. 679–705.

Stern, P. C., Young, O. R., and Druckman, D. (eds) (1992), *Global Environmental Change: Understanding the Human Dimensions* (Washington, DC: National Academy Press).

Taylor, P. J., and Buttel, F. H. (1992), 'How Do We Know We Have Global Environmental Problems?' *Science and the Globalisation of Environmental Discourse*, 23 (3), pp. 405–16.

Thacher, P. S. (1991), 'Multilateral Cooperation and Global Change', *Journal of International Affairs*, 44, pp. 433–55.

Turner II, B. L., Kasperson, R. E., Meyer, W. B., Dow, K. M., Golding, D., Kasperson, J. X., Mitchell, R. C., and Ratick, S. J. (1990), 'Two Types of Global Environmental Change: Definitional and Spatial-Scale Issues in Their Human Dimensions', *Global Environmental Change*, 1, pp. 14–22.

WRI (World Resources Institute), UNEP (United Nations Environment Program) and UNDP (United Nations Development Program) (1990), *World Resources 1990–1991: A Report* (New York: Oxford University Press).

WRI (World Resources Institute), World Bank, and UNDP (United Nations Development Program) (1985), *Tropical Forests: A Call for Action* (vols 1–3) (Washington, DC: World Resources Institute).

Yearly, S. (1992), *The Green Case: A Sociology of Environmental Issues, Arguments and Politics* (London: Routledge).

Yearly, S. (1996), *Sociology, Environmentalism, Globalisation: Reinventing the Globe* (London: Sage Publications).

5 Governance and the Postnational Policy Process

ROGER SIBEON

The theoretical and methodological framework sketched below is a sensitizing perspective that, I suggest, is a suitable basis for developing a sociology of governance that critically engages the idea of globalization. The chapter falls into two parts, the first being a short description of the theoretical framework, the second focusing on globalization and the construction of a contemporary sociology of postnational governance. *Anti-reductionist sociology* is the name that I have given to a theoretical and methodological framework that I am currently developing (Sibeon 1997a; forthcoming) as part of an interest in the sociology of public policy and governance (Sibeon 1996, 1997b). In this sub-field there are good reasons for drawing not only on sociology but on recent work in the disciplines of political science and of public policy and policy analysis; this is reflected in the interdisciplinary flavour of the second part of the chapter.

ANTI-REDUCTIONIST SOCIOLOGY

Anti-reductionist sociology's starting point is critique of four theoretical deficiencies that feature all too frequently in social science. These are *reductionism*, a procedure that attempts – in the first or (Althusserian) last instance – to reduce the complexities of social life to a single unifying principle of explanation (Lyman and Scott, 1970, p. 16; Hindess, 1986a, 1986b) such as 'rational choice', 'capitalism', 'race', 'gender', 'post-Fordism', or 'globalization'; *essentialism*, which presupposes a necessary unity or homogeneity of social phenomena such as the state, law, education, or of taxonomic collectivities like 'women', 'men', 'black people', 'white people', or social classes; *reification*, which involves the attribution of agency to entities that are not actors or agents; and functional *teleology*, an expression which refers to illegitimate attempts to explain the causes of social phenomena in terms of their effects. Anti-reductionist sociology emerges via critique of these illegitimate forms of analysis, and employs critique as a basis for the development of a set of concepts that constitute an integrated theoretical and methodological framework. This process of critique and concept formation involves large-scale synthesis that draws critically on several theoretical schools. These include microsociology (Joas, 1987); Elias's (1978) figurational sociology; Berger's constructivist sociology (1969; Berger and Luckmann, 1972); Foucault's (1980) sociology of power, and post-Foucauldian conceptions of governance (Rose and Miller, 1992); actor–network theory and translation sociology as developed by Callon (1991) and Latour (1991), and Law's (1994) sociology of ordering; Hindess's (1986a, 1986b, 1988, 1996) anti-reductionist perspective, which refers to actors, forms of thought, interests, social relations, the conditions of action, and power; Giddens's ideas (1984, 1993) on time-space and his theory of structuration; notions of indeterminacy and time-space variability that until recently have been aligned with (but which are not exclusive to) postmodern theorizing; and recent work – pertaining to agency/structure and micro–macro – that forms part of the post-postmodern 'return to sociological theory' (McLennan, 1995) associated with, for example, Bryant (1995), Layder (1993, 1994), Holmwood (1996), Stones (1996) and Mouzelis (1991, 1995).

Significant concepts in anti-reductionist sociology are agency, structure (the conditions of action) and social chance; micro–macro; and time-space, together with social networks and the idea of materials and material-diffusion. Let us begin with *agency*. My conception of agency borrows from Hindess's (1986a, p. 115) definition of an actor as an entity that, in principle, is capable of formulating and acting upon decisions. Actors in terms of this definition may be individual human actors (whom I refer to as *individual actors*), and *social actors* (ibid.) or 'supra-individuals' (Harre, 1981, p. 141). The term 'social actor' refers to organizations; and also to families, committees and some other small-scale micro groups (Harre, 1981, p. 144, pp. 150–2). Thus, social actors are, for example, committees (such as the Cabinet, or a local tenants' association committee) and organizations of various kinds including, for instance, central government departments, private firms, local authorities, professional associations, the church, trade unions, and organized pressure groups. Taxonomic collectivities such as social classes, 'men', 'black people', 'white people', or 'women', are not actors: this is because they are social aggregates that 'have no identifiable means of taking decisions, let alone of acting on them' (Hindess 1988, p. 105). Nor are social movements actors, despite claims to the contrary by, for example, Touraine (1981) and Munck (1995).

Having defined agency, it should be observed that the 'conditions-of-action' (Betts, 1986, p. 41) or, put more simply, 'social conditions' (Hindess, 1986a, pp. 120–1) may be thought of as the element *structure* in terms of my conception of agency/structure. For example, in policy sectors such as, say, education, penal affairs, or health, the relevant conditions of action within which actors operate are likely to include political, bureaucratic and professional discourses; the degree of consensus or conflict within the policy sector; contingent events that have implications for the policy sector in question; the state of the economy; public opinion and the mass media; international capital flows, and so on. Social conditions/the conditions of action to a greater or lesser extent, influence actors' forms of thought, decisions and actions, and, depending on the circumstances, facilitate or constrain actors' capacities to achieve their objectives. The conditions of action are not structurally predetermined; empirically they should be investigated in terms of an interpretively 'open' (ontologically flexible) methodological orientation (Stones, 1996; Sibeon, 1997a, pp. 2–5). Implicit in these remarks is the view that social conditions are contingently produced/reproduced or contingently transformed or eliminated. However, as well as the concepts *agency* and *structure* (social conditions), sociology should employ the idea of *social chance*. This refers to contingent and indeterminate phenomena (Smith, 1993) that are unplanned and which – unlike phenomena that constitute 'structure' – do not extend widely across time and/or social space, though some chance happenings may become institutionalized across time and/or space and thereby become a part of 'structure' (Sibeon, 1997a, pp. 8–9). In effect, by social chance I mean the unplanned outcomes of *interactions* between agency, structure (social conditions), and social chance (Abrams, 1982, p. 273; Betts, 1986, p. 60): another way of putting this is to say that agency, structure, and social chance tend to have mutually shaping influences one upon the other (Sibeon, 1996; forthcoming).

A balanced analytical procedure in terms of agency/structure modifies conventional structural notions by drawing on the various theoretical components that are synthetically re-worked to constitute anti-reductionist sociology. One of these components that builds on formulations referred to earlier, is to do with use of both a *social integration* perspective (the study of agency/actors and social relations – whether co-operative or conflictual – between actors) and a *system integration* perspective (this refers to the study of relations between roles/positions and social institutions) (Mouzelis, 1995, 1997; Archer, 1996). Also of importance in my framework is micro–macro (Ritzer 1990) and the concept of 'social networks'. In anti-reductionist sociology, closely related to the idea of social networks is the concept *materials*. Following Callon and Latour (1981, p. 284) and Latour (1986), I employ the term 'materials' in a general way to include a wide variety of discourses (for example, religious, technical, professional, or political discourses or any combination of these), laws, rules, some types of resources, written materials, and policies, together with value expressions, social practices, and typifications of the kind that are ordinarily associated with the routines of everyday life. It is a short step from the idea of materials to the idea of *material diffusion* (Fararo, 1992): materials are potentially mobile phenomena that travel across social space and time (Braithwaite, 1994; Law, 1986, p. 32). The time-space distance that they 'travel' and the extent to which the material – for example, the spatial and temporal movement of material across a national or transnational policy network – remains the same (or is altered in some way, or perhaps killed-off) *during* the course of its travel, are not necessary effects of the social totality; rather, they are empirically contingent time-space outcomes of diachronic and synchronic interactions between agency, structure (social conditions/the conditions of action), and social chance.

TOWARDS A SOCIOLOGY OF POSTNATIONAL GOVERNANCE

It hardly need be said that analysis of postnational governance cannot properly be undertaken in isolation from the idea of 'globalization', which is examined below as a precursor to the later analysis of governance in a postnational context. In linking the idea of governance to globalizing processes let us begin by noting that the globalization thesis suggests that there is a high level of global connectedness of phenomena, a diminution of the significance of territorial boundaries, and a lessening of the significance of the national level of governance. However, some writers who are keen to promulgate the globalization thesis display a tendency to exaggerate the scale and/or the intensity of globalization; to assume, in reductionist and essentialist fashion, a social development (globalization) that is relatively unified and undifferentiated in terms of its impacts upon politics and policy; and to replace conceptions of agency and the time-space variability of structure (social conditions) by ontologically crude and reified notions of globalization as a massively 'objective', inexorable and irreversible process (Bretherton, 1996). A problem with approaches of this kind is that they are reductionist and essentialist in the terms defined earlier, and they also deploy a mixture of functional teleology and reification. Whether and in what form general social patterns (such as 'post-industrialism' or 'globalization') exist, and with what consequences, are empirical matters that cannot be decided on *a priori* theoretical grounds; such patterns are not structurally predetermined and their impacts on political institutions and upon policy sectors (education, health, social services, trade policy, and so on) may be variable and uneven (Williams, 1994). Thus there are good reasons – once reductionist, essentialist and reified theories are abandoned – for holding to the view that 'globalization' should be seen as a non-directional, interactive and open-ended period of social change (Albrow, 1996).

The conception of globalization set out above has an affinity with my approach to the study of postnational governance. First, however, it is necessary to say something about governance *per se*, this being a concept that conventionally has national rather than transnational connotations. The expression 'government' is commonly associated with sovereign nation-states and the rights of *governments* to determine the conduct of certain activities within their geographical territories and to carry out, for example, administrative tasks or to delegate those tasks to various agencies that are closely controlled and co-ordinated from 'the centre'. In contrast, *governance* is the management of networks that are comprised of a variety of state and non-state actors (the latter include, for example, private firms, voluntary-sector organizations, interest groups, trade associations, and professional bodies). Under conditions of governance, rather than government, the element of management is more in the nature of a negotiable and interactive process of 'steering' than of top-down management control exercised from a central position (Kickert, 1993). The relative shift away from traditional, hierarchical forms of state-centred public administration is a factor in political scientists' increased interest in 'policy network' analysis (M. J. Smith 1993); put at its simplest, a policy network is an array of state and non-state actors – including social ('organizational') actors – who jointly participate in policy formulation and its implementation. The growing salience of governance is a reflection of increased complexity in the policy environment, including politico-cultural transition away from conventional binary thought (state/ society, plan/market, public/private) and movement towards governance networks that are modifying traditional forms of the state/civil society distinction. Governance in the sense that I have just described has in recent years become a feature of public policy and public administration *within* nation-states; it has also, however, become a feature of transnational governance. Globally there is some movement away from state-dominated service provision, and transition toward a 'mixed economy' of public policy in which state, voluntary-sector, and commercial actors interact in the planning and delivery of what in the past had often been regarded as essentially 'state' services (electricity, water, telecommunications, social services, and so on). McGrew uses the expression 'global governance' (1997, p. 15) to describe formal and informal linkages between transnational 'governmental' organizations such as the United Nations and the European Union, and non-governmental actors. McGrew's account of *global* governance should, however, be tempered by an awareness that world-regional groupings of states or 'blocs' are themselves forms of (transnational but not necessarily global) governance, and these blocs – such as the European Union (EU), the North American Free Trade Area (NAFTA), and the Asia Economic Co-operation Forum (APEC) – are in some respects a defensive *reaction* against globalization, a reaction designed to protect the countries in question against the vagaries of global competition (Imber, 1997).

In the remainder of the chapter, drawing on the preceding observations on globalization and governance and the theoretical framework outlined earlier, a part of my concern will be to show that recent advances – made by, in particular, political scientists and public-policy academics – in the study of European postnational governance are available to those whose interest is the study of postnational governance in non-European and global contexts. In Europe, the European Union (EU) is, of course, a key supranational organization that has significant implications for the European policy process (Meny et al., 1996) and for the relation of Europe to other world-regional blocs (Smith, 1996). However, in acknowledging transnational tendencies, we should avoid exaggerated claims that national-level policy making is no longer significant. The nation-state continues to be an important element within the policy process and this is as true of the formulation of foreign policy (Jones, 1991) as it is for 'domestic' policy. To say that the issues which enter the policy agenda have an increasingly global dimension to them, is not to say that policy decisions and their implementation are necessarily global: 'The policy agenda may be global, but decision-making and delivery remain national' (Parsons, 1995, p. 235). For example, the European Union is not entirely supranational; as Schmidt (1996) observes, numerous researchers have indicated that while the policy process in some European policy sectors (for example, telecommunications) is largely supranational, in other European policy sectors (such as electricity) the policy process is to a large extent intergovernmental. Globally the reality is that relatively few transnational organizations are available at the decision-making and implementation stages of the policy process (Parsons, 1995, pp. 242–3). Let me provide an illustration of the point that Parsons is making. Given the existence of nation-states' different cultural and political traditions and un-identical economic circumstances, and given that national actors play a part in shaping welfare policy and its implementation, it is hardly surprising that there should be major differences between, for example, the Japanese, Swedish and British welfare states (for an analysis of these differences, see Gould, 1993).

In acknowledging that globalization has implications for governance, it is important to recognize that as well as *transnational* and *national* policy dimensions of the kind that I have just referred to, it is also necessary to consider *subnational* governance. The idea of locale and spatial variation, as well as being part of postmodernists' predilection for 'local narratives' (Krokidas, 1993, p. 534), is increasingly featured in empirical studies of subnational spatial variation (for example, variation from one local authority to another) in the development and implementation of policies, including local policies developed in response to transnational socio-economic processes associated with de-industrialization, unemployment, and urban deprivation (Harloe et al., 1990). An aspect of the contemporary emphasis accorded to locale, spatial variation, and subnational governance, is the growing recognition of the significance of regions in the policy process (Amin and Thrift, 1995); in Europe, this is reflected in the EU's commitment to the development of regional policy (Bew and Meehan, 1994).

It should be clear from the foregoing that there are problems both with traditional state-centric orientations and with crude 'globalization' approaches that emphasize only the transnational or that exaggerate its significance. In contrast, an anti-reductionist sociology of *postnational* governance recognizes the importance of subnational, national, and transnational policy processes. These levels of policy process are not embedded in a unified social totality. They are relatively autonomous – that is, events and processes at one level do not determine happenings at another level – although there may well be contingently sustained linkages between them. The operation of multiple levels of the policy process is further complicated by the increasing emphasis on policy networks as mechanisms of governance. For instance, transnational European policy networks – of the kind composed of subnational actors (for example, local authorities or regional bodies) from each of the member states – are to some extent becoming more autonomous of national governments, although the extent of any such autonomy is in part a function of whether the transnational networks in question are tightly integrated policy communities, or relatively loosely-knit issue networks composed of a large number of actors none of whom have acquired a great deal of political influence (M. J. Smith, 1993). Indeed, European governance is becoming considerably more intricate in ways that I do not have the space to explore fully here (Richardson, 1996a, 1996b). Complex combinations of 'vertical' and 'lateral' relationships and cross-sectoral interactions are increasingly becoming a feature of European postnational governance. In Europe the idea of separate hierarchical 'tiers' or 'levels' of government (local, regional, national, European) is being 'complemented and challenged' (Bennington and Taylor, 1993, p. 129) by forms of governance which evolve from postnational policy networks that coalesce around overlapping and interlocking 'spheres' of governance as well as separate 'tiers' (levels) of government (ibid.).

It is partly the growing interest in transnational governance that has resulted in a steadily expanding literature on patterns of European governance. The development of the European Union has been a special factor in this. In looking beyond Europe, a distinction that is not altogether different from the previously mentioned supranational and intergovernmental forms of European governance, is the distinction between corporative and regulative methods of policy co-ordination. Genschel and Werle (1993), in their account of international governance relating to telecommunications, adopt Common's (1961) distinction between corporative and regulative modes of policy co-ordination. The corporative mode is where nation-states set up a transnational organization and transfer certain national sovereign rights to it, so that states agree to be legally bound by decisions of the transnational actor. The transnational actor, in other words, is empowered to act on behalf of the states. While the corporative model tends to lead, at least within the policy sector in question, towards a structure that exhibits some of the features of what might be called a transnational 'hierarchy', the regulative mode, though it might involve the creation of a new transnational organization for adminis- trative, legal, or advice-giving purposes, does not rest on a transfer of sovereign rights to a new supranational organization; rather, a set of formally binding rules is agreed among states, rather like an inter- national law or treaty. The regulative mode of international co- ordination within a particular policy domain or issue area is very often referred to as an international 'regime'.

Undoubtedly, the notion of a 'regime' has some analytical value (Thrift, 1994). However, for reasons referred to earlier in the chapter, a focus on transnational policy networks affords a particularly fruitful method for investigating postnational governance. At the transnational level, some policy spheres (for example, international financial systems) are more highly globalized than others. This is illustrated in Thrift's (1994) account of international financial systems. I am unable here to engage fully with Thrift's interesting and wide-ranging paper. However, I shall mention one of his empirical interpretations, which concerns not only globalized networks but also two theoretical foci – micro–macro and time-space – that I mentioned in the first section of the chapter. Thrift (1994) convincingly demonstrates that international systems based largely on electronic communication and the rapid global diffusion of large amounts of data, do not necessarily result in a drastic lessening of the importance of actors, nor of localized social relations which include face-to-face relations in micro-settings. On the one hand, it is true that the international financial system – within which global electronic networks have become increasingly important – has to some extent become 'disembedded from place' (1994, pp. 25–7). But on the other hand, transnational financial networks generate a vast amount of data and also generate a range of meanings surrounding the possible interpretation of those data, so that, paradoxically, inter- personal exchanges in meetings to negotiate, discuss, interpret, and act upon the data, assume special importance (ibid.). This refers not only to ongoing operations; in special circumstances, face-to-face contact is necessary so as to enable the relevant actors to respond quickly to events (1994). These locales and meeting places – which may be thought of, in Law's (1994, p. 104) terminology, as 'ordering centres' that process information – are sometimes 'cosmopolitan' (Thrift 1994, p. 26), with participants from many different countries. Notice that there is here a version of a micro–macro dialectic in which the cogni- tive and decisional outcomes of these meetings feed back into the 'disembedded' electronic space that is associated with the international financial communication system (ibid.). The idea that there is a dialectical relation between policy materials and their social contexts, also relates to an observation that was made in the first section of the chapter, where I briefly referred to the relative spatial mobility and temporal durabilities of the various materials that circulate across locales and across networks: although I cannot pursue this here, it is worth noting that insufficient attention has been given to the development of conceptual and methodological tools for the purpose of examining material diffusion processes (Fararo, 1992) that operate across transnational contexts (Braithwaite 1994).

CONCLUDING OBSERVATIONS

Investigation of postnational governance in the explicitly anti-reductionist terms set out earlier, is not very far advanced. A number of writers involved in the study of globalized politics and governance have in varying degrees addressed at least some of the issues discussed in this chapter; see, for example, Albrow (1996), Axford (1995), Held (1995), Hirst and Thompson (1996). Some of these studies are excellent in their own terms. However, they are not, at least in terms of the development of anti-reductionist conceptual schemes designed for the particular purpose of engaging in analysis of policy processes under the highly complex conditions of postnational governance, as advanced as the work undertaken by writers concerned specifically with the European policy process (see Anderson and Eliassen, 1993; Meny et al., 1996; Richardson, 1996b). This state of affairs is perhaps a reflection of the unusual nature of the European Union and the almost unique complexity of the multi-tiered and multi-sphere forms of European governance that I alluded to earlier, and a reflection of the responses of policy theoreticians and researchers to that complexity. In regard, then, to the investigation of globalization and governance, I suggest that the approaches referred to earlier with reference to studies of European governance have wide application in the study of postnational governance across a range of global contexts. In these respects I suggest, also, that the theoretical and methodological framework that I call *anti-reductionist sociology*, though still relatively underdeveloped (Sibeon, 1996, forthcoming), is potentially capable of making a significant contribution to the development of a contemporary sociology of postnational governance.

REFERENCES

Abrams, P. (1982), *Historical Sociology* (Ithaca: Cornell University Press).

Albrow, M. (1996), *The Global Age* (Cambridge: Polity).

Amin, A., and Thrift, N. (1995), 'Institutional Issues for the European Regions: From Markets and Plans to Socioeconomics and Powers of Association', *Economy and Society*, 24 (1), pp. 41–66.

Anderson, S. S., and Eliassen, K. (eds) (1993), *Making Policy in Europe: The Europeification of National Policy-making* (London: Sage).

Archer, M. (1996), 'Social Integration and System Integration: Developing the Distinction', *Sociology*, 30 (4), pp. 679–99.

Axford, B. (1995), *The Global System: Economics, Politics and Culture* (Cambridge: Polity).

Bennington, J., and Taylor, M. (1993), 'Changes and Challenges Facing the UK Welfare State in the Europe of the 1990s', *Policy and Politics*, 21 (2), pp. 121–34.

Berger, P. (1969), *The Social Reality of Religion* (London: Faber and Faber).

Berger, P., and Luckmann, T. (1972), *The Social Construction of Reality* (Harmondsworth: Penguin).

Betts, K. (1986), 'The Conditions of Action, Power, and the Problem of Interests', *The Sociological Review*, 34 (1), pp. 39–64.

Bew, P., and Meehan, E. (1994), 'Regions and Borders: Controversies in Northern Ireland about the European Union', *Journal of European Public Policy*, 1 (1), pp. 95–113).

Braithwaite, J. (1994), 'A Sociology of Modelling and the Politics of Empowerment', *British Journal of Sociology*, 45 (3), pp. 444–79.

Bretherton, C. (1996), 'Introduction: Global Politics in the 1990s', in C. Bretherton and G. Ponton (eds), *Global Politics: An Introduction* (Oxford: Blackwell).

Bryant, C. (1995), *Practical Sociology: Post-empiricism and the Reconstruction of Theory and Application* (Cambridge: Polity).

Callon, M. (1991), 'Techno-economic Networks and Irreversibility', in J. Law (ed.), *A Sociology of Monsters: Essays on Power, Technology and Domination* (London: Routledge).

Callon, M., and Latour, B. (1981), 'Unscrewing the Big Leviathan: How Actors Macro-structure Reality and How Sociologists Help them to Do So', in K. Knorr-Cetina and A. V. Cicourel (eds), *Advances in Social Theory and Methodology: Towards an Integration of Micro- and Macro-Sociology* (London: Routledge).

Commons, J. R. (1961), *Institutional Economics: Its Place in Political Economy* (Madison: University of Wisconsin Press).

Elias, N. (1978), *What is Sociology?* (London: Hutchinson).

Fararo, T. J. (1992), *The Meaning of General Theoretical Sociology: Tradition and Formalization* (Cambridge: Cambridge University Press).

Foucault, M. (1980), *Power/Knowledge* (New York: Pantheon).

Genschel, P., and Werle, R. (1993), 'From National Hierarchies to International Standardization: Modal Changes in the Governance of Telecommunications', *Journal of Public Policy*, 13 (3), pp. 203–25.

Giddens, A. (1984), *The Constitution of Society* (Cambridge: Polity).

Giddens, A. (1993), *New Rules of Sociological Method* (2nd edn, Cambridge: Polity).

Gould, A. (1993), *Capitalist Welfare Systems: A Comparison of Japan, Britain and Sweden* (London and New York: Longman).

Harloe, M., Pickvance, C., and Urry, J. (eds) (1990), *Place, Policy and Politics: Do Localities Matter?* (London: Unwin Hyman).

Harre, R. (1981), 'Philosophical Aspects of the Micro–Macro Problem', in K. C. Knorr-Cetina and A. V. Cicourel (eds), *Advances in Social Theory and Methodology: Towards an Integration of Micro- and Macro-Sociologies* (London: Routledge).

Held, D. (1995), *Democracy and the Global Order: From the Modern State to Cosmopolitan Governance* (Cambridge: Polity).

Hindess, B. (1986a), 'Actors and Social Relations', in M. L. Wardell and S. P. Turner (eds), *Sociological Theory in Transition* (London: Allen and Unwin).

Hindess, B. (1986b), 'Interests in Political Analysis', in J. Law (ed.), *Power, Action and Belief: A New Sociology of Knowledge?* (London: Routledge).

Hindess, B. (1988), *Choice, Rationality and Social Theory* (London: Unwin Hyman).

Hindess, B. (1996), *Discourses of Power: From Hobbes to Foucault* (Oxford: Blackwell).

Hirst, P., and Thompson, G. (1996), *Globalization in Question* (Cambridge: Polity).

Holmwood, J. (1996), *Founding Sociology? Talcott Parsons and the Idea of General Theory* (London and New York: Longman).

Imber, M. (1997), 'Geo-governance without Democracy? Reforming the UN System', in A. McGrew (ed.), *The Transformation of Democracy?* (Cambridge: Polity).

Joas, H. (1987), 'Symbolic Interactionism', in A. Giddens and J. Turner (eds), *Social Theory Today* (Cambridge: Polity).

Jones, W. S. (1991), *The Logic of International Relations* (7th edn, New York: Harper Collins).

Kickert, W. (1993), 'Complexity, Governance and Dynamics: Conceptual Explorations of Public Network Management', in J. Kooiman (ed.), *Modern Governance: New Government–Society Interactions* (London: Sage).

Krokidas, A. (1993), Review, *Sociology*, 27 (3) pp. 534–6.

Latour, B. (1986), 'The Powers of Association', in J. Law (ed.), *Power, Action and Belief: A New Sociology of Knowledge?* (London: Routledge).

Latour, B. (1991), 'Technology is Science Made Durable', in J. Law (ed.), *A Sociology of Monsters: Essays on Power, Technology and Domination* (London: Routledge).

Law, J. (1986), 'On Power and its Tactics: A View from the Sociology of Science', *The Sociological Review*, 34 (1), pp. 1–38.

Law, J. (1994), *Organizing Modernity* (Oxford: Blackwell).

Layder, D. (1993), *New Strategies in Social Research: An Introduction and Guide* (Oxford: Polity).

Layder, D. (1994), *Understanding Social Theory* (London: Sage).

Lyman, S., and Scott, M. (1970), *A Sociology of the Absurd* (New York: Appleton Century Crofts).

McGrew, A. G. (1997), 'Globalization and Territorial Democracy', in A. G. McGrew (ed.), *The Transformation of Democracy?* (Cambridge: Polity).

McLennan, G. (1995), 'After Postmodernism: Back to Sociological Theory?', *Sociology*, 29 (1), pp. 117–32.

Meny, Y., Muller, P., and Quermonne, J-L. (1996), 'Introduction', in Y. Meny, P. Muller, and J-L. Quermonne (eds), *Adjusting to Europe: The Impact of the European Union on National Institutions and Policies* (London: Routledge).

Mouzelis, N. (1991), *Back to Sociological Theory: The Social Construction of Social Orders* (London: Macmillan).

Mouzelis, N. (1995), *Sociological Theory: What Went Wrong? Diagnosis and Remedies* (London: Routledge).

Mouzelis, N. (1997), 'Social and System Integration: Lockwood, Habermas, Giddens', *Sociology*, 31 (1), pp. 111–19.

Munck, G. (1995), 'Actor Formation, Social Co-ordination, and Political Strategy: Some Conceptual Problems in the Study of Social Movements', *Sociology*, 29 (4), pp. 667–85.

Parsons, W. (1995), *Public Policy* (Aldershot: Edward Elgar).

Richardson, J. (1996a), 'Policy-making in the EU: Interests, Ideas and Garbage Cans of Primeval Soup', in J. Richardson (ed.), *European Union: Power and Policy-making* (London: Routledge).

Richardson, J. (ed.) (1996b), *European Union: Power and Policy-making* (London: Routledge).

Ritzer, G. (1990), 'Macro–Micro Linkages in Sociology: Applying a Metatheoretical Tool', in G. Ritzer (ed.), *Frontiers of Social Theory: The New Syntheses* (New York: Columbia University Press).

Rose, N., and Miller, P. (1992), 'Political Power Beyond the State: Problematics of Government', *British Journal of Sociology*, 43 (2), pp. 173–205.

Schmidt, S. (1996), 'Sterile Debates and Dubious Generalizations: European Integration Theory Tested by Telecommunications and Electricity', *Journal of Public Policy*, 16 (3), pp. 233–71.

Sibeon, R. (1996), *Contemporary Sociology and Policy Analysis: The New Sociology of Public Policy* (London: Kogan Page and Tudor).

Sibeon, R. (1997a), 'Power Agency/Structure and Micro–Macro: An Excursus in Anti-reductionist Sociology', paper presented to British Sociological Association Annual Conference, April, University of York.

Sibeon, R. (1997b), 'Anti-reductionist Sociology and the Study of Postnational Governance', paper presented to Third European Conference of the European Sociological Association, August, University of Essex.

Sibeon, R. (forthcoming), *Sociological Theory Today*.

Smith, M. (1993), 'Changing Sociological Perspectives on Chance', *Sociology*, 27 (3), pp. 513–31.

Smith, M. (1996), 'The EU as an International Actor', in J. R. Richardson (ed.), *European Union: Power and Policy-making* (London: Routledge).

Smith, M. J. (1993), *Pressure, Power and Policy: State Autonomy and Policy Networks in Britain and the United States* (London: Harvester).

Stones, R. (1996), *Sociological Reasoning: Towards a Post-modern Sociology* (London: Macmillan).

Thrift, N. (1994), 'A Phantom State? International Money, Electronic Networks, and Global Cities', paper presented to the Centre for Social Theory and Comparative History, June, UCLA.

Touraine, A. (1981), *The Voice and the Eye: An Analysis of Social Movements* (Cambridge: Cambridge University Press).

Williams, F. (1994), 'Social Relations, Welfare and the Post-Fordism Debate', in R. Burrows and B. Loader (eds), *Towards a Post-Fordist Welfare State?* (London: Routledge).

Part III
Synergetic/Discrepant Differences

6 New Orientalisms, Global Capitalism, and the Politics of Synergetic Differences:
Discursive Construction of Trade Relations between the USA, Japan and the East Asian NICs
NGAI-LING SUM

INTRODUCTION

Edward Said has enriched our understanding of 'othering' by insisting that the relationship between the Orient and the Occident has been produced as part of a discourse articulated by Western colonial powers – a discourse 'of power, of domination, of varying degrees of a complex hegemony' (1978, p. 5). Following Said, some scholars in first-generation critical international relations[1] have examined Western foreign-policy discourses about non-Western others through such binaries as 'East–West', 'Occident–Orient' ('West–rest'), 'insider–outsider', and 'order–threat'. Drawing on an 'Asian-Pacific' case study and an articulation of trade-competitiveness-development discourses in the post-Cold War era between the USA, Japan and the East Asian newly-industrializing countries (hereafter NICs), this chapter proposes a second-generation approach that criticizes and re-examines the unclear boundaries implied in these dichotomies. It thereby broadens the range of 'others' to be examined, highlights the variety of discourses deployed to construct difference and otherness, and analyses the politics of difference involved in these various constructions. In particular, it suggests three 'new kinds of Orientalism' that go beyond the alleged 'clashes of civilizations' between 'East' and 'West'. I also re-introduce structure into what is predominantly an agent-centred mode of analysis. Thus I consider: the structural context(s) in which particular discursive formation(s) become dominant, the structural and discursive selectivities which influence how the narrative possibilities inscribed in different discursive formations

99

are re-invented/hybridized, and how social forces tend to relocate themselves in the 'politics of synergetic differences'. It is these structural and strategic moments operating in the current globalization–regionalization dialectic that allow trans-border identities and strategies to emerge and react back on that dialectic.

DIFFERENT TYPES OF OTHER AND THREE 'NEW KINDS OF ORIENTALISM'

The politics of difference begins with the explicit and implicit construction of boundaries between 'West and rest' or 'self and other'. These demarcate nation(s) and communities on the inside from real or potential enemies and, more generally, 'others' on the outside (Walker, 1995, p. 305). The latter are depicted as different in terms of discourses of inequality, danger, threat, and so on. Such discourses are important referents in examining trade strategy, economic/political development, race, gender, class, religion, etc., enabling others to be portrayed as 'unfair', 'dangerous', or 'inferior'. Going beyond such binary views of inside/outside, this chapter argues that not only are there *different types of other on the outside*, there can also be *different types of other on the inside*. This argument blurs some of the demarcations beloved of critics of Orientalism and casts doubt on the simple 'othering' of the Orient by those in the Occident. It demands closer attention to internal/external differentiations within and across discursive fields and to the micro-physics of power enabling global and regional hegemonic viewpoints to maintain their influence through the continual re-articulation of insider/outsider distinctions. Indeed the very plurality and heterogeneity of these distinctions may be a source of strategic flexibility because it extends the repertoire of legitimate actions and alliances. These points can be illustrated from at least three 'new kinds of Orientalism' evident in the discursive construction of trade relations between the USA, Japan and the East Asian NICs.

Types of Other

The two main types of other are outsiders and 'internal others'. They may be adjudged equal or unequal. Equal outsiders are deemed close to the hegemon's time/space and are not differentiated in inferior–superior terms. Few cases exist. One example would be US–EU trade-negotiation discourse: this seldom deploys an essentializing evaluative rhetoric even as it criticizes specific trade practices. This case is irrelevant to 'new Orientalism'. Far more prevalent are discourses about unequal outsiders. They are otherized through evaluative 'superior–inferior' and 'fair–unfair' cultural–textual schemata and categories of difference. This subtype occurs in a first kind of 'new Orientalism' found in America's 'neo-liberal' trade discourse with Japan in the post-Cold War era.

'Internal others' are defined as 'others' in terms of hegemonic discourses prevailing in the social formation to which they allegedly belong. Equal 'internal others' are deemed to occupy the same time/space as the hegemon and their difference is seen in relatively non-antagonistic terms. They draw on the same discursive repertoire as the hegemonic centre but offer alternative accounts on similar issues by inverting the otherizing cultural categories/explanations promoted by the latter. Unequal 'internal others' may be seen (or see themselves) as within the self-defined time/space of the (Eastern) hegemon. Their inequality is constructed through 'superior–inferior' and 'leader–follower' categories of the latter. In general, where the 'otherized' (whether internal or external) exist as real subjects (rather than as figments of fevered hegemonic imaginations), there are significant incentives for social forces to reposition themselves strategically and/or turn such 'otherizations' to their advantage. These types of 'internal otherness' are illustrated with case studies on the second and third 'new kinds of orientalism': respectively, the US's equal 'internal others' and their idea of 'economic nationalism', and Japan's unequal 'internal others' and its re-invention of the 'flying geese' discourse (see Table 6.1).

Three 'New Kinds of Orientalism'

After the Cold War, 'discourses of danger' have been re-deployed from the geo-political to the geo-economic sphere. They are now voiced in international trade, competitiveness, and development relations. In this context, 'neo-liberal' trade discourses about the USA and Japan can be interpreted as a technology of power for 'otherizing' Japan and defining it as deviating from the 1980s' 'universal free trade' model. 'Neo-liberalism' was first championed by Reagan and Thatcher and by US-dominated organizations such as the World Bank and IMF. It eulogizes market-friendly development, minimal states, and free trade, and identifies these principles with the USA. Thus the

Table 6.1　*Types of other and 'new kinds of Orientalism'*

	Equal	Unequal
'External Other'	External and close to the western hegemon's self-defined time/space (US–EU trade dialogue)	External but inferior to western hegemon's time/space (*Old Orientalism and first 'new kind'*)
'Internal Other'	Same time/space as the Western hegemon	Inferior and within the (Eastern) hegemon's self-defined time/space
	Non-antagonistic alternatives by inverting the otherizing cultural categories (*Second 'new kind of Orientalism'*)	(*Third 'new kind of orientalism'*)

'free trade' discourse was deployed under Reagan and Bush to other-ize 'external others' (e.g., Japan) as acting 'unfairly'. They are now entrenched in GATT–WTO discourses. Such discourses illustrate a first kind of 'new Orientalism'. This involves *a set of economic narratives centred around the prevailing values/norms, governmentalities, and time/space of the US hegemon and deployed to otherize powers which are derogated as different and somehow unequal (e.g., because they are culturally inferior, less 'rational', less 'modern', or marginal to American interests and spheres of influence)*. Thus Japanese economic and political institutions and practices are not only seen as different from those in the USA but are also regarded as 'unfair' and antagonistic to US interests. Geo-economic narratives of 'free trade' thereby serve to impose new (Western) standards of economic 'rationality' on (Eastern) others to enhance the growth of an open/multilateral global/regional trading system. And, until these 'others' (including Japan) modify their trading and organizational practices, they are condemned for their 'unfair' behaviour.

This 'neo-liberal trade' narrative was challenged in the mid-1980s by a group of equal 'internal others' in the USA. Dubbed as 'revisionist', they offer a very different account of US–Japan relations. They construct 'the American Self/Japanese Other' in and through propositions such as 'Japan is not Western' or 'Japan as threat'; and claim that 'American decline can be reinvigorated by economic nationalism' or, later, by 'techno-nationalism'. Given the mass of literature (both sophisticated and populist) on this topic, this chapter focuses on those the *Wall Street Journal* (1990) called 'the Gang of Four' (Johnson, van Wolferen, Fallows, and Prestowitz). Their work illustrates a second kind of 'new Orientalism'. This involves *heterodox economic–cultural discourses centred around the values/norms, procedural and substantive rationalities, and time/space of the West's equal 'internal others', which are deployed to interpret relevant 'external others' (e.g., Japan) not only as different but also as threatening the values, interests, and superiority of the hegemon on its own ground.* Of particular interest here is how these particular new-Orientalist discourses have been extended and re-combined in Japan and the USA alike to underpin new trade-policy alliances and strategies.

Japan has selectively integrated the heterodox economic discourses of US scholars into its own self-understanding. Thus a body of 'anti-bashing' literature counteracts 'neo-liberalism' and its critique of Japanese trade practices. More recently, Johnson's 'developmental state' narrative has been remapped onto Japanese time and space. One could even claim that this amounts to a kind of 're-invented Orientalism'. A similar selective articulation of heterodox or 'revisionist' themes has occurred in the USA. This is especially clear in the re-articulation of 'trade', 'high-tech Japan' and, later, 'competitiveness' discourses promoted by Tyson (1992). These are used to redefine the American 'self' (reflected in the debate over 'who is us?') in the face of Japanese threats to American prosperity. Her idea of 'managed trade' signifies a defensive 'self' that is seen from the veiwpoint of the high-tech sectors. This new narrative has resonated in the Clinton administration and was consolidated as part of his regime of economic truth at least up to 1993.

Around the same time as the USA began constructing 'Japan as threat', the 1985 Plaza Accord between G5 ministers of finance engineered a massive revaluation of the yen and reduced Japanese price competitiveness in export markets. In response Japan sought to reposition itself in East Asia not just in terms of deepening the intra-regional division of labour but also through the selective re-interpretation of Akamatsu's idea of 'flying geese'.[2] Thus Japanese research institutes (such as JETRO amd Nomura) now suggest that Japan can lead the flight of other East Asian NICs to industrial success. This illustrates a third kind of 'new Orientalism'. This involves *a development discourse centred around the prevailing values/norms, governmentalities, and time/space of Japan that assigns a follower identity to the East's unequal 'internal others' (e.g., NICs) – claiming that their interests are best realized by entering the Japan-led framework as junior partners.* This discourse creates Eastern unequal 'internal others' and leads to a cultural otherization of East Asian economies reminiscent of Western Orientalism.

A STRATEGIC–RELATIONAL APPROACH TO THREE 'NEW KINDS OF ORIENTALISM' IN THE POST-COLD WAR ERA

Structural and Strategic Contexts of the Post-Cold War Era and US–Japan Trade Conflicts

Two broad trends in the global political and economic order help to contextualize the three 'new kinds of Orientalism'. First, the end of the Cold War and disintegration of the Soviet Bloc has changed the geo-political security game from a bipolar to a multipolar one. In East Asia, Japan and China, respectively, the current and emerging regional hegemons have joined the sole remaining global hegemon (the USA) in an effort to redefine their geo-political identities and interests. Secondly, in the increasingly dominant geo-economic sphere, an acceleration of globalization/regionalization has reinforced tendencies towards global disorder. This chapter concentrates on changes in geo-economic relations between the US, Japan, and East Asian NICs, and their links to key textual redefinitions of their identity and interests.

Previously, American preoccupation with the Cold War (and maintaining anti-communist cohesion within the American alliance system) led it to overlook key aspects of its partners' trade and investment practices. Thus, whilst Western Europe was generally expected to comply with free-trade principles of the US-led GATT regime, certain exceptions were made in East Asia as part of the USA's geo-political strategy for the region. Although Japan entered GATT and has developed intense trade and investment relations with the USA, geo-political considerations led the American government to resist domestic business pressure and exclude Japan from the demand for reciprocal trading concessions. Indeed, despite the increasing imbalance in US–Japanese trade relations, there was little serious threat to such exemptions until the 1980s.

This was when the more general threat to US economic dominance entailed in the changing global economy led to increasing American concern about US–Japanese economic relations – especially as Japan's increasing success in re-inserting itself in the world economy was combined with America's declining capacity to adjust to global competition. Accordingly, concerns were raised about Japanese trade barriers (e.g., the domestic and overseas role of *keiretsu*) and growing trade imbalances – which saw the 1980 deficit of US$ 7 billion grow by 1994 to some US$ 55 billion (see Table 6.2).

The Structural/Discursive Selectivities and First/Second 'New Kinds of Orientalism' in the USA

These trade imbalances prompted conflicts. The 'Japanese other' was redefined from the early 1980s onwards and 'reciprocity' was demanded. The new discourse went beyond the otherization of Japan under Nixon (Leaver, 1989, pp. 430–2). For, uniquely, it links Japan to the very economic identity of the USA and its need to reposition itself in the new global economy. This is reflected in various artistic terms (e.g., 'multilateralism', 'liberalization', 'developmental state', 'technology policy') that can be flexibly re-deployed to construct both the 'Japanese other' and the 'American Self'. This section explores these re-interpretations in terms of the first and second 'new kinds of Orientalism'.

Table 6.2   *USA's commodity trade deficits with Japan (US$ billion)*

1987	52.1
1988	47.6
1989	45.0
1990	38.0
1991	38.5
1992	43.7
1993	50.2
1994	55.0

Source: US Department of Commerce, Survey of Current Business.

The structural/discursive selectivities of the multilateral trading order: first 'new kind of Orientalism'

The GATT/WTO regime privileges 'neo-liberalism' in defining a 'fair' multilateral trading order. In the 1980s, the multilateral regime was disrupted by a relative decline of US domination in world trade. Growing trade deficits with Japan prompted Congressional and wider social disquiet about 'unfairness'. This was articulated in terms of 'restrictive practices' (on agricultural products) and 'structural barriers' maintained by Japanese firms to protect domestic markets (such as the *keiretsu* system, which restricts entry by foreign firms). Such discourses not only criticize Japan as 'unfair' but do so in an 'otherizing' manner. They contrast Japanese conduct with a (newly constructed) American 'liberal self' and call for 'national fairness', 'reciprocity' and 'level playing fields' in trade relations with the USA (Kudrle, 1995, pp. 168–71).

Of interest during this period is how the USA has strategically connected its new-found 'liberal self' with protectionist tendencies in its trade relations with Japan. This contradictory 'American liberal-protectionist self' can be seen in the promotion since the 1980s of a policy of 'managed trade' (i.e., negotiated market shares). This includes two sets of international legal practices. The first concerns the management of exports (e.g., 'voluntary export restraints' (VERs) and 'anti-dumping provisions'); and the second covers the expansion of (US) markets abroad (e.g., 'voluntary import expansions' (VIEs) and the 'Super 301' unfair-trade law – Sjolander, 1994, p. 46). This articulation of 'protectionism' with neo-liberal 'unfairness' creates a symbolic and material space in which Japan can be 'otherized' as departing from 'liberal' standards; but, at the same time, it permits the USA to normalize its 'protectionist' practices. Examples of practices targeted at different sectors of Japanese industry under the Bush and Reagan administrations are:

1982	Automobile VERs
1984	Steel VERs
1985	Machine tool VERs
1986	Semiconductor VIEs
1988	'Super and Special 301s'

The 'otherization' of Japan as 'unfair' can be seen in the Bush administration's upgrading of 'Section 301' (i.e., Chapter 1 of Title III of the

US Trade Act of 1974) to become 'Super 301'. Section 301 was intended to deal with complaints about goods; Super 301 was extended to include a non-exhaustive list of US-defined 'unfair' practices (e.g., workers' rights and inadequate anti-competitive policy regimes). In May 1989 President Bush, under serious Congressional pressure, invoked 'Super 301' to define Japan as 'trading unfairly' in supercomputers, telecommunication satellites, and wood products.

This US redefinition and broadening of possible areas of 'unfairness' can be seen as *the first 'new kind of orientalism'*. It rests on economic narratives centred around 'fair/unfair' trade policy/practices unilaterally defined by the USA to serve the interests of the 'American self' against the 'Japanese other'. It provides a discursive framework and sanctions for the USA to condemn countries which are supposedly departing from 'liberal' standards; and it legitimates the American self-image as 'liberal-protectionist'. This paradoxical (if not self-contradictory) identity is evident in the view of Senator Max Baucus, Chair of the International Trade Subcommittee of the Senate Finance Committee, that: '[o]ur trading partners must realize that the US is firmly committed to opening markets. ... If we cannot open those markets through the GATT, we will use Section 301' (*International Trade Reporter*, 9, January 1990, p. 60).

The emergence of the equal 'internal others' in the West: a second 'new kind of Orientalism'

The 'American liberal-protectionist self' co-exists with a non-liberal construction of American interests by its equal 'internal others'. Beginning with Chalmers Johnson (1982), an alternative interpretation of Japanese economic power has been developed which 'revises' the 'neo-liberal' accounts of capitalist development (whether in America or Japan) and tries to 'otherize' Japan from this viewpoint. This 'revisionism' (*Business Week,* 1989) covers a wide range of sophisticated and populist literature. But I will concentrate here on writers whom The *Wall Street Journal* describes in a telling (and 'otherizing') simile as the 'gang of four' (i.e., Johnson, van Wolferen, Fallows, and Prestowitz).[3] These writers, through their rather different concerns with state, culture, and international strategies, deploy the following constructions in contrasting the 'Japanese other' and 'American self': (a) 'Japan as different' (i.e., non-Western); (b) 'Japan as threat or danger'; and (c) an 'economic nationalist' interest for the US.

First, Johnson, a professor of political science at the University of California, San Diego, offers a Eurocentric account of the specificity of post-war Japan. This was first presented in his influential book *MITI and the Japanese Miracle* (1982). Without reflecting on its relevance to an East Asian context, Johnson deploys the Enlightenment institutional triplet of 'market economy', 'civil society', and 'sovereign state'. Denying that Japanese development is explicable in terms of simple market forces or a distinctive Japanese culture, he grounds it in a distinctive form of 'state' which dates from the Meiji period. But the Japanese 'developmental state' is analysed in Eurocentric terms as institutionally autonomous from market forces and as intervening from outside and above the market to pursue a political project. In a manner alien to America's liberal-market traditions, this consensus-building interventionist state has long promoted 'strategic industries'. This is especially clear in the use by the Ministry of International Trade and Industry (MITI) of special tax incentives, cheap loans, and access to export financing to encourage the dramatic ascent of different high-tech industries (e.g., steel, automobiles and electronics). This statist reading of Japan's uniqueness has ambivalent implications for defining America's own identity and interests. It could be used to reinforce the sense of superiority based on a liberal self-identity; or to undermine that feeling by noting how an allegedly inferior developmental model threatens US interests. Thus it could legitimate demands for liberalization and de-regulation in Japan or demands for a similarly effective system of state support for industry in the USA. Caricatures of Johnson's work have often been invoked since the late 1980s in support of various attempts to redirect US economic policy towards a neo-mercantilist and/or interventionist position.

Karel van Wolferen and James Fallows construct (albeit in somewhat different ways) 'Japanese otherness' in terms of specific Japanese cultural traits. Van Wolferen, a Dutch journalist and long-time resident of Japan, argues in *The Enigma of Japanese Power* (1989) that Japan's system is a 'truncated pyramid' with overlapping hierarchies that is 'out of control'. An article in *The National Interest* (1991) reinforces this claim. Van Wolferen notes that there is no final arbitrator among the overlapping hierarchies of the bureaucratic–Liberal Democratic Party–business alliance. He deploys metaphors such as 'a juggernaut with no brakes' and 'kings without power' to portray 'Japan as threat' to the 'legal international framework' (1989, p. 431).

James Fallows, Washington editor of *Atlantic Monthly*, penned two articles for his journal (1989a; 1989b) and a book, *More Like Us* (1989c). These argue that 'Japan is different'. Rejecting state-centred analyses, he refers this to such essential Japanese qualities as being 'tribe-like', 'lacking universal principles', and adopting a 'situational morality' (1989a, pp. 46–51). Fallows claims that such features prompt US–Japan conflict because Japan lacks real respect for universal free-trade/laissez-faire rules. These threats are hard to resist because of the inherent 'individualist beliefs' of America; the 'American self' could never become like the 'Japanese other' and thus defend itself in like manner (1989c, p. x). In a second article, however, Fallows advocates an 'economic nationalist' identity for the USA, suggesting that it should 'contain Japan' by resorting to 'managed trade' (negotiated market shares) and 'managed competition' (1989b, pp. 63–4).

Clyde Prestowitz, a former trade negotiator, invoked Johnson's arguments to reorient US economic strategy. Johnson had suggested that the Japanese state regards geo-economic goals and industrial performance as akin to national security (Johnson, 1982, p. 21; Johnson *et al.*, 1989, p. 102). In turn Prestowitz suggested the US state had been preoccupied with Cold War geo-political and laissez-faire goals and that, in undermining American industrial and technological leadership, this had contributed to economic decline. He also claimed that Japanese investment in the USA was a form of colonization and seriously threatened American identity and interests. A research institute established by Prestowitz even concludes that the American auto industry can best be saved from the Japanese threat by offering low-interest loans diverted from military R&D funding.

The 'revisionism' of the 'Gang of Four' rests on a 'Japanese otherness' constructed in and through a curious mix of positive and negative images. On the one hand, we find positive evaluations of state/strategic policies/high-tech (future technology); and on the other, negative judgements concerning a 'system out of control'/'lacking universal principles'. These positive and negative features can be condensed into the image of 'Japan as threat' and the concomitant call for remapping the 'American self' in terms of 'economic nationalism'. These discourses, created and popularized by America's equal 'internal others', constitute *a second 'new kind of Orientalism'*. Drawing on a mixture of Enlightenment categories and heterodox economic–cultural discourses, these equal 'internal others' interpret Japanese 'difference' as a threat to the values and interests of the hegemon which requires the latter to adapt or perish.

Strategic and Discursive Repositionings of the US and Japan

Challenged by these reciprocal constructions of the 'Japanese other' and the 'American self', both sides have been seeking to redefine their identities/interests/strategies economically and politically.

Japan's repositionings and the discourses of 'Japanese uniqueness'

Faced with this double otherization by hegemonic Western powers and their equal 'internal others', there have been two successive responses in Japan. First, Japanese forces have contested the otherizing discourse by producing 'anti-bashing' literature to counteract 'neo-liberalism' and claims of Japanese 'unfairness'. This is reflected in diplomatic literature warning against 'emotionalism' and 'hysteria', and pleas, on the part of Watanaba Taizo of the Foreign Ministry and Prime Minister Kaifu, for 'calmer attitudes'. The above diplomatic talks co-existed with more nationalistic claims that critics of Japan are racists. This can be seen from Japanese intellectual magazines (e.g., *Chuo koron*) that were filled with articles on America's conceptions of the 'yellow peril'. Other materials include Shintaro Ishihara and Akio Morita's booklet entitled *The Japan that Can Say 'No'* (1989). This argued Japan's superiority over the US in technology and that Japan should further its own interests and stop being threatened by the US. The publication of these materials attracted much attention and provoked economic nationalism; but they hardly contributed to the effective strengthening of Japan's negotiating position – let alone an alternative hegemonic discourse (of the kind envisaged in Woo-Cumings, 1993, p. 143).

The second phase is more interesting and intellectually more challenging. It involves transforming the debate over the 'Japanese uniqueness' (in terms of, for example, the Japanese model of capitalism and society) into a potent weapon of empowerment. One form that it takes is that of linking Japanese time and space to the positive aspects of the West's heterodox economic discourses on 'Japanese otherness' (e.g., Johnson's earlier idea on the 'developmental state'). This can be seen in Keizo Nagatani's paper on 'Japanese Economics: The Theory and Practice of Investment Coordination' (1992), which aims to re-invent a 'Japanese self' and to re-position in the trade conflict by, first of all, refuting negative discourses from the West on Japan (e.g., charges laid by Fallows and van Wolferen) and re-articulating the positive ones (e.g., the 'statist' discourse) to the historical time and global space of Japan. Such re-invention and re-articulation can be seen in the following account on 'Japanese economics', where Nagatani invokes the idea of a 'visible hand' (statist as opposed to market growth) to epitomize Japanese development strategies (i.e., 'government-guided industrialization', 'modernization through its fiscal authority and financial industry', and 'close government–business partnership') (1992, p. 192) since Meiji Restoration. In particular, he hopes

> to bring out the essence of 'Japanese Economics' that has shaped Japan's economic policies over the past 120 years. Contrary to the claim by Western critics, it is my belief that Japanese economic policies and strategies are based firmly on principles and quite consistent with the framework of their doctrines and therefore that knowing Japanese Economics is useful for the Westerners not only to better understand Japan but to cope more effectively with her. ... Whereas Western Economics is natural – scientific, impersonal, non-historical, static and universal, Japanese Economics is social – scientific, game-theoretic, historical, dynamic and relative. These doctrinal differences naturally lead to different policy formulas and different styles of policy making, the most notable difference having been in the area of investment policy. Whereas Westerners believe that people's free choice over assets in the market place will produce an efficient and socially desirable pattern and pace of capital accumulation and that governmental intervention in this process will necessarily entail distortions and waste, the Japanese believe that economic growth and development do not come naturally, that different forms of capital have different effects on economic growth and development, and that a proper sequence of investment must be designed and implemented by a 'visible hand' in order to succeed.   (1992, p. 178)

In relation to global time and space, he adds that Japan is a 'latecomer' and a 'follower' that 'must devise its own survival technique ... in a world already endowed with dominant players and rules written by them' (1992, p. 188). This creation of the 'latecomer/follower' identity not only enables Nagatani to distinguish Japan's trajectory from the West; but also creates an alternative discursive space – 'Japanese economic' – that might enable Japan to reposition itself in the politics of difference in the global economy.[4] Table 6.3 summarizes the two discursive formations regarding 'Japanese' and 'Western' economics.

Table 6.3 *Two discursive formations regarding Japanese and Western economics*

'Japanese Economics'	'Western Economics'
A number of dominant economies	US as the dominant economy
Latecomer and follower mentality	Hegemon mentality
Active rationality in setting goals	Market rationality
Second-best solutions	First-best solutions to constraints
Biological view of the national economy	Physical view of the national economy
State active in economic management	Free trade
Equilibrium through the art of organizing people	The efficiency of competitiveness
Co-operation and co-ordination	Competitive individualism
Long-term prosperity	Short-term efficiency

Source: Compiled by the present author on the basis of Nagatani's work.

This vignette illustrates a strategic hybrid that links the ambivalent 'statist discourse' of the West's equal 'internal others' to Japan's time and space. Apart from Nagatani's work, there is a flood of hybridized narratives that are related to Japan's 'unique' forms of capitalism (e.g., Gerlach's 'alliance capitalism', Eisuke Sakakibara's 'non-capitalist market economy', and Mark Fruin 'network capitalism'). This reconstruction of the 'Japanese self' demonstrates a kind of 're-invented orientalism' that creates intersubjective spaces that are still embedded in its construction of 'uniqueness' but are not too divorced from Western understanding. These hybrid identities are polyvalent because they can be interpreted in many ways: (a) by (post)colonial actors as a tendency towards the building of an 'Asian' identity and/or to further its economic role in the area; (b) by the 'West' as a tendency towards *auto-Orientalism* (even Occidentalism) in otherizing them in return (Lie, 1996, p. 11);[5] and/or (c) as contributing towards a move away from a 'neo-liberal' form of capitalism, which celebrates convergence around a single model (that of Atlantic market capitalism), to an 'Asian-Pacific' kind.

The US's repositionings and the discourses of 'competitiveness' in the Clinton administration

In the face of Japanese success, the yawning Japan–US trade deficit, and the emerging projection of the 'Japanese Self' on the international scene, equal 'others' in the US have sought to redefine American interests in the face of 'Japan as threat'. In some cases they conclude that the USA should force Japan to become more like America but should itself seek to become more like Japan. This solution denies Japanese 'uniqueness' (except in so far as Japan pioneered the idea) and paradoxically implies that the USA could reduce Japanese imports by importing the Japanese model itself. The most obvious indicators of this strategy are recommendations by the US's research institutes for it to strategically evolve and selectively consolidate a 'new' 'techno-economic' approach that emphasizes 'managed trade', 'competitiveness', 'high-technology policies', and 'factory-level Japanization'. These ideas were adumbrated in the writings of Fallows and Prestowitz; but they were deepened and matured into strategic positions in two representative texts published by the Berkeley Roundtable on International Economy (BRIE), and the Massachusetts Institute of Technology (MIT) respectively.

In one of BRIE's earlier books, edited by Johnson, Tyson and Zysman, *Politics and Productivity: How Japan's Development Strategy Works* (1989), there are five key features which are said to contribute to Japanese economic success. They comprise: (a) a pattern of industrial 'catch-up' shaped by policies of import substitution and export promotion; (b) government agencies such as MITI exerting substantial efforts to build a Japanese position in advanced technologies; (c) an industrial and manufacturing organization that builds on flexibility rather than simply mass/volume production; (d) a dense network of businesses around trading companies and banks (i.e., *keiretsu*); and (e) the role of high-technology policies and state policies in promoting competitiveness. This statist/neo-mercantilist conception of Japan is important because it is bound up not only with American perceptions of Japan; but also with American perceptions of the 'self', especially regarding Japan's 'success' and how it 'threatens' the US.

One particular perception is offered in Laura Tyson's book *Who's Bashing Whom? Trade Conflict in High-Technology Industries* (1992), which links the 'success of Japan' with 'US high-tech sectors'. Focusing on sectoral performance, she calls for a 'strategic vision' to develop a 'credible commitment to maintain American strength in high-technology industries' (1992, p. 288). She then defines the American 'self'/interests in terms of 'competitiveness' and advances the following micro-economic claims: (a) the American government can facilitate 'competitiveness' by raising the quality of public education, increasing the efficiency of infrastructure, making markets, creating high-wage jobs, and promoting 'strategic/high-tech' industries, etc.; and (b) adverse trends in competitiveness are reversible through 'managed trade', which may encompass 'any trade agreement that establishes quantitative targets on trade flows' through a result-oriented trade strategy and 'Framework' Talks with Japan (1992, pp. 296, 264).

This remapping constructs a more protectionist, interventionist, and 'techno-nationalist' identity and strategy for the US. This new narrative has found resonance in economic and political circles. Economically, for example, it serves the micro-electronic industry's lobbying for support to high-tech industries. Politically, Clinton was keen to advance a new 'frontier myth' in his election programme. This aimed to expand American 'competitiveness' in a global age and the Tysonian discourse helped to privilege this 'competitor' identity and strategy. This was evident when Tyson was appointed as the Chair of Clinton's Council of Economic Advisors and 'competitiveness', 'managed trade' and 'technological initiatives' became part of his regime of economic truth in 1993.

Discursively, there was a clear remapping of the regimes of economic truth between the Bush and Clinton administrations through a shift in the image of Japan and its implications for rebuilding the 'American self'. This new 'self' has not gone unchallenged (cf. Krugman's neo-liberal rebuttal, 1994); nor has the intended 'industrial policy' been at all fully or effectively implemented (Froud et al., 1996a). However, what is crucial, in identity terms, is the interpenetration of the Japanese 'other' with the American 'self' in and through the language of 'competitiveness'.

Concurrently, management and business literature attributes Japanese competitive advantage to its production techniques. Thus a recent and influential MIT study, co-authored by James Womack, Daniel Jones and Daniel Roos, *The Machine that Changed the World* (1990), ascribed the success of Japan's automobile industry to a 'lean

Table 6.4 *Economic truth in the Bush and Clinton administrations*

Clinton's regime of economic truth	Bush's regime of economic truth
Trade policy is linked to domestic economic policy to strengthen the competitiveness of domestic industry	Links between trade policy and domestic economic policy are not strong
Expansion of exports from US via VIEs (i.e., strategic/managed trade)	Controls of imports to US via VERs
Priority for 'high-tech' industries	Priority for consumers
Important role for government	Important role for private sector
Importance of Asian-Pacific	No general policy on Asia
'Multi-track' (combining global, regional and bilateral approaches)	Unclear 'multi-track approach'

Source: Adapted from T. Sasaki and Y. Shimane (1994), p. 80, Table 10.

production system' which is allegedly superior to Fordist mass production. It is even hailed as a 'global symbol of a new era' (1990, p. 277) and coded in a 'manufacturing infrastructure' language that prioritizes a response through 'factory-level Japanization' (e.g., lean production, just-in-time supply system, and total quality management) in the USA. Synergetic discourses of 'learning from Japan' are also combined with Americanized rhetorics of differences from Japan, and accounts of 'Japanization' as 'a fallen idol' for the US (or elsewhere) (e.g., Froud et al., 1996b). This conjunctural articulation of synergy and differences begins to remap another US–Japan discourse – this time on the factory level. This micro-economic narrative of 'synergetic differences', when coupled with Tysonian discourses on 'competitiveness', allows for further interpenetration of the Japanese 'other' with the American 'self'. Despite their complementary and contradictory aspects, these complex and interpenetrative sets of discourse are (re-)circulated and (re-)constructed by politicians, think-tankers, journalists, business strategists, and social scientists to (re-)create, in a selective manner, a new intersubjective space-time to be known as the 'Asian-Pacific'.

The Construction of Unequal 'Internal Others' in Asia: A Third 'New Kind of Orientalism'

Around the same time as the USA began constructing 'Japan as threat', the 1985 Plaza Accord engineered a massive devaluation of the yen. Saddled with uncompetitive export prices and rising domestic labour costs, and fearing greater protectionism in US and European markets, Japan has been searching for new production sites in East Asia. These have proved fruitful for the re-deployment of the 'flying geese' narrative. As a 'model of development', the 'flying geese' was first proposed by Akamatsu Kaname (1896–1974) as an economic and industrial theory with practical implications for Asian development. As a discursive construction, it was used in a militaristic form to legitimize the 'Japanese Greater East Asian Co-prosperity Sphere' during the Second World War. At the height of the domination of the trans-Atlantic partnership in the 1960s, this theory was further developed by Kojima and Okita to re-present Japan and South-East Asia as laggard 'geese' attempting to 'catch up' with the Euro-American leaders (cf. Korhonen, 1994).

In the mid-1980s, the 'catch up' image shifted from Euro-America to the Asian region. In this regard, the *'new flying geese'* construction was strategically twisted to remap/redefine the relationship between Japan and other Asian countries. This re-interpretation was promoted by technocrats (e.g., Saburo Okita) as well as Japan-related research institutes such as JETRO and Nomura. A key step in this strategic redefinition was coded in the language of synergy and the image of a flock of 'flying geese'. Japan (as the leader of the flock) spearheads the formation, which is followed by the four NICs, six ASEAN (Association of South-East Asian Nations) economies, and the post-socialist bloc as next to have taken off. This 'flying geese' metaphor re-presents the growth trajectory in a deterministic manner in terms of a movement from traditional to modernized economic orders. It privileges Japan as the industrial leader and involves the product-cycle metaphor of Japan shifting its sunset industries to its East Asian NIC 'flock'. This developmental trajectory envisages the latecomers replicating the experience of the countries ahead of them in the formation. Thus, Japan guides the 'flock of geese' in its techno-economic 'flight to success' but each member of the flock follows under its own independent flight power but following the staging points of Japan (Sum, 1996, pp. 225–31).

As a strategic re-invention of the 1980s, the 'flying geese' narrative implies: (a) a hierarchy promoting the image that the US and Japan guide/lead the 'flock'; and (b) a realignment of the East's unequal 'internal others', that is, economies less developed than the Japanese exemplar, to a follower position. As a Japan-centred discursive representation, it has the effect of creating a leader–follower relationship that maps Japan to the former and the other Asian countries to the latter. In this regard, the Asian countries are otherized as 'synergetically inferior' and become the unequal 'internal others' of Japan. This creation of Eastern unequal 'internal others' demonstrates otherization effects pertinent to the politics of difference in Western Orientalism. In particular it suggests that there is *a third 'new kind of Orientalism'* constructed in and through a development discourse centred around the prevailing values/norms, governmentalities, and time/space of Japan that assigns a follower identity to the East's unequal 'internal others' and claims that their interests will best be realized by entering into a Japan-led framework as junior partners. As a form of domination in the economic–cultural sphere, this may mean the 'synergetic subordination' of the East Asian NICs to Japanese economic practices that are promoted by its foreign direct investment, overseas development assistance, and overseas security investment.[6] Thus the transfer of Japanese sunset industries to the East Asian NICs and from the latter to other Asian economies is constructed to be mutually beneficial to a new 'Asian-Pacific'.

SOME CONCLUDING REMARKS: 'NEW KINDS OF ORIENTALISM' AND GLOBAL CAPITALISM

Two main sets of remarks can be drawn about 'new Orientalism' and global capitalism. The first set concerns the search for a plurality of discourses for representing the culturally-embedded politics of international trade in and beyond East Asia. These remarks seek to transcend the singular conception of 'first-generation' Orientalism by highlighting the unclear boundaries between Western hegemonic forces and the West's equal 'internal others', the latter and the West/East, and the East's regionally hegemonic forces and their unequal 'internal others'. Thus this chapter has tried to complexify the politics of difference and its hybrid discursive forms by introducing three 'new kinds of Orientalism'. Bhabha's idea of 'hybridity' is useful because it highlights the unclear boundaries of the inside/outside (1984, 1994). But this idea can also be criticized on two grounds. First, Bhaba does not clearly explain how more complex differences and their hybrids are constituted. And, secondly, he largely ignores the relation between hybrids and power-relations, the identity struggles involved therein, and the possibility of turning 'otherization' to one's advantage.

My second set of remarks concerns hybridity/difference/synergy, power-relations, and the nature of capitalism. My case studies adopt a more integral analysis of the political economy of synergetic differences by relating the re-imagination/re-positioning of identities to the complex, unfolding dialectic of globalization–regionalization. Newly emerging (or re-vivified) identities, interests and strategies which combine elements from different discourses and material terrains may be re-articulated in the new global (dis)order. For example, Japan's appropriation of the 'statist/Japanese economics' narratives and America's 'techno-economic' discourses on 'competitiveness' and 'factory-level Japanization' may create a new intersubjective space-time of the 'Asian-Pacific'. This new identity and vision may shape the design of institutions to remap social relations beyond the space-time dominated by the 'neo-liberal' paradigm of Anglo-American capitalism. Hybrid identities such as 'Asian-Pacific' may re-order complementarities and difference among different national economies, social processes, and material frameworks across borders. Such re-ordering is often mediated by actors who move across/between spaces to co-ordinate production, finance, trade, culture across/within different sites. These movements of people include different forms of labour, including migrant labour, legal and illegal, refugees, and permanent tourists who thereby get involved not only in (re-)making the spatial division of labour/knowledge, but also in reaffirming/challenging its strategies of exploitation, subjugation and domination.

NOTES

1. Dalby (1990); Walker (1993, 1995); Campbell (1992, 1994); O Tuathail (1993, 1996).
2. The metaphor was originally used to legitimize the 'Japanese Greater East Asian Co-Prosperity Sphere' in terms of 'emancipating' East Asia from Atlantic domination. This connotation is absent today.
3. For an in-depth study of the sophisticated and populist writings on this issue, see O Tuathail (1993).
4. Complementing Nagatani's work is more recent literature emphasizing the specificity of Japanese capitalism. Thus Eisuke Sakakibara (1993)

portrays Japan as a 'noncapitalist market economy'; and Mark Fruin (1992) usefully distinguishes American 'market capitalism' from Japanese 'network capitalism'.

5. Lie is right that constructing Japanese 'uniqueness' may be a kind of 'auto-Orientalism'; and that the way it is hybridized and represented is better described as 're-invented Orientalism'. But I disagree that it constitutes Occidentalism. For auto-Orientalism is the search for the self and is at most a defence against Orientalist thinking; conversely, Occidentalism is an Eastern style of thinking not about the East itself but about the 'West'.

6. On these economic–political practices, see Arase (1994) and Sum (1997).

REFERENCES

Arase, D. (1992), 'Public–Private Sector Interest Coordination in Japan's ODA', *Pacific Affairs*, 67 (2), pp. 171–99.

Arase, D. (1994), *Buying Power: The Political Economy of Japan's Foreign Aid* (Boulder, CO: Lynne Reinner).

Bhabha, H. K. (1984), 'Of Mimicry and Man: the Ambivalence of Colonial Discourse', *October*, 28, pp. 125–33.

Bhabha, H. K. (1994), *The Location of Culture* (London: Routledge).

Campbell, D. (1992), *Writing Security* (Manchester: Manchester University Press).

Campbell, D. (1994), 'Foreign Policy and Identity: the Japanese "Other"/American "Self"', in S. Rosow, N. Inayatullah, and M. Rupert (eds), *The Global Economy as Political Space* (Boulder: Lynne Rienner), pp. 147–70.

Dalby, D. (1990), *Creating the Second Cold War: The Discourse of Politics* (London: Pinter).

Drysdale, P. and Garnaut, R. (1993), 'The Pacific: An Application of a General Theory of Economic Integration', in C. F. Bergsten and M. Noland (eds), *Pacific Dynamism and the International Economic System* (Washington: Institute for International Economics), pp. 183–224.

Fallows, J. (1989a), 'Containing Japan', *Altantic Monthly*, May 1989, pp. 40–54.

Fallows, J. (1989b), 'Getting Along with Japan', *Altantic Monthly*, December 1989, pp. 53–64.

Fallows, J. (1989c), *More Like Us* (Boston: Houghton Mifflin).

Fallows, J., Johnson, C., Prestowitz, C., and K. van Wolferen (1990), 'The Gang of Four Defend the Revisionist Line', *US News and World Report*, 7 May 1990, pp. 54–5.

Froud, J., et al. (1996a), 'Sinking Ships? Liberal Theorists on the American Economy', *Asia Pacific Business Review*, 3 (1), pp. 54–72.

Froud, J., et al. (1996b), 'A Fallen Idol? Japanese Management in the 1990s', *Asia Pacific Business Review*, 2 (4), pp. 20–43.

Fruin, Mark (1992), *The Japanese Enterprise System: Competitive Strategies and Co-operative Structure* (Oxford: Clarendon Press).

Gerlach, G.L. (1992), *Alliance Capitalism* (Berkeley: University of California Press).

Ishihara, S. and A. Morita (1991), *The Japan that Can Say 'No'* (New York: Simon and Schuster).

Johnson, C. (1982), *MITI and the Japanese Miracle* (Stanford: Stanford University Press).

Johnson, C., Tyson, L., and J. Zysman, (eds) (1989), *Politics and Productivity: How Japan's Development Strategy Works* (Berkeley: Ballinger Publishing).

Korhonen, P. (1994), 'The Theory of the Flying Geese Pattern of Development and its Interpretations', *Journal of Peace Research*, 31 (1), pp. 93–108.

Krugman, P. (1994), 'Competitiveness: A Dangerous Obsession', *Foreign Affairs*, March/April 1994, pp. 28–44.

Kudrle, R. T. (1995), 'Fairness, Efficiency, and Opportunism in US Trade and Investment Policy', in D. Rapkin and W. Avery (eds), *National Competitiveness in a Global Economy* (Boulder: Lynne Rienner), pp. 153–78.

Leaver, R. (1989), 'Restructuring in the Global Economy: From Pax Americana to Pax Nipponica?', *Alternatives*, XIV, 4 pp. 429–62.

Lie, J. (1996), 'Theorizing Japanese Uniqueness', *Current Sociology*, 44 (1), pp. 5–13.

Nagatani, K. (1992), 'Japanese Economics: The Theory and Practice of Investment Coordination', in J. Roumasset and S. Burr (eds), *The Economics of Cooperation: East Asian Development and the Case for Pro-Market Intervention* (Boulder: Westview), pp. 175–200.

O'Tuathail, G. (1992), 'Critical Geopolitics and Development Theory: Intensifying the Dialogue', *Transactions: Institute of British Geographers*, 19, pp. 228–38.

O'Tuathail, G. (1993), 'Japan as Threat: Geo-economic Discourses in the USA–Japan Relationship in US Civil Society, 1987–1991', in C. William (ed.), *The Political Geography of the New World Order* (London: Belhaven), pp. 181–209.

O'Tuathail, G. (1996), *Critical Geopolitics* (Minneapolis: University of Minnesota Press).

Prestowitz, C. (1989), *Trading Places: How We are Giving our Future to Japan and How to Reclaim It* (New York: Basic Books).

Reich, R. (1990), 'Who is Us?', *Harvard Business Review*, 68 (1), pp. 53–64.

Said, E. (1978), *Orientalism* (London: Routledge and Kegan Paul).

Said E. (1986), 'Orientalism Reconsidered', in *Europe and Its Others*, vol. I, ed. F. Baker, P. Hulme, M. Iversen, and D. Loxley (Colchester: University of Essex), pp. 12–29.

Sakakibara, E. (1993), *Beyond Capitalism: The Japan Model of Market Economics* (Lanham: University Press of America).

Sasaki, T., and Shimane, Y. (1994), 'The New Dynamics of the Asian Economy', *Japan Research Quarterly*, 3 (3), pp. 50–88.

Sjolander, C. T. (ed.) (1994), 'The Discourse of Multilateralism: US Hegemony and the Management of International Trade', in C. Sjolander and W. Cox, *Beyond Positivism: Critical Reflections on International Relations* (Boulder: Lynne Rienner), pp. 37–58.

Sum, N.-L. (1996), 'The NICs and Competing Strategies of East Asian Regionalism', in A. Gamble and A. Payne (eds), *Regionalism and World Order* (London: Macmillan), pp. 207–46.

Sum, N-L. (1997). '"Embeddedness" and "Geo-Governance" of Cross-Border Regional Modes of Growth: Their Nature and Dynamics in East Asian Cases', in A. Amin and J. Hausner (eds), *Beyond Markets and Planning: Third Way Approaches to Transformation* (Cheltenham: Edward Elgar), pp. 159–95.

Tyson, L. (1992), *Who's Bashing Whom? Trade Conflict in High-Technology Industries* (Washington: Institute for International Economics).

van Wolferen, K. (1989), *The Enigma of Japanese Power* (New York: Vintage).

van Wolferen, K. (1991), 'No Brakes, No Compass', *The National Interest*, 25, p. 5.

Walker, R. (1993), *Inside/Outside: International Relations as Political Theory* (Cambridge: Cambridge University Press).

Walker, R. (1995), 'International Relations and the Concept of the Political', in K. Booth and S. Smith (eds), *International Relations Theory Today* (Cambridge: Polity), pp. 306–27.

Womack, J., Jones, D., and Roos, D. (1990), *The Machine that Changed the World* (New York: Macmillan).

Woo-Cumings, M. (1993), 'East Asia's America Problem', in M. Woo-Cumings and M. Loriaux, *Past as Prelude: History in the Making of a New World Order* (Boulder: Westview Press).

7 Reviewing the Western Spectacle: Reflexive Globalization through the Black Diaspora

BARNOR HESSE

> *Modern imperialism was so global and all-encompassing that virtually nothing escaped it; besides as I have said, the nineteenth-century contest over empire is still continuing today. Whether or not to look at the connections between cultural texts and imperialism is therefore to take a position in fact taken – either to study the connection in order to criticize it and think of alternatives for it, or not to study it in order to let it stand, unexamined and presumably unchanged.*

(Edward Said, 1993, pp. 80–1)

INTRODUCTION

How can we develop contemporary concepts of globalization which understand its intricate association with modernity's imperialisms? Perhaps the beginning of the answer lies in how we think about space: *the final frontier*. What imperialism means in the discourse of globalization can be seen in screen versions of science fiction. These regularly re-cycle a compelling trinity of familiar themes: the conquest of space, the alien invasion and the close encounter. Does it stretch the imagination too much to suggest that these scenarios of 'otherness' draw upon long-established motifs in the West's imperial culture? These include Europe's sixteenth-century invasion of the Americas; the nineteenth-century colonial conquest of India, Africa and the Pacific; and the twentieth-century Western nationalist opposition to 'non-European' immigration. Hollywood science fiction is one of the few areas in social life where the possibility of a single world consciousness is both assumed and procured. Invariably cultivated as a discourse of globalization, it seems to be underpinned by a distinctly European formation of imperialism which is disavowed[1] and promoted by an evangelical faith in an apparently self-effacing universal liberalism.

What concerns me in this chapter is not so much the social phenomenon of globalization, but the formation of the discourse through which globalization is conceptualized. The theoretical problem I want to confront resides in the tendency Anglo-American social theories of globalization have to reprise rather than review the narrative of the Western spectacle. Such approaches seldom consider that distinctions between the West and the 'non-West' or between Europe and 'non-Europe' harbour more complex issues concerning the formation of modernity than those of contemporary socio-geographic polarities. It is almost as if the theoretical discourse of globalization is in thrall to the specular consumption of an esteemed western enterprise that rarely attaches any cultural or political significance to its imperial formation. We can see this in Anthony Giddens's valuable, albeit passing remarks on Western and non-Western frames of modernity:

> Is modernity peculiarly Western from the standpoint of its globalizing tendencies? No. It cannot be, since we are speaking here of emergent forms of world interdependence and planetary consciousness. The ways in which these issues are approached and coped with, however, will inevitably involve conceptions and strategies from non-western settings.   (Giddens, 1990, p. 175)

These remarks are less critical than at first appears. Giddens's approach to understanding the formation of globalization relies on specifying four institutional dimensions: the nation-state system, the world military order, the international division of labour and the world capitalist economy (Giddens, 1990, pp. 71–8). Yet the context in which he conceptualizes these as institutions of globalization seems unconcerned with the cultural logic and power-relations that imposed and created Western and non-Western assemblages. Is it unreasonable to recall that the modernity of our worldly interdependence was imperial in its formal contours and remains globally racialized[2] in its specular provenance? Failure to recall this leads to an inability to understand the formative role of European racism in Western societies. Some of what needs to be recalled has been summarized by Nicholas Thomas where he describes the colonial formation of modernity:

In effect, modernity itself can be understood as a colonialist project in a special sense that both the societies internal to the Western nations, and those they possessed, administered and reformed elsewhere, were understood as objects to be surveyed, regulated and sanitized.   (Thomas, 1994, p. 4)

The implications of avoiding these racialized markings of globalization are significant. They result in a recurrent conceptual repression where Western imperial culture is left unexamined (Said, 1993), and insinuatively the social formations of Western racisms are reproduced unchallenged and unchanged (Rattansi and Westwood, 1994).

There are three main arguments that I intend to make in this chapter. These can be summarized as follows. First, the critique of racialized globalization as a discourse requires a profound disruption of the Western spectacle, which confines theories of globalization within the horizon of an undisputed 'European planetary consciousness' (Pratt, 1991) and disregards the possibility of alternative representations of the planet. I argue for the exposition rather than repression of how the discourse of globalization is racialized. I illustrate the value of my approach through a deconstruction[3] of formulations drawn from Roland Robertson (1992), a leading social theorist of globalization, who seems to exemplify much of what I want to contest. Secondly, I argue that in order to avoid these conceptual repressions it is important to identify forms of reflexive globalization capable of comprehending the social legacies of the two European colonial empires (Pagden, 1995).[4] Reflexive globalization describes the logic of post-colonial[5] discourses constituted as critiques of and alternatives to the discrepancies[6] of European imperialism in Western culture. Finally, I argue that one form of reflexive globalization which has attempted to break the spell of the Western spectacle's stultifying world vision, expresses itself through modernity's cross-cultural formations. In particular I argue that the cross-cultural formation of the Black diaspora contains reflexive dimensions of globalization that expose part of the complex institution of European racism in modern Western formations. Black diaspora reflexivities attempt to overcome the particularist emancipatory, rationalistic and aesthetic ideals of the West, where these have been complicit with the culture of imperialism. As we shall see, it is the conceptual exclusion of this type of reflexive globalization that facilitates the Western spectacle's dazzling recurrence in the discourse of globalization.

REPRESSIVE DISCOURSE OF WESTERN GLOBALIZATION

The formation of the contemporary consciousness of the world as a whole is a significant Western cultural development. This more than anything has attracted the designation 'global culture' (Featherstone, 1991). Its uniqueness is taken to reside in that it signifies neither the culture of the nation-state nor a world culture but the globalization of cultural processes that transform the meaning and configuration of different nations. In various forms these sustain world-wide exchanges and flows of goods, people, information, services and images. This global process has also been described as a 'third culture' (Featherstone, 1991) because it facilitates extremely diverse cultural flows (e.g., lawyers, accountants, fast-food distributors, popular cultures). It needs to be recognized however, that third cultures do not only emerge as the mediating spaces between the national and the international, they are also consolidated by their status as exemplars of Western culture in their capacity as regulators of the confluence between the hegemonies of Europeanness and the subordinations of non-Europeanness. What I am suggesting is that, despite its obvious value as a concept, the idea of third cultures nevertheless conceals a theoretical problem. Although it acknowledges the incidence of cultural differences ethnographically in the universal dimensions of globalization, it also represses any reference to the colonial configuration of that ethnography. Here then lies the principal focus of my concern.

Perhaps the clearest and most sustained analytical demonstration of this repressive approach occurs in the work of Roland Robertson (1992). According to Robertson:

> Globalization as a concept refers both to the compression of the world and the intensification of consciousness of the world as a whole. The processes and actions to which the concept of globalization now refers have been proceeding, with some interruptions, *for many centuries*. (Robertson, 1992, p. 8; emphasis added)

This is the basis of an account that defines globalization almost exclusively as a progressive and hegemonic form of Western expansion and civilization (Robertson, 1992, pp. 58–9). But it traces in its wake, through Robertson's occasional references: the beginnings of globalization's trajectory in late fifteenth-century Europe's geographical surveys; the late nineteenth-century consolidation of 'international society' which considers the 'admission of non-European countries';

the early twentieth-century 'crystallization of the Third World'; and the late twentieth-century Western experience of the strains and complexities of multiculturalism, polyethnicity and civil rights (Robertson, 1992). These are incidental themes for Robertson because he argues against the 'strong temptation for some to insist that the single world of our day can be accounted for in terms of one particular process or factor such as "westernization", "imperialism" or, in the dynamic and diffuse sense, "civilization"' (Robertson, 1992, p. 55). The conceptual rejection of these global structures is especially noteworthy because it signifies a consistent theoretical exclusion of the racialized dimensions of globalization. What Robertson's account provides is an explanation of Europe's Western pre-eminence in the world without recourse to the formation of imperialism.

A clear illustration of this occurs where Robertson argues that globalization 'involves comparative interaction of different forms of life' (1992, p. 27) as if these were respectively distinguished by distinct histories of autonomous development. Robertson simply represses any reference to the cross-cultural formation and colonial historicity of that interaction:

> In an increasingly globalized world there is a heightening of civilizational, societal, ethnic, regional and, indeed individual, self-consciousness. There are constraints on social entities to locate themselves within world history and the global future. Yet globalization involves the diffusion of the expectation of such identity declarations. (Robertson, 1992)

Robertson is concerned to argue that 'globalization theory is an elaboration of civilizational analysis' (Robertson, 1992, p. 129) because he wants to rescue civilization as a concept from its problematic career and use it in a 'neutral way to refer to the major sociocultural and symbolic centers in world history' (Robertson, 1992, p. 115). Hence he argues that it became a key dimension of the globalization process at a 'critical historical moment' (Robertson, 1992), which not only referred to the richness and depth of formally organized cultures but expressed a legally regulative idea that informed the criterion of acceptance into 'international society'. But even though Robertson accepts that during the nineteenth century it operated as a 'standard of civilization' that governed the admission of Africa and Asia into Europe's construction of international society, he seems to regard the prevailing institution of imperialism and assumptions of European superiority as incidental or inconvenient matters of fact. This enables him to argue that 'even though there was much unjust treatment and racism' (1992, p. 124) it is hard to ignore the role of European standards and political discourses in the demands of African and Asian people for equality of rights in international law. The suggestion is that these incursions of liberalism within 'non-Europe' somehow assuaged the imperial impositions and domination of Europe. Within this glib historicity Robertson proposes as a contemporary perspective, a 'move beyond the Western-centredness of classic civilizational analysis' (1992, p. 136) in which the analysis of the 'problem of globality' (1992, p. 137) requires that 'we "allow" civilizations to identify themselves both historically and contemporaneously' in encounters that define the world as 'a single place' (1992). But can this definition of the world as a single place continue to operate within terms and assumptions that deny the deeply layered connections between European standards of civilization and corresponding statutes of colonialism?

Although Robertson does not mention it, European expansionism begins in the fifteenth century with the so-called discovery and colonization of the Americas, accompanied by the destruction and segregation of native Americans and the transportation of enslaved Africans to labour on cotton, sugar and tobacco plantations. As C. L. R. James (1938) and Eric Williams (1944) argued long ago, the factory processing of these raw materials, underpinned by the late eighteenth-century's rapid industrialization of production methods in Europe, stimulated competitive investment, catalysed advantageous trade terms and foreign exchange and made international cities of previously port towns. This not only established the basis of the Atlantic economy (Curtin, 1990; Solow, 1991), it increasingly compressed the worldly inter-relatedness and relative consciousness of three continents (Europe, Africa, the Americas) within a distinctive governmental nexus of racial hierarchy, economic exploitation and colonial aesthetics across three centuries.

It has been suggested that the first period of European colonial empires ends about 1830 (Pagden, 1995); although if we take into consideration the abolition of the last remnants of slavery in the United States and Brazil, the period extends well into the 1860s and 1880s. The second period of European imperialism begins in the early eighteenth-century (Pagden, 1995) and is consolidated in the 1780s when the first signs of a decline in the stability and profitability of a slavery-based Euro-global economy appear. This period inaugurates the history of European occupations in Asia, Africa and the Pacific and continues into the second half of the twentieth-century. It leaves in its trail distinct racialized forms of globalization that accrue directly from this 'final phase' of European imperialism. In this sense racialized globalization developed in the context of distinctive political forms, transportation routes and transnational lines of communication. What needs to be underlined here as a way of understanding the historical conduit of modern forms of globalization is that over a period of four and a half centuries the European colonial processes 'changed dramatically the human geography of the planet' (Pagden, 1995). In other words the imperial globalization of a European planetary consciousness established the world dominance of western capitalism, the ubiquity of the nation-state, the subaltern construction and dehumanization of 'non-Europe' and the governmental authority of Western legislation and media. Each of these structures has been strategically effective in regulating the systemic racialization of modernity and in instituting the global dispersal of European hegemony.

What Robertson's whole approach neglects to conceptualize is how the modern (European) taxonomy of peoples and places was achieved through the global ascription of 'comparative anatomies' (Wiegman, 1995) which defined a process of racialization that valorized European bodies and pathologized 'non-European' bodies. In other words the Enlightenment's determination of 'race' as an epistemological category (see Eze, 1997), the generic European colour visualization of the body (e.g., 'red', 'black', 'brown', 'white') is coterminous with classifying the exclusive meaning of respective locations in geography, history, culture, politics (e.g., Native American, African, Asian, European). What can be defined as European racism also emerged through this global process of racialization. It was expressed as a logic of racialized governmentality[7] (e.g., regulation, violation, civilization, exploitation, representation) that invested in the colonial determination of asymmetrical values, entitlements and obligations accorded to differentially racialized populations. In the formation of modernity, Europe and its hegemonization of the West (Pieterse, 1994), this political formation of racism (i.e., racialized governmentality) has been one of the primary legacies in the construction of global culture. It inhabits a compass of developments that Robertson's depiction of globalization inescapably underwrites as a conceptual exclusion, yet paradoxically at the same time these developments seriously undermine the presuppositions of his avowed conceptual formulations.

It is now important to consider what it is about theoretical discourses of globalization that precludes them from incorporating the imperial dimension. In thinking about the racialization of globalization we need to take seriously the question posed and answered by Aime Cesaire in his discourse on colonialism:

> has colonization really placed civilizations in contact? Or if you prefer, of all the ways of establishing contact, was it the best? I answer no. And I say that between colonization and civilization there is an infinite distance.   (Césaire, 1972, p. 11)

It is the erasure of the visibility and meaning of this infinite distance that marks the extent and scope of the Western spectacle. What this erasure signifies is a failure in social theory to conceptualize the implications that arise from the excess of imperialism over the imprint of liberalism in the horizon of global culture. This discrepant formation of globality can only be addressed by taking seriously the pervasiveness of the Western spectacle.

THE WESTERN SPECTACLE

In this context the Western spectacle puts the best possible spin on the aesthetic pre-eminence and political ubiquity of European discourses in world culture. The spectacle is inscribed in an invariable conceptual equation between a hegemonically white European visualization of the world and its representation as a legitimate or coherent social formation. This Western sight-seeing is conveyed and reinforced through forms of visual legislation and optical meanings that euphemize imperial sensibilities. Its conceptual organization can be summarized as the discourse of 'the West and the Rest' (Hall, 1992).

According to Stuart Hall, once the 'West' is understood as a historical rather than a geographical construct, it becomes possible to identify at least four ways in which it functions as a concept. First, it describes a way of thinking about societies categorized as 'Western' and 'non-Western'. Secondly, as a 'system of representation' it is a package of various images displayed in 'verbal and visual language' which 'condenses' different features into a 'composite picture' of what different societies and cultures mean (Hall, 1992, p. 277). Thirdly, it makes available a 'standard or model of comparison' (Hall, 1992) to explain the social distance and cultural difference between 'the West' and the 'non-West'. Finally, it 'provides criteria of evaluation against which powerful positive and negative features cluster' (Hall, 1992) to define an exalted 'West' and a pathologized 'non-west'. What we need to appreciate from this analysis is the significance of the Western idea as a dominant 'organizing factor in a system of global power relations' (Hall, 1992, p. 278). In representing the dominance of the 'West' as the consequence of intrinsic European qualities and exclusive internal developments, it defines the conventional terms in which the literary and visual discourses of globalization are given meaning. Circulating in the commodification and dissemination of images, voices, texts, memories, histories and fantasies, these terms rehearse and stage the globalization of the West as a superior, consensual, liberal, universal civilization.

My understanding of this formation of 'West' and 'non-West' as the Spectacle is also based on the ideas of Guy Debord (1994), who argues: 'The Spectacle appears at once as society itself, as a part of society and as a means of unification. As a part of society, it is that sector where all attention, all consciousness converges' (Debord, 1994, p. 12). The Spectacle is a discursive organization of an imaginary social representativeness that rests on a cultivated social exclusiveness. It defines the social as a theatre of visual and vocal representation where desires of engagement and participation are consummated through acts of identification, understood as the privileged consumption of universal recognition. The more the Western spectacle is contemplated in these terms, the less the lives rendered invisible or less valuable by it, actually seem to resemble part of what is significant about social life itself.

But it is not simply this 'concrete manufacture of alienation' (Debord, 1994, p. 23) that the spectacle produces, but the disavowal of its colonial formation and hegemony. It inserts a soft-focused lens on the history of the West's exploitation and dehumanization of 'non-Europe' and consequently blurs the relation between contemporary manifestations of racism and the constitutive contamination of liberal-democratic values. How this emerges is as important as how it is sustained. Debord suggests that it is the fetishization of and fascination with the commodity that inaugurates the regime of the spectacle: 'The spectacle corresponds to the historical moment at which the commodity completes *its colonization of social life*' (Debord, 1994, p. 29; emphasis added). Consequently the world we 'see' and valorize is the world of the commodity, where social life is advertised and packaged for immediate contemplation and anticipatory consumption by the spectacle's chosen histories, cultures and peoples. It is a commercial for Europeanized global hegemony.

It is ironic that Debord employs the term 'colonization' in relation to commodification since this itself is particularly significant in the Western hegemony of the world. It is only through the accruing racialized formation of meaning that the Western spectacle can globalize the 'non-European' ('non-white') other, outside the chosen people, as irredeemably deficient, deviant and disorderly. Invariably narrowly cast as an outsider, an inferior, a threat, a margin, an amusement, an exoticism, an after-thought; the 'non-European' as 'non-white', and vice-versa, is situated within the imperial vision and governmental landscape of an idealized Western panorama and paranoia. It is through the perpetual construction of this Western spectacle as a mode of 'perceptual and conceptual government' (Thomas, 1994), which ignores the imperial formation of the West, that modernity is collapsed into the trope of progress, and racialized globalization is identified with a natural world order.

It may be useful to understand the Western spectacle as a decontextualized symptom of racialized globalization. The work of Anne McClintock (1995) supplies a valuable perspective in understanding the formation of this symptom. McClintock suggests that an 'epochal shift' occurred in the culture of European imperialism during the last decades of the nineteenth-century. A movement from scientific racism to a commodity racism was instituted through 'specifically Victorian forms of advertising and photography, imperial expositions and the museum movement', which were able to convert the 'narrative of imperial Progress into mass-produced consumer spectacles' (McClintock, 1995, p. 33). Crucial to the establishment of this popular culture was the commodity itself that circulated within households as both an imperial window on the world and the palpable fetish of a self-acclaimed superior civilization. The expansion and distribution of images and narratives through mass advertising and the celebration of brand names, traded on depictions of inferiorized 'non-European' otherness and their transparent incorporation into civilization through the consumption of everyday commodities like biscuits, toothpaste or soap. From the 1850s onwards this spectacle was engraved in the packaging, marketing and distribution of 'evolutionary racism on a hitherto unimagined scale' (McClintock, 1995, p. 209). It invested the 'aesthetic space around the commodity with the commercial cult of empire' (McClintock, 1995, p. 213) and Europe with the virtue of a panoptic vision (cf. Pratt, 1991).

The Western spectacle is conceived although not born at this moment; paradoxically it requires for its spectacular development the active forgetting of the imperial formation of the West, which is provided by a white amnesia (Hesse, 1997a). This occurs in the post-1945/post-colonial period of institutional decolonization. White amnesia accentuates the obliteration from the heritage of modern Western institutions explicit memories that situate European identities and national cultures in the imperial discourses that constituted them. The conceptual repressions of white amnesia represent the articulatory power of racism as inscribed in a displaced, if not discredited, hardly remembered imperial regime. What emerges therefore in the apparent natural birthing of the Western spectacle is a governmental division of the world into two parts, 'one of which is held up as a self-representation to the world and is superior to the world' (Debord, 1994, p. 220). In the Western spectacle we find the cultural elevation of the West over the 'non-West' and the aesthetic subordination of 'non-whiteness' to whiteness. This visual regime is 'the opposite of dialogue' (Debord, 1994, pp. 13–17). It promotes a specular unthinkability which evades recognition of its complicity with imperialism or racism and resists accountability to those post-colonial cultures of modernity which incorporate as part of their raison d'être a distinctive reflexive globalization.

THE DISCOURSE OF REFLEXIVE GLOBALIZATION

The Western conceptual disavowal of globalization as racialization is not immune to a counter-reflexivity. This is because reflexivity describes an intrinsic concern with the production and accountability of knowledge in relation to its social or political usefulness. Giddens (1990) has argued that reflexivity is a defining characteristic of the recurrent constitution of human action because it subjects human behaviour to a horizon of self-monitoring. However, the experience of reflexivity in modernity is radicalized because the revision of conventions and social practices applies continuously to all aspects of life; it involves the 'presumption of wholesale reflexivity' and this includes the 'reflection upon the nature of reflection itself' (Giddens, 1990, p. 39). Reflexivity in the context of modernity then subverts both reason and certainty in knowledge since we can never be sure that 'any given element of that knowledge will not be revised' (Giddens, 1990). This idea has been extended and developed by Ulrich Beck (1997) in what he describes as 'reflexive modernization'. It describes a radical questioning of modernity in relation to its origins and its possibilities.

Reflexive modernization is 'permeated with the knowledge that the future cannot be understood and withstood in the conceptual framework of the past' (Beck, 1997, p. 14). What Beck seems to be arguing is that reflexive modernization not only calls the classical formulations of industrial society into question, it even questions the form that questioning has conventionally taken. It is possible to develop these conceptual resources to identify in the questioning of modernity a questioning of imperialism. In this way we can illuminate an expositional form of reflexive globalization. It is nurtured by a post-colonial desire and sensibility that arise from the marking of a 'time-lag' (Bhabba, 1994) in the cultural constitution of modernity. The time-lag accrues from the values and histories conferred upon metropolitan Western societies which exclude from contemporary relevance the colonial and slave histories because they contravene the idea of universally applied values (e.g., liberty, equality, tolerance). Although Europe's metropolitan and colonial cultures co-existed at the time of the formation of modern values, within the Western spectacle historically recurrent issues raised by the formerly colonized and enslaved appear to bear little or no relation to the democratic meanings enshrined in the current, expansive direction of Western societies. With the exposure of this modernist time-lag a post-colonial sensibility emerges with the question, 'who defines this present from which we speak?' (Bhabba, 1994, p. 244).

As part of this post-colonial critique I want to argue that Aimé Césaire (1972) offers an almost paradigmatic exposition of reflexive globalization. It is a discourse on colonialism which provides a critical interrogation of the modes through which the components of imperialism and racism, concealed by the Western spectacle, continue to shape the globalization of the world, even though this influential formation is discursively repressed. Although Césaire does not use the term globalization, his frequent references to European and Western civilization in relation to the cultures of the world implies the concept. Césaire suggests it is through the critiques of those subjugated as 'non-Europeans' and 'non-whites' that the imperialism of Western culture is exposed as using idealized principles to represent the globalization of the colonial project variously as: evangelicalism, philanthropy, conquering disease, pushing back the boundaries of knowledge, the glorification of God, or extending the rule of law (Césaire, 1972).

Only within the cognitive emancipations of post-colonial discourses can reflexive globalization affirm its theoretical significance. Using

Césaire makes it possible to specify five related aspects of reflexive globalization which indict the Western spectacle's display of 'humanity reduced to a monologue' (Césaire, 1972, p. 57) and insert a critical questioning of white amnesia. First, reflexive globalization analyses the decivilizing and brutalizing impact of imperialism on the construction of Europe and its hegemony over global culture. Secondly, it exposes the extent to which Europe tolerates and accepts the violations of 'non-European' people by Europe, even though this violates European principles of humanism. Thirdly, as a critique of globalization's complicity with imperialism, it highlights the relation of liberal and democratic concepts to a history that has been 'sordidly racist' (Césaire, 1972, p. 13). Fourthly, it reflects on the principles of legitimization established to expropriate and exploit 'non-European' peoples for public or global purposes. Finally, it can be said to monitor the continuing impact of colonialism on modernity, which takes the globalized form of racism in Western societies. What I am suggesting here is that reflexive globalization envisages the euphemistic and sanitizing logics of the Western spectacle. It constitutes both an exposition of the Western spectacle's conceptual repression of its imperial and racial formations as well as a critique of the continuing modulated effects of that formation.

DIASPORA FORMATIONS AND REFLEXIVITY

The continuing incidence of racism in Western societies (Rattansi and Westwood, 1994), which inhabits the realm beyond the Western spectacle, provides a context in which the significance of diaspora as a recurrent transnational and cross-cultural formation emerges as a conduit of reflexive globalizations. These migratory formations of globally dispersed populations are increasingly specifying the historical and cartographic entwining of all representative, dialogical and visually interactive cultural identities (Brah, 1996). Diasporas are symptomatic of globalization because they emphasize the multiplicity of different linkages and interconnections that transcend the nation-states and societies that comprise the modern world system (cf. McGrew, 1992). They constitute part of what represents a challenge to the nation-state in its present form because they are increasingly implicated in transnational networks of economic, political and cultural transactions irreducible to its inclinations. The idea of diaspora, however, needs to be distinguished initially at the empirical level from

the reductive geographical descriptions o
For example, Gerard Chaliend and Jean-P.
that diasporas can be defined in relation to
indicators. First, there is the question of the
which dispersal takes place, as for instance th
religious and/or ethnic collectivities, precipitate
political. Secondly, there is the development of a
which disseminates accounts of the history associat
of dispersion and forms the basis of a cultural he.　　　displaced population. Thirdly, there is the desire of a wi.　urvive as a
community or a minority through the transmission of a cultural heritage. Fourthly, there is the impact of temporality where the passage
of time testifies to the vibrancy and longevity of the displaced population's social survival, cultural adaptations and recognition of being
part of a diaspora (Chaliend and Rageau, 1995). The empirical idea of
diaspora incorporates a profound reference to a centre or home, from
which the dispersion occurs; raises questions of who travels, when,
how and under what circumstances; and accentuates the politics
invested in the distinctions between diasporic locations and 'home'
locations (Grewal and Caplan, 1994; Brah, 1996).

The *critical* relation of diaspora to globalization in modernity,
however, can only be revealed if we move beyond its empirical designation. Avtar Brah (1996) has provided a number of important theoretical clarifications which suggest that the empirical description of
diaspora as a process must be further distinguished from the concept
of diaspora, which 'places the discourse of "home" and "dispersion" in
creative tension, inscribing a homing desire while simultaneously critiquing discourses of fixed origins' (Brah, 1996, pp. 192–3). In addition
she introduces the idea of diaspora-space as a genealogical form of
analysis which addresses the contested interface between local,
national and transnational social encounters. This formulation can be
used to contextualize various discursive imprints of globalization since
it describes the political and cultural cohabitation of migrants and
their descendants together with those constituted and represented as
indigenous. It is through diaspora-space that the entanglement and
intertwining of histories of dispersion with those of entrenchment produces distinct cultural and political forms of reflexivity. Diaspora-
space is the site where 'the native is as much a diasporian as the
diasporian is the native' (Brah, 1996, p. 209). In this sense Britain is a
diaspora-space in so far as it is reflexively constituted as a dialogical
setting in which social forms are disclosed through contested and

interactions between differently ethnicized diasporas that both the white governmental (Hesse, 1997a) and diverse cultural representations of national identity (Hesse, 1997b).

A number of these features arise in the representational significance of the modern Black diaspora in late twentieth-century Britain. Generally however, the category of diaspora has been used empirically by Black historians and cultural theorists to provide a focus for the modern slavery dispersal and colonial displacement of populations of African descent since the end of the fifteenth century throughout and beyond the so-called 'New World'. It signifies the historical geographies of a globalized identity structured through cultural proliferation and racial dislocation (Harris, 1982; Conniff and Davis 1994). This can be developed to suggest that the Black diaspora is a transnational and cross-cultural structure of movements, dialogues, reflections and dispositional elective affinities (Gilroy, 1997).

Within the intensified consciousness of the world as a Western spectacle, the reflexive globalization of the Black diaspora has been conceptually initiated through two recurrent idioms of its intellectual and popular discourses. First, through cultural *metonyms,* where diasporic representations of various experiential shades of Black skin are invested with *symbolizing affinities* that connect the dispersed representations and reminiscences of modern African genealogies. The perspectives supplied by cultural metonyms indict prevailing accounts of globalization which normalize the colonial historicity and racism of Europe in relation to people of African descent. Secondly through *political metaphors,* reflexive globalization in the Black diaspora signifies diverse expressive circumventions of racism, interrogations of democracy and restitutions of Black bodily integrity in Western cultures and politics. These political metaphors affirm accountable valorizations of Black being in modernity and expose the liberal–colonial doubleness (Bhabba, 1994) of Western democracies.

Reflexive globalization in this emancipatory context criss-crosses and constitutes the 'Black Atlantic' network of aesthetic practices, cultural exchanges and political communications (Thompson, 1983; Gilroy, 1993) that institute, transform and circulate Black identities, visuals, musics and discourses. This is why the reflexive globalization of the Black diaspora in Britain begins with contemporary intellectual and popular interpretations of the slavery experience and their residual implications for everyday life in Western cultures. It extends to the cultivations of the meanings attached to the Black subaltern experience of modernity as an imperial consequence of European colonialism in Africa and the Caribbean; racist exclusion and subordi-nation in the United States and Europe; and the twentieth-century Black migratory and settlement experience in Britain together with its regionalized accentuations (Hesse, 1993). It also involves the retrieval and affirmation of African histories and philosophizing discredited by Western culture (Mudimbe, 1989; 1994), and the transformation of Western national cultures through empowering Black political, cul-tural and existential practices (see Gordon, 1997). At this point it becomes important to specify what gives rise to this complex forma-tion and the development of specific reflexivities in the modern Black diaspora.

Time-Space Compression in the Black Diaspora

So far I have suggested that the reflexivities of the Black diaspora have been diversely shaped and variously induced by the global modalities of slavery, imperialism and racism. What I want to discuss here is how these articulations can be best understood by reference to the time-space compression of the Black diaspora. According to David Harvey (1989) time-space compression refers to the social con-struction of a global sensation in which the pace of life seems to speed up, as spatial frontiers and geographies can be rapidly crossed in a variety of ways and the experience of time as duration in the world shortens in diverse modes of social being. Consequently social life is increasingly defined on the reflexive learning curve of 'how to cope with an overwhelming sense of compression of our spatial and tempo-ral worlds' (Harvey, 1989, p. 240). We need, however, to extend the concept of time-space compression beyond Harvey's tendency to reduce it to those aspects of the Western world privileged in a hege-monic European imagination. As Doreen Massey (1994) argues, time-space compression needs to be understood in differential and even oppositional terms, since it 'must have been felt for centuries, though from a very different point of view by colonized peoples all over the world' (Massey, 1994, p. 147). This suggests that we need to raise par-ticular questions about the different causes of geographical mobility and variable senses of time and place in the contemporary discourses of globalization, as well as factoring in the experiential differences of 'race', gender, class and ethnicity (Massey, 1994).

In both political and cultural terms the Black diaspora is profoundly implicated in the global sense of a shrinking and shifting world that increasingly provides either little or precarious respite from racialized inequities and injustices in avowedly liberal-democratic polities (Gilroy, 1993; Bhabba, 1994; Rattansi and Westwood, 1994). This suggests that the sociological concept of 'risk' (Beck, 1997; Giddens, 1990), which points to ever-present, over-arching threats or hazards to social life across the planet, needs to recognize the Westernized colonial risk to 'environmental racism' (Macionis and Plummer, 1997). In this social context of risk Black people have continually mobilized challenges to social exclusion, civil-rights violations, cultural devaluation, economic impoverishment and racial victimization (see Marable, 1985, 1988).

The incidence of 'risk' across the Black diaspora exposes the logic of its time-space compression. This involves what I have referred to elsewhere as the Black temporality of the cut (Hesse, 1993). It describes a discontinuous temporality in which contemporary Black experiences are variously and repetitively cut back to their historical, colonial dimensions; it is an engaged, re-interpretative formation of racialized time sensibilities which subvert the shallow depth of remembrance in Western social life as well as accelerating the desire for social change. As a consequence, everyday Black diasporic subjectivities are frequently de-stabilized by symbolic reminders of the unresolved racialized injustices of modernity.

This also has consequences for the meaning of Black subjectivity. It underlines a constitutive split in the social construction of Black identities; a split between two different temporalities of subjectivity distinguished by Edouard Glissant (1989) as 'reversion and diversion'. For the presence of Black identities in the social conditions of displacement reversion signifies the obsession with origins, it permanently 'consecrates' the idea of returning to the geographical, historical and cultural significance of Africa. Diversion however is a countervailing temporality, it is an inducement to face the future in the prevailing conditions and engage with the contemporary Western implications of racialized displacement (cf. Glissant, 1989). The forms of reflexive globalization which flow from these cross-cutting temporalities can be defined in three specific ways. First, an anti-slavery reflexivity that enunciates the axiological restitution[8] of humanity and integrity to Black embodiment in the context of human diversity. Secondly, an anti-colonial reflexivity that affirms the national sovereignty or communitarian edification[9] of Black people's lives, livelihoods and cultural heritage. Thirdly, an anti-racist reflexivity that challenges the unequalized acquisition and restrictive benefits of democratic citizenship available to Black populations in Western societies.

Each of the reflexive logics which emerge and overlap in these modalities represents the impact of time-space compression on the Black diaspora. As meditative and expressive forms they resonate through everyday discourses. Whether through Black musics, newspapers, stage productions, art exhibitions, community discussions, radio, cinema, novels, monographs, telephone conversations, church services, stand-up comedy; these reflexive logics resource memories, exposés and elaborations of the racialized grounds of social action which circulate in the global formation of Western institutions and identities. It is here that the politics and cultures of diasporic interventions produce and sustain Black identities, in an antagonistic relation to the global, governmental institution of Western culture (Hesse, 1997b). Or, as Stuart Hall puts it, in relation to Black cultural politics:

The attempt to snatch from the hidden histories another place to stand in, another place to speak from ... that moment is an extremely important moment. It is a moment which always tends to be over-run and to be marginalized by the dominant forms of globalization. (Hall, 1991, p. 35)

The reflexivities implied in this diasporic formation not only express a desire to avoid the representational annihilation of Black identity in modernity, they provide a distinctive interpretation of the meaning of globalization and attempt to shatter the chimerical idealizations of the Western spectacle.

CONCLUSIONS

In thinking about the reflexive globalization of the Black diaspora in relation to theoretical discourses of globalization, it is important to consider how and why it continues to contest the unresolved inequities and injustices which are constitutive of racialized discrepancies in Western societies. Although these pervade and contaminate the organic ideals of Western cultures and politics they are regularly disavowed in the Western spectacle of globalization. This means coming to terms with the formation of the Black diaspora within and beyond modernity's subaltern processes, requiring an alternative account of racialized modernity and its globalization. Reflexive globalization exposes, through the interventions it facilitates around the circumvention and interrogation of Western identities, cultures and politics (see Hesse, 1997b), the prevailing unquestioned racialized conceptions of globalization in which there is no discernible difference between the world and the Western spectacle. Reflexive globalization, where it is expressed and where it is acknowledged, serves as an urgent reminder that it is still: 'the West that studies the ethnographies of the others not the others who study the ethnography of the West' (Césaire, 1972, p. 54).

ACKNOWLEDGEMENTS

I would like to thank both Avtar Brah and Denise Noble for their patience and critical insights in providing detailed comments on earlier versions of this chapter.

NOTES

1. Disavowal describes the process or logic through which particular issues, events or themes are consistently ignored and excluded from the realm of commentary or acknowledgement and therefore repressed from view.
2. Racialization here is used in a global sense to describe the representation of the world as if it naturally coincided with the Western hegemonic distinction between the ascribed visual meanings of European and 'non-European' bodies and the characteristics attributed to their respective cultures. In this context the signifier Europe or European is not necessarily continental-bound, it also refers to a certain Western centralizing Eurocentrism (Sayyid, 1997) that represents imperialized countries like the United states, Canada and Australia as steeped in unquestionably white European foundations. Consequently, racialization also signifies the world diversity of human cultures in the reductive terminology of 'white' and 'non-white', where the latter as a category implies secondariness and subordination.
3. The quasi-methodological role of 'deconstruction' (see Gasch, 1994) in social theory is to identify within a discourse or an analysis areas of inconsistency and undecidability in relation to the logic of the argument. This is in order to reveal at least two things. First, significant issues or themes connected with the analysis which are repressed or treated insignificantly by the analysis, yet incidentally referred to in the analysis (e.g., 'race' and imperialism in relation to globalization). Secondly, the methods or 'decisions' which are used to produce the intentional outcome of the argument despite the existence of inconsis-

tencies and alternative interpretations. In this sense deconstruction is a subversive yet revelatory analytical approach.

4.   It needs to be remembered that the time-period and meaning of modernity coincides with the institution of European colonialism in the Americas from the late sixteenth-century onwards and the age of high imperialism in the nineteenth-century consolidation of European colonialism in India, the Pacific and Africa.

5.   There is considerable debate about the meaning of the post-colonial (see Williams and Chrisman, 1993). My use of it here is not intended to convey the idea that we are now in that chronological era of superseded colonial formations; but rather to suggest the post-colonial is a theoretical and political intervention which attempts to expose and contest the limitations of imperial conceptuality (Said, 1993). It is a thinking at the limits (Hall, 1996) which reveals the complex cultural and political interplay between imperial and subaltern discourses (Bhabba, 1994) and articulates the form of emancipatory representations and strategies (Parry, 1994).

6.   The concept of 'discrepancy' refers to inconsistencies of meaning or contradictions of principles within a discourse or formation (e.g., racism in relation to liberal-democracy) which are tolerated as if insignificant, left unexamined and held not to put into question the overall ideals of the discourse (e.g., liberty and equality). I have dealt with this at length elsewhere (see Hesse, 1997b).

7.   Michel Foucault's concept of governmentality describes the relationship between power and knowledge in the regulation of all forms of personal, social and political conduct (see Burchell et al., 1991). It is used here to suggest that racism is developed as a relation of governance between bodies racialized as hegemonic and subordinate (e.g., European and 'non-European' bodies). See also Hesse (1997a).

8.   This describes the significance in Black diasporic cultures of venerating and valorizing the modern relevance of African-derived or inspired values, knowledges and identifications, despite the West's exclusive portrayal of Africa as savage, exotic, unstable and poverty stricken. See also Hesse (1993).

9.   This describes the emphasis placed on empowerment through community formations and values in the development of Black movements for civil liberties, social justice and economic liberation. See also Hesse (1993).

REFERENCES

Beck, U. (1997), *The Reinvention of Politics: Rethinking Modernity in the Global Social Order* (Oxford: Polity Press).

Bhabba, H. (1994), *Locations of Culture* (London: Routledge).

Brah, A. (1996), *Cartographies of Diaspora* (London: Routledge).

Burchell, G., Gordon, C. and Miller, P. (eds) (1991), *The Foucault Effect: Studies in Governmentality* (London: Harvester and Wheatsheaf).

Césaire, A. (1972), *Discourse on Colonialism* (New York: Monthly Review Press).

Chaliend, G., and Rageau, J.-P. (1995), *The Penguin Atlas of Diasporas* (Harmondsworth, UK: Viking).

Conniff, M. L., and Davis, T. J. (1994), *Africans in the Americas: A History of the Black Diaspora* (New York: St Martin's Press).

Curtin, P. (1990), *The Rise and Fall of the Plantation Complex: Essays in Atlantic History* (Cambridge: Cambridge University Press).

Debord, G. (1994), *Society of the Spectacle* (New York: Zone Books).

Eze, E. C. (ed.) (1997), *Race and the Enlightenment* (Oxford: Blackwell).

Featherstone, M. (ed.) (1991), *Introduction in Global Culture: Nationalism, Globalization and Modernity* (London: Sage).

Gasche, R. (1994), *Inventions of Difference* (London: Harvard University Press).

Giddens, A. (1990), *Consequences of Modernity* (London: Polity Press).

Gilroy, P. (1997), 'Diaspora and the Detours of Identity', in K. Woodward (ed.), *Identity and Difference* (London: Sage).

Gilroy, P. (1993), *The Black Atlantic: Modernity and Double Consciousness* (London: Verso).

Gilroy, P. (1987), *There Ain't No Black in the Union Jack* (London: Unwin Hyman).

Glissant, E. (1989), *Caribbean Discourse* (Charlottesville, VA: University of Virginia Press).

Gordon, L. R. (ed.) (1997), *Existence in Black: An Anthology of Black Existential Philosophy* (London: Routledge).

Grewal, I. and Caplan, C. (eds.) (1994), Introduction, in *Scattered Hegemonies* (London: University of Minnesota Press).

Hall, S. (1996), 'When was the "Post-colonial?" Thinking at the Limit', in I. Chambers and L. Curti (eds), *The Post-Colonial Question* (London: Routledge).

Hall, S. (1992), 'The West and the Rest: Discourse and Power', in S. Hall and B. Gieben (eds), *Formations of Modernity* (London: Polity Press).

Hall, S. (1991), 'The Local and the Global: Globalization and Ethnicity', in A. D. King (ed.), *Culture, Globalization and the World System* (New York: Macmillan).

Harris, J. (ed.) (1982), *Global Dimensions of the African Diaspora* (Washington, DC: Howard University Press).

Harvey, D. (1989), *The Condition of Postmodernity* (Oxford: Basil Blackwell).

Hesse, B. (1997a), 'White Governmentality: Urbanism, Nationalism, Racism', in S. Westwood and J. Williams (eds), *Imagining Cities: Signs, Scripts, Memories* (London: Routledge).

Hesse, B. (1997b), 'It's Your World: Discrepant M/Multiculturalisms', *Social Identities*, 3 (3), October.

Hesse, B. (1993), 'Black to Front and Black Again: Racialization through Contested Times and Spaces', in M. Keith and S. Pile (eds), *Place and the Politics of Identity* (London: Routledge).

James, C. L. R. (1938/1980), *Black Jacobins* (London: Allison and Busby).

McClintock, A. (1995), *Imperial Leather: Race, Gender and Sexuality in the Colonial Conquest* (Routledge: London).

McGrew, A. (1992), 'A Global Society', in S. Hall, D. Held and T. McGrew (eds), *Modernity and its Futures* (London: Polity Press).

Macionis, J. J., and Plummer, K. (1997), *Sociology: A Global Introduction* (London: Prentice Hall Europe).

Marable, M. (1988), *African and Caribbean Politics* (London: Verso).

Marable, M. (1985), *Black American Politics* (London: Verso).

Massey, D. (1994), *Space, Place and Gender* (Cambridge: Polity Press).

Mudimbe, V. Y. (1994), *The Idea of Africa* (London: James Currey).

Mudimbe, V. Y. (1989), *The Invention of Africa* (London: James Currey).

Pagden, A. (1995), *Lords of All the World: Ideologies of Empire in Spain, Britain and France c.1500–c.1800* (London: Yale University Press).

Parry, B. (1994), 'Resistance Theory/Theorising Resistance or Two Cheers for Nativism', in F. Barker, P. Hulme and M. Iverson (eds), *Colonial Discourse/Postcolonial Theory* (Manchester: Manchester University Press).

Pieterse, J. N. (1994), 'Unpacking the West: How European is Europe', in A. Rattansi and S. Westwood (eds), *Racism, Modernity and Identity* (London: Polity Press).

Pratt, M. L. (1991), *Imperial Eyes* (London: Routledge).

Rattansi, A., and Westwood, S. (1994), *Racism, Modernity and Identity* (London: Polity Press).

Robertson, R. (1992), *Globalization* London: Sage).

Said, E. (1993), *Culture and Imperialism* (London: Vintage).

Sayyid, B. (1997), *A Fundamental Fear: Eurocentrism and the Emergence of Islamism* (London: Zed Books).

Solow, B. (ed.) (1991), *Slavery and the Rise of the Atlantic System* (Cambridge: Cambridge University Press).

Thomas, N. (1994), *Colonialism's Culture* (London: Polity Press).

Thompson, R. F. (1983), *Flash of the Spirit: African and Afro-American Art and Philosophy* (New York: Vintage Books).

Thompson, V. B. (1987), *The Making of the African Diaspora in the Americas, 1441–1990* (London: Longman).

Wiegman, R. (1995), *American Anatomies* (London: Routledge).

Williams, E. (1944), *Capitalism and Slavery* (London: André Deutsch).

Williams, P. and Chrisman, L. (eds) (1993), *Colonial Discourse and Post-colonial Discourse* (London: Harvester and Wheatsheaf).

8 Globalization, the Pope and the Gypsies
THOMAS A. ACTON

All modern states are nation-states

(Giddens, 1993, p. 311)

Why is globalization theory so fascinating? In part, at least, because it legitimizes questions very different from those addressed by political theory and the sociology of politics before they found the writings of Wallerstein (1974) or Sklair (1991). But that fascination endures precisely because the norm of political analysis is that bluntly expressed by Giddens above. If we look, however, at some recent developments in globalization theory, and the way these fit with international Romani politics, as a case study, we may come to see that the view of globalization as a new process in the history of the world is misleading; that it is the nationalization of the sixteenth century that has always been an aberrant and anti-human ideological process requiring violence and the use of force against the innocent to maintain its cognitive hold.

For any sociologist or historian involved with Romani Studies over a long period, Giddens' presentation of the ideology of the nation-state as though it were a set of definitions which could assist sociological understanding, closely followed by a failure to realize the racist nature of Marshall's theory of citizenship (Giddens, 1993, p. 313), is likely to arouse emotions which go beyond irritation into outrage. The virtue and the genius of Giddens, however, is that by presenting a conventional wisdom so concisely, he sometimes gives exactly what we need to contradict, in order to understand the difficulties in our own thought. Who is to say, as the post-Giddensians will undoubtedly assert, this is not within the great man's obscurer purposes?

This chapter works around the proposition that any presentation of a political entity as a nation-state is a self-serving racist deception. I have presented elsewhere (Acton, 1994) a general account of the cognitive difficulties that the failure by European thought to address the endemic nature of genocidal activity within states defining themselves as national presents to Romani Studies. There, I argued that West

European Gypsy history has to be understood as a story of two geno-cides, rather than one of continuous, undifferentiated persecution. Of course, ethnic conflict and discrimination have never actually ceased; but they are cyclical in intensity. The development of the nation-state and of agricultural capitalism in the sixteenth-century brought at first exclusionary, and then genocidal, policies to a crisis. England, and many other states, made it a capital crime merely to be a Gypsy. The classic 'Gypsy way of life' was the result of the survival strategies of Gypsy groups isolated within West European political units, taking them down a different road of social development from that of the much larger enslaved Romani communities of the Balkans, or the small taxation-collectives of the Baltic region. Then, from the late nineteenth-century, a different kind of assimilative, homogenizing European racism emerged, equally unable to accept the Jewish ghetto or the Gypsy caravan as tolerated exceptions from the norm. The way of life which was created after the first genocide was rendered non-viable by the Nazi genocide, the most extreme example of European anti-Gypsyism. We have to explain, however, why European thought has not repudiated anti-Gypsyism in the same way as it has repudi-ated anti-Semitism. The answer lies in the failure to analyse the conse-quence of sixteenth- and seventeenth-century genocides against Gypsies, which left them in the position that Jews would be in today, had the Nazis won. This failure leaves Western politicians unable to realize they they are the heirs of unrepentantly genocidal states. For a British Labour politician like Roy Hattersley (1997), for example, his racist slurs against 'gypsies' are as unimportant as a joke about 'fairies'. There is no general European apology to the Gypsies, as there is to the Jews. Good anti-racists may fail to realize that Gypsies are an ethnic community, or series of ethnic communities. People are ignorant, because knowledge would entail an intolerable delegitima-tion of European nation-states.

I hope in this chapter, however, to go beyond previous attempts to present globalization theory as a way out of this impasse. I want, rather, to suggest that the immediate attractiveness and theoretical glamour of globalization theory occurs primarily because the preva-lence of nation-state ideology has obscured those facets of our common human experience which globalization theory brings to the fore. In the chapter that follows we will see the Pope, and Gypsies both lettered and unlettered, who may never even have heard of Sklair, seizing on the terminology of an explicitly sociological theory, for their own purposes. I hope thereby to discount the novelty of globalization concepts, and present the possibility of a discourse within which, from a longer perspective on human history, it is the theory of the nation-state we see as an aberration in collective human self-representation.

GLOBALIZATION THEORY AND NEW SOCIAL MOVEMENTS

In fact Sklair (1995) presents us with a possible account of how globalization theory may offer to transnational 'new social movements' the tools with which to theorize their own existence, although he also suggests that there are great difficulties in the way of their doing so effectively. He points to the failure of the older trade union and socialist international movement ('the global organization of labour') to oppose transnational capitalism effectively, and suggests that oppositional 'new social movements' (feminism, environmentalism, consumer protectionism) are equally constrained to local disruption in any effective opposition. To sum up a rather dense argument, after making the now commonplace starting-point distinction between 'international' (that which operates within more than one nation-state) and 'transnational' (that which operates beyond the constraints of the nation-states), Sklair (1995, p. 500) asserts that the dominance of global capitalism has to be theorized through three building blocks: 'the *transnational corporation,* the characteristic economic form of economic transnational practices, a still evolving *transnational capitalist class* in the political sphere, and in the culture-ideology sphere, *the culture-ideology of consumerism*'. He goes on (p. 508) to assert that just because these are global, each of them can 'only be effectively challenged locally by those who are prepared to disrupt their anti-social practices'. Thus, in globalization theory, that which is 'transnational' is strongly contrasted to that which is 'international'. 'International organizations' are formed by the linking together and co-operation of analogous organizations within separate nation-states, and are dependent on the reality of the nation-state. 'Transnational organizations' are those which are autonomous but exist on, or have spread to, the territory of more than one nation-state, but are not part of the structure of those nation-states. So, for example, 'transnational corporations' are very hard for nation-states to control because they can easily shift profits, production and top personnel to the state territory which offers them the most favourable regime.

GYPSIES AND THE TRANSNATIONAL

The word 'transnational' thus becomes the buzz-word of this thinking. Whether or not Sklair (1995) is right in insisting that effective resistance to the world-system must start locally, pan-Gypsy activism (or Romani nationalism or the International Romani movement, however one terms the array of Gypsy politics) has jumped on the buzz-word 'transnational'. For example, a new organization, the Scottish Gypsy Traveller Association (SGTA), held a 'Transnational Conference and Festival' in October 1996. Scottish Gypsies such as Willie Reid (1993) had for some time criticized the Scottish particularism associated with the School of Scottish Studies and Hamish Henderson (1992, p. 174), which tried to incorporate the folklore of the Scottish Travellers as though it were merely an aspect of Scottish culture, denying or minimizing its Romani roots. By inviting Gypsies from North America and Eastern Europe to their conference, the SGTA were bringing the rest of the (Gypsy) world into play to combat Scottish assimilationism.

A current application by UNITE (United Nomads for Integrated Transnational Education) for planning permission for a Gypsy caravan site in Essex seeks to add planning value by promising to include a classroom for 'transnational education'. I am not an innocent bystander in this process; I was co-opted onto its steering committee. I have been discussing these concepts with Gypsy activists myself, acting, I suppose, as a kind of sociological gun-runner, liberating theoretical small arms and discourse grenades that Gypsy intellectuals and activists can detonate among the complacent officialdom of the local and national state. But I am hardly alone in this; every sociologist involved with Gypsy politics finds him or herself doing this, especially those sociologists such as Nicolae Gheorghe in Romania or Ken Lee in Australia, who are Romani themselves.

Such terminology finds favour only because Gypsy organizations can add effectiveness to their action by a transnational strategy. The relations of the Gypsy political movement with the Roman Catholic Church provide a particularly interesting example of this.

Lobbying the Vatican

I have discussed elsewhere (Acton 1979; 1997) general social and political aspects of the relations between Gypsy groups and organized religion. To cut a long story short, during the 1980s the former paternalist–racist–missionary approach of the Roman Catholic Church to

Gypsies came under criticism because of its perceived failure to stem the tide of conversions from Catholicism to Pentecostalism. In Rome the leading Italian scholar-priest working with Gypsies, Bruno Niccolini, led a different strategy, of learning from Pentecostals instead of demonizing them, and of endorsing broader social objectives, and so seeking relations with Gypsy political organizations to equal that which Gypsy Pentecostals had built up locally, particularly in France. These approaches were pursued not only through one of the Vatican's house journals (Niccolini 1990), but also through the publications of the Roman Catholic Gypsy organization and journal *Lacio Drom* (Karpati, 1992). The changes of state system in Eastern Europe in 1989 liberated a whole new cohort of Romani intellectuals eager to take advantage of this, in particular the brilliant Romanian sociologist and activist Nicolae Gheorghe, himself a dark-skinned, black-eyed Gypsy, but also the son of a policeman, pupil of the greatest Romanian sociologist, Henri Stahl, and a long-term aide to traditional Romanian Gypsy leaders, and now one of the heroes of Isobel Fonseca's travel book *Bury Me Standing* (1995).

The confluence of these interests took place at a conference organized by the Centro Studi Zingari in Rome, looking at Gypsy politics in general, and given the grandiose title *East Facing West* (Karpati, 1992). Part of the not-so-hidden agenda of that conference was to gain the formal support of the Roman Catholic Church at the highest level for the political strategies of the International Romani Union, represented there by two of its leading members Rajko Duric and Nicolae Gheorghe, and a number of their supporters. In this attempt they were as successful as they could possibly have hoped to be.

The Pope's Response

On 26 May 1991, the Pope delivered a discourse (Wojtyla, 1991) to a two-thirds Gypsy audience who included Pentecostals and members of other religions, as well as Catholics. An English translation of the original Italian discourse is given in Appendix to this chapter. This discourse was obviously formulated in the first instance in response to a political agenda; but it is also a formal statement with theoretical, and spiritual and sociological implications of greater complexity and depth than any previous Papal statement on Gypsies, and constituted a definitive breach with previous paternalistic and anti-political stances. The implications also go beyond the theorization of Gypsy politics. It refers to Gypsies as:

a minority which knows no territorial limits and which has repudiated armed struggle as a means of imposing its will; a minority paradigmatic in its transnational dimensions which brings together in a
single cultural community people dispersed around the world and
diverse in race, language and religion.

This text holds out the possibility, through a radical critique of the
pretensions of nationality, of a fresh understanding of the meaning of
catholicity or universality, and therefore of the nature of a catholic
Christianity itself.

The third and fourth sections of the discourse carry the political
message. There is a condemnation of 'marginalization and violent discrimination', asserting that acceptance should not depend on assimilation, but that Gypsies have the right to be 'recognized as an ethnic
minority, with rights to a distinct cultural identity, and with a language
of your own', and to a nomadic life if they so choose. This affirmation
is not left hanging in a moral vacuum, but is linked to an endorsement
by name of the then most important Romani political organization,
the Romani Union, and to encouragement for a political response
from lawmakers to the Romani Union's demands. Effectively the
Pope has put his weight behind the processes of negotiation with
Gypsies of the European Community and the Conference on (now
Organization for) Security and Co-operation in Europe (CSCE; now
OSCE). Indeed, Romani Union activists were separately assured that
the Vatican would use diplomacy within the CSCE to raise the issue of
violence against Gypsies in Eastern Europe. In other words, the
Vatican promised to lend its transnational clout to the transnational
strategy of a 'new social movement'. Politically, Gypsy activists could
hardly have asked for more. This suggests perhaps, that despite
Sklair's pessimism, a new social movement can go beyond local disruption of elites and ideologies to utilize the logic of transnational
activities within international organizations against ethnic oppression.

The Pope's text also made a subtle intervention in the politics of the
Romani Union itself by describing it as 'a flowing together of national
and local associations of Rom'. This was a clear endorsement of 'feder-
alists' who wished to see the Romani Union adopt a more federal
structure, recognizing the autonomy of local constituent organizations,
in place of the more authoritarian Praesidium-dominated structure
inherited from the influence of 'democratic centralism'. The thrust
would have been imperceptible to anyone not familiar with the issues.
One may speculate that the Pope may not quite have realized what his

advisers had led him to say. The parallel with the Roman Catholic Church itself as a transnational organization remains unstated but must occur to some readers at least. The church too seeks to construct 'a single cultural community' out of 'people dispersed around the world and diverse in race, language and religion'. Should it perhaps also be seen as 'a flowing together of national and local associations' rather than a centralized, authoritarian hierarchy? As much as any text issued from the Vatican, this text shows the ineluctable movement of the Roman Catholic Church, through its endorsement of political democracy, away from its own authoritarian tradition to a far more congregational understanding of the governance of the church.

The political and religious radicalism of this text regarding Gypsies is not left as a specific exception to the general order of things, which affects only Gypsies, but is grounded in a more universal theoretical and spiritual approach, which specifically draws on globalization theory to describe Gypsies as a 'transnational' minority. The Pope accepted this neologism from the advisers who offered it to him after discussions with Romani Union members, including Nicolae Gheorghe. It was in fact rather an eerie experience to have been discussing these phrases at the beginning of the week while the Romani Union representations to the Vatican were being prepared, and then to hear them fall from the Pope's lips at the end of the week. What is their significance?

CHALLENGING THE NATION-STATE

To say that Gypsies are a 'transnational' minority, rather than a 'national' or even an 'international' minority, is to say that they are a phenomenon, a people in their own right, not to be defined simply in contrast to the ethnic majorities in one or several states (cf. Acton and Gheorghe 1993). This implies that there are structures of political rights anterior to, and transcending, the existence of the nation-state; it repudiates the Hobbesian insistence of Renaissance Europe that the nation-state is the seat of all sovereignty. The Pope has been brought to assert that nation-states do not have the right to deal with Gypsies – and by implication, any ethnic minority – as though they were a purely 'internal problem'.

The arguments deployed by Nicolae Gheorghe (1997) elsewhere show how, from a Romani point of view, he evokes Gypsy politics as instantiating forms of transnationalism; this politics is:

something that is lacking in the world at present when the issue of national minorities is played out in intergovernmental politics. At present, the basic framework of such intergovernmental politics is that nation-states make representations to other states when something affects members of their 'nation' who live as a minority in those other states. This adversely affects minorities such as the Roma who have no such resource, no 'fatherland' to back them up. We still have to work out an adequate concept under which Roma can be recognized as a subject of international law protection. ...

The discourse of national minorities is another way to reproduce and to reinforce the nation-state. The fact that the nation-states are so generous now with these 'minorities' is just one device to reinforce the legitimacy of these states as ethnic states, states which actually belong to an ethnic 'majority'. So, ethnic minority policies are exhibited as if in a display cabinet, like a showcase in international politics to make sure that the Council of Europe and the western democracies think that things are good in eastern Europe. ...

Are there any alternatives to this? Let me present my own political utopia, in which I must acknowledge the influence of Liégeois's book *Mutation Tsigane* (1976). It is that of transnationalism. ... How can we try to conceptualize the situation of Roma being a dispersed people, non-territorially-based, and distributed across many countries and so on? Why have I used the word 'transnational' from the array of concepts which are on offer to describe 'non-territorial' or 'cross-statal' or 'dispersed' minorities? The idea, the meaning, is to indicate that we can evolve in a different way to nation states and national minorities. I wish to assert that we can build up an ethnic dynamic and a new image by reference to and in interaction with non-national institutions or supra-national institutions.

From here comes the energy of working through the Council of Europe, the European Community and the United Nations, trying to explore this niche which is provided by supra-national institutions, which can contribute towards a new form and identity which is formed in this dynamic and not that of the nation-states.

(Gheorghe, 1997, pp. 155–61)

The Roman Catholic Church itself is paradigmatically transnational. But the compromise by which it survived the sixteenth-century Reformation was the acceptance in practice of the primacy of the nation-state. The medieval principle of Canossa (where the Holy Roman Emperor submitted on his knees to Papal authority) was reversed, and Catholic French and Spanish kings were to have the same say in determining the leadership of their 'Roman' Catholic state churches as English monarchs in their established Protestant church. Anglican and Lutheran state churches became as authoritarian and violent as Roman Catholicism in the oppression of nonconformist Christians who held to visions of a reformed and autonomous universal Christendom. The Papacy itself acquired de facto Italian nationality. But if Christianity was the biggest ideological victim of the nation-state, Gypsies and Jews, people without territory, were its greatest physical victims.

The historic compromise between church and nation-state is fundamentally repudiated in this text. Gypsies are not cited as an exceptional case, but rather as a paradigm, possessors of characteristics which we all should have, harbingers of the Gorbachevian dream of a 'common home' which the Pope cites in defiance of the reality of the vicious backwash of territorial nationalism currently ravaging Eastern Europe.

Even more extraordinarily, the text, although it defends and affirms Romani ethnic identity, does not rely on constructing an ethnic nationalism to counterpoint territorial nationalism. Instead it acknowledges that the Romani movement brings together 'in a single cultural community people ... diverse in race, language and religion'. This is a truth Gypsy nationalists often find hard to come to terms with, in their desire to standardize the Romani language, or to postulate a single essential or original Romani race or culture, to recast a common history into the type of myth of common origin that ethnic majorities of nation-states have tended to write as their historical heritage.

Of course it is not so: the ancestors of the Romani people who left India were probably of diverse cultural and phenotypic origin even then, drawn together outside India only by their ability to communicate in a Prakritic *lingua franca*. Since then there has been a continuous process of ethnic fragmentation and reconstruction alongside a wide range of other ethnicities. This text presents this diversity not as a weakness, but as a strength. The 'single cultural community' is no less authentic, no less legitimate because it is explicitly a social construction. Even our most cherished cultural traditions were once a fresh creation. Gypsies are not just another new nation; the Romani political movement is here presented as constituting a new paradigm. The implication is that, as at the time of the beginning of the Christian church itself, God is choosing those who are poor, oppressed and despised to transform our general understanding of reality. Our humanity itself is shown to be socially constructed and therefore capable of moral amendment, even in something apparently so deep-rooted as half-a-millennium's racism against Gypsies. The test thus becomes not only a charter for Romani activists within the Roman Catholic Church, but an important item in the collection being compiled by Romani Union diplomacy of declarations in favour of the Rom from international organizations such as the OSCE, the European Union, the Council of Europe and UNESCO (Danbakli, 1994).

Such an approach has to be seen as coming not just out of the immediately preceding discussions between Romani Union representatives and Vatican officials, but out of the whole dialectical interaction between the developing forms of new Gypsy religious and political organizations and established power structures – a globalized politics which has risen to contradict national politics, in the same way that Gypsy organization in the 1960s tried to use national politics to contradict local politics (Acton, 1974). The Pope's discourse is therefore both a product of, and an example of, what can be seen as the tendency to a 'normalization' of the relations between Gypsies and world religions, as well as advocacy of it. But perhaps before this discourse it was not so apparent quite how much such a normalization will undermine accepted ideas of political normality, if anti-Gypsy racism is actually to be deconstructed.

A sociologist involved with Gypsies cannot continue to see the nation-state as an emblem of Giddensian modernity or even postmodernity. The nation-state defined itself from the sixteenth-century onwards not only by the fortified external frontier, but by attacking the aliens, such as Gypsies and Jews, within. The cultural residue of these events can be analysed as a pathological aberration, rather than the norm, if we think of 'globalization' not as something new, but as a restoration of the primacy of the universal (or transnational) in moral analysis which was disrupted by the political forms engendered by the transition from feudalism to capitalism.

REFERENCES

Acton, T. (1974), *Gypsy Politics and Social Change* (London: Routledge and Kegan Paul).

Acton, T. (ed. S. Cranford), (1979) 'The Gypsy Evangelical Church', *The Ecumenical Review* (Journal of the World Council of Churches), vol. 31 (3), pp. 289–95.

Acton, T. (1994), 'Modernization, Moral Panics and the Gypsies', *Sociology Review,* vol. 4 (1) (September), pp. 24–8.

Acton, T., and Gheorghe, N. (1993), 'Minority, Ethnic, National and Human Rights', in M. Reidy and S. Udodesku (eds), *A Call for a New Community* (Geneva: World Council of Churches).

Acton, T. (1998), 'Mediterranean Religions and Romani People', *Journal of Mediterranean Studies,* 7 (1), pp. 37–51.

Danbakli, M. (1994), *On Gypsies: Texts Issued by International Institutions* (Toulouse: Centre Régional de Documentation Pédagogique de Midi-Pyrénées Interface Collection).

Fonseca, I. (1995), *Bury Me Standing* (London: Chatto).

Gheorghe, N. (1997), 'The Social Construction of Romani Identity', in T. Acton (ed.), *Gypsy Politics and Traveller Identity* (Hatfield: University of Hertfordshire Press),

Giddens, A. (1993), *Sociology,* 2nd edn (Cambridge: Polity).

Hattersley, R. (1997), 'The Open Road Leads only to the Internet', *Guardian,* Monday 14 April, p. 20

Henderson, H. (1992), *Alias MacAlias* (Edinburgh: Polygon).

Karpati, M. (ed.) (1992), *Est e Ovest a Confronto sulle politiche regionali e local versi I Rom* (Rome: Centro Studi Zingari).

Liégeois, J.-P. (1976), *Mutation Tsigane* (Paris: Presses Universitaires de France).

Niccolini, Don B. (1990), 'L'Opera Nomadi e la Promozione umana degli Zingari di fronte ai compiti della Chiesa (riassunto)', in Report of the Third International Meeting for the Pastoral Care of Travelling People, 7–9 November 1989, Vatican City, *People on the Move* (Journal of the Pontifical Commission for the Pastoral Care of Migrants and Itinerant Peoples), Anno XX, no. 56, pp. 123–33.

Reid, W. (1993), 'Scottish Gypsies/Travellers and the Folklorists', paper given to the Economic and Social Research Council Seminar on Romani Studies, 9 September, University of Greenwich.

Sklair, L. (1991), *Sociology of the Global System* (London and Baltimore: Harvester and Johns Hopkins University Press).

Sklair, L. (1995), 'Social Movements and Global Capitalism', *Sociology,* vol. 29 (3), pp. 495–512.

Wallerstein, I. (1974), *The Modern World System* (New York: Academic Press).

Wojtyla, K. (Pope John Paul II) (1991), 'Di fronte alle minoranze etniche si consolodi una cultura dell'accoglienza e della solidarieta', *L'Osservatore Romano,* CXXI (223) (27 September).

APPENDIX

(Translated from the Italian of *L'Osservatore Romano,* Friday 27 September 1991.)

The Holy Father attends a conference organized by the Centro Studi Zingari.

'The Presence of Ethnic Minorities should Encourage Tolerance and Solidarity'.

The new climate that has been created in the world allows an enlargement of the understanding and responsiveness of political institutions towards the rights of ethnic minorities. None the less, much needs to be done in order to encourage a genuinely tolerant and solidaristic society. This was what the Holy Father said to an international conference organized by the Centro Studi Zingari. Below is the discourse pronounced by the Holy Father.

Dear Brothers and sisters,

1. It gives me particular joy to welcome you here today, 2 September, on the 26th anniversary of the first meeting between you and Paul VI, of blessed memory.
   Accompanied by certain Conciliar Fathers, the Pope was making a pilgrimage to your camp in Pomezia, when he eloquently asserted the duty that the Church owes to the whole human family. Faithful to the teaching of our redeemer, the Church remembers that the human race, with all its different sections seeking to gain a sincere understanding of each other, must think to build its common future within which the dignity of every person is respected, including those who are as yet still marginalized. This can be postulated as both a condition and a guarantee of a renewed era of solidarity and peace.
   To mark this 'memorable day', Paul VI solemnly enthroned the Madonna Queen of the Gypsies and blessed your tradition of pilgrimages to most of the principal Marian sanctuaries of the world.

2. That day, 26 September 1965, was indeed an important development of the pastoral activity of the Church towards your people.
   That first contact was followed by others, especially on the occasion of the international conferences organized by the Pontifical Council for the Pastorate of Migrants and Itinerants in 1980 and 1989. But there have also been other contacts, during those years, during pastoral visitations of the Roman diocese, and during pilgrimages to various countries of the world such as recently at Szombathely in Hungary.
   This present audience is singularly interesting. The Centro Studi Zingari, based in Rome, is celebrating its 25th anniversary and has marked this auspicious occasion with a conference which has for the past few days discussed the theme 'East facing West: Regional and Local Gypsy Politics', with the participation of representatives of Gypsy organizations and experts from almost all European countries and also of other nations world-wide.
   I wish to give my affectionate thanks to you all, indicating especially Monsignor Giovanni Cheli, President of the Pontifical Council for the Pastorate of Migrants and Itinerants, who kindly briefed me on various aspects of your reality.
   And I think equally cordially of Monsignor Bruno Niccolini, President of the Centro Studi Zingari, who carries pastoral responsibility for

nomads in Rome, and also of Dr. Mirella Karpati, editor of *Lacio Drom Review*, and of Mr Rajko Duric, President of the World Romani Union, and his colleagues.

I also thank for their presence the Hon. Flaminio Piccoli, president of the Italian parliamentary foreign affairs commission, and the Hon. Beatrice Medi, deputy mayor of Rome City.

3. I know how important it is for you to defend the culture of your people and make known the traditions of your people. I can assure you that the Church faithfully guards and encourages in depth the reasons and ideal motivations of [i.e. stemming from] your history.

You are engaged in the task of affirming the essence of your social and cultural identity; you wish to safeguard the diversity of life, ethnicity, culture and modes of travelling which make you distinct. The family constitutes for you the natural location for ethnic consciousness, as the centre of all your being, the solid and irreplaceable nucleus of the organization of your community.

Looking at the generosity you show in handing on life [i.e. having children] we share your concern for preparing the future of the young generation, developing the best of your traditions in a fertile dialogue with other peoples.

The religiosity which permeates your daily life must be admired, and recall to us that God calls on all of you who are believers to bear witness, in accordance with your own cultural identity, to the vocation and mission proper to a Christian calling: to be aware that we are all, all the time, on the road towards the heavenly country.

4. Your history has been marked by marginalization, and also by episodes of violent discrimination. But we have now reached a moment in history which, even if some of its aspects are complex and contradictory, presents also for you as never before specific hopeful possibilities. The fall of barriers which seemed till very recently inviolable offers the possibility of a new dialogue between Peoples and Nations. Minorities are seeking to be recognized as such, with the freedom of their own responsible self-determination, and the desire to participate in the destiny of humanity as a whole.

In this revitalized scenario of hopes and plans, you are also invited to contribute to the building of a more fraternal world, of an authentic 'common home' for us all. You constitute a minority which knows no territorial limits and which has repudiated armed struggle as a means of imposing its will; a minority paradigmatic in its transnational dimensions which brings together in a single cultural community people dispersed around the world and diverse in race, language and religion.

Your dispersion has led in our own time to a movement towards reunification in one large organization, the Romani Union, itself a flowing together of national and local associations of Rom. Thanks to these structures you may hope to succeed more easily in being recognized as an ethnic minority, with rights to a distinct cultural identity, and with a language of your own. At the same time you are asserting the right to be citizens on an equal level with all others in the country in which you choose to live.

Today, political organizations in the community are beginning to give a greater understanding and responsiveness to these aspirations of yours, and for this purpose certain legislative measures are gradually being put forward, although much remains to be done in order that the earth should consolidate an authentic culture of welcome and solidarity.

5. You, dear friends, have been able to survive many trials in the past because you believed and hoped in God and because of the very strong links which bind you together. Now on these same values of faith and community you are called to build your future, transcending the insidious inroads of consumerism and personal pleasure-seeking (i.e. the ethics of the 'me generation'), following what is so fundamental to your life: respect for man as the 'image and glory of God' (1 Cor. 11:7).

I prophesy that this conference of yours will increase in you the desire to construct, with ever greater openness and generosity, a society sensitive to the over-riding human and spiritual values, such as justice, fraternity and peace.

I confide to the Lord, the true creator of Peace for the nations, all your projects for good, assuring you that I will remember you in my prayers.

The Virgin Mary, Queen of the Gypsies, will sustain and accompany you always.

My greetings of blessing to you all.

Part IV
Migration and Globalization

9 Analysing the Political Economy of Migration: the Airport as an 'Effective' Institution of Control

ROBERT MILES

INTRODUCTION

Airports are worlds of the present and especially of the future. As institutions, they embody in their existence and operation the process of globalization. In so doing, they play a significant role in the organization of ethnicity and in the confirmation and transcendence of nationalism. They do all this in the course of organizing the movement of large numbers of people through a confined space in very short periods of time. The British Airports Authority, which owns seven UK airports through which 71 per cent of UK air passenger traffic and 81 per cent of cargo passed in 1995 (BAA plc, 1995), has witnessed in recent years a continuous expansion in the number of passengers handled: 63.7 million in 1988, 77.7 million in 1993 and 87.7 million in 1995 (BAA plc 1988, 1993, 1995).[1] The company itself sees future growth to be a function of globalization (BAA plc, 1995, p. 2):

> This growth in traffic is related to economic recovery in the UK and the health of the global economy. We expect demand for air travel to keep growing well into the 21st century, especially against a background of increasing global interdependence and steady growth in developing countries.

These passenger statistics provide a simple measure of volume but fail to identify a central feature of the structure of airports. Airports are spatially organized to classify and separate different categories of traveller: they provide an excellent opportunity to observe the practice

161

and consequences of the institutional organization of social differentiation and exclusion.

Class differentiation is reproduced in airport organization. In so doing, airports echo the practice of airline companies which distinguish between at least two and usually three different categories, which can be loosely described as First, Business and Tourist classes. One consequence is the provision of privileged space for First and Business class passengers. At London Gatwick Airport, the Fast Track facility provides a priority route through the airport for first and business–class passengers, for example. Universally, special lounges are created, access to which is controlled by swipe cards, for such passengers, separating them from tourist–class passengers and providing a wide range of facilities and services not available to the latter.

Airports also differentiate between nationals and aliens, partly through the dichotomy between domestic and international passengers. For the former, at least when they pass through the domestic terminal, the airport is little more than an expression of the ability to move quickly from one part of the nation-state to another and therefore an expression of how small, in space and time, the nation-state has become. For the latter, when passing through the international terminal, the airport is not only an expression of how small the world has become but it also serves as the site of a national frontier, across which movement is regulated by the state. It is therefore a reminder not only of national identity, but also of the passenger's juridical status in the international order. The latter refracts the current balance of economic and political power within the world capitalist economy, in so far as that balance shapes decisions about who may pass across that frontier, and on what conditions. These decisions are also shaped by and reproduce, racism and sexism.

So airports, like seaports (which have a much longer history), are the sites of migration control and therefore of state power. In the case of an island such as Britain, they have been until very recently the only legally recognized point of transfer into and out of the territory controlled by the UK state. The geographical status of an island does enhance the state's power to control the movement, not only of people but also of capital and commodities: land borders are notoriously more difficult to monitor and control, as the UK state recognizes through its experience with the border between the UK and the Republic of Ireland on the island of Ireland. With the opening of the Channel Tunnel, it has become a moot point as to whether Britain is still an island, but the fact that the Tunnel provides only a rail link with the continent of Europe through a very confined space ensures that state control over the people and the commodities that move through it remains equivalent to that exercized at airports and sea-ports. Crossing the border to France from the UK still requires the migrant to give up to an organized (and partially privatized) system of transportation the power and responsibility to move him or her.

MIGRATION CONTROL AND RACISM: THE RESEARCH LEGACY

Within British academic research, the analysis of migration and of state controls over migration has focused largely upon determining whether the logic and method of control can be described as racist and, more recently, sexist (e.g., Miles and Phizacklea, 1984; WING, 1985). This limited focus is easily explained. The development of what was once known as the sociology of 'race relations' was shaped by a constant interaction with the evolution of England's or perhaps Britain's 'race relations problem' between the late 1950s and the mid-1970s. In so far as the 'race relations problem' was understood, within its own terms, to be a consequence of migration, then the solution to the problem was sought in seeking to control migration, or rather the migration of 'coloured people'. There was, after all, a certain kind of logic to the 'race relations problematic' (Miles, 1993a, pp. 110–11, 129). Successive UK governments enacted legislation to control migration, the key legislation commencing with the Commonwealth Immigrants Act of 1962 and ending with the Immigration Act of 1971. Subsequent legislation has only refined and elaborated the principles established in law during this short period. Specifically, this legislation was passed to abolish the right of entry of certain categories of migrant while extending to others the right to enter the UK without restriction (see Dummett and Nicol, 1990; MacDonald, 1991).

One of the more difficult aspects of the retreat from Empire was to ensure that 'our own kith and kin' would be able to migrate to the UK without constraint (even if they were nationals of other, independent nation-states) while 'coloured people' who were British subjects were deprived of a long-standing right to enter and settle in the Motherland. In one sense, this was not difficult to achieve: legislation could be, and indeed was, drafted to draw the necessary distinction. But if the technical matter of legal drafting was easily resolved, the need to obscure what was really being done was more difficult: the legitimate fear of being accused of discrimination motivated by racism, recognized within the state as early as 1947, ensured that legislation first drafted in the early 1950s was not finally enacted until 1962 (Joshi and Carter, 1984; Harris, 1987; Carter, Harris and Joshi, 1987). And it was a Labour government which did most to make explicit the racist distinction that was partly hidden in the Commonwealth Immigrants Act of 1962, when it passed the Commonwealth Immigrants Act of 1968, withdrawing from UK passport holders the right to enter Britain if they did not have grandparents born in the UK.

As someone who has made some contribution to this analysis of UK immigration legislation and policy, I have no doubt that it was and is correct to claim that both have been shaped by racism and sexism since 1945. Indeed, a similar claim can be made about legislation and policy during the first half of the twentieth century (Dummett and Nicol, 1990). But this is not all that can be said. The immigration legislation of the twentieth century has also embodied class discrimination (Miles, 1993b). Moreover, I now wonder whether the eagerness to describe the legislation and its implementation as racist has obstructed the development of a wider political economy of migration and of migration control. So deep-rooted is the opposition to the UK state's immigration policy on this particular dimension that it has become more or less automatic to lay the charge of racism in response to each new state initiative since 1962. This 'reflex reaction' is evident in the contrast between the virtual academic silence concerning the migration implications of the Prevention of Terrorism Act and in the academic clamour to support the Fortress Europe thesis, a thesis that rather simplistically translates the analysis of UK migration policy onto the wider stage of the European Union, which has been struggling with the issue since the late 1980s (Miles, 1993a, pp. 194–216).

THE CHANGING CONTEXT FOR INTERNATIONAL MIGRATION AND MIGRATION CONTROL

In the light of this British research tradition, I am again advocating the development of a more comprehensive political economy of international migration and thereby a political economy of migration control (cf. Miles, 1993a, pp. 107–27). An analysis of the current conjuncture will need to consider two structural processes which will shape the future. The first has been much discussed: in the context of the growth of transnational corporations and the associated intensification of competition within the capitalist world economy, various economic and political forces are undermining the existence of the sovereign nation-state, at least as it was idealized in nineteenth-century nationalist theory. One strategic response to these developments has been the creation of regional economic and political alliances of nation-states with the objective of, first, restructuring capital located within their territories to sustain or improve its capacity to compete within the world capitalist economy, and secondly, of mediating the impact of the world economy upon the economic and social conditions within those nation-states.

The European Union is one instance of such regionalization and supra-nationalization within and of the capitalist world economy. It was founded by the Treaty of Rome in 1957, which committed its signatories to the abolition of restrictions on the movement of persons, services and capital, a commitment given legislative substance in the Single European Act, which came into effect on 1 January 1993. The removal of controls on the movement of people, commodities and capital within the EU has proceeded unevenly but, nevertheless, this is a process that will inevitably continue to constrain the extent to which member states act autonomously. The implications for the state's claimed 'natural right' to control the movement of foreign nationals across its borders, in the light of the commitment to facilitate the unrestricted movement of not only capital and commodities but also people, have been widely discussed throughout the EU in the light of the signing and implementation of the Schengen Treaty (e.g., Miles and Thränhardt, 1995).

Secondly, the scale and velocity of the migration of people across international borders has increased dramatically in the past thirty years: this is less commonly remarked upon. These international migrations include movements of people seeking to take up residence in a nation-state other than the one from which they derive their juridical status as a national, short- and long-term movements in connection with professional and business practice or to sell labour power, and movements related to leisure and tourism. This categorical diversity requires a reflection on British common sense and academic conceptions of the meaning of 'immigration', and on their problematic interrelationship: our analytical categories cannot be derived uncritically from common sense.

The post-1945 'immigration debate' in Britain has presumed a narrow conception of immigration: consistent with the formal dictionary definition, immigration is understood as the movement of people across the national boundary with the objective of permanent settlement in the

UK. In the light of the actual intentions of those British subjects who entered the UK from the Caribbean and the Indian subcontinent in the late 1940s and early 1950s, and of subsequent evidence of return movements, it is in fact problematic to conceive even of this movement holistically as an immigration in this strict sense. Even though a large proportion of those who arrived during this period did subsequently take up permanent residence in the UK, this was the outcome of a process, one element of which was the imposition of legal controls on what had previously been the right of unrestricted movement into and out of the UK for British subjects: the result was that many migrants became settlers. Indeed, political and public attention has been so preoccupied with the abolition of this right for British colonial subjects under the apparently neutral category of 'immigration control' that it has failed to acknowledge that some migration legislation (most notably the Immigration Act of 1971), justified by reference to the shibboleth of 'strict immigration control', has in fact granted many millions of foreign nationals (including nationals of EU member states) new rights of entry into the UK (Dummett and Nicol, 1990).

It is perhaps more meaningful to commence analysis with the categories of international migration and international migrant, because these make no presumption about settlement: they refer solely to the spatial movement of people across national boundaries. Where the world's territory is divided into nation-states and where it continues to be presumed that a particular juridical status as a national is unique, exclusive and consequential (Brubaker, 1990) (although this has been significantly modified by the formation of supra-national units such as the EU), such movement (irrespective of its motives and intentions) necessarily confronts the state with the issues of intervention and control: for the state, the arrival of nationals who belong to other nation-states requires a decision as to whether or not to allow them to enter the territory it dominates and, if permission to enter is granted, the terms of entry. It is in the interstices between migrants' intentions and state decisions that we can derive a typology of different categories of international migration.

The sheer volume of movement across international borders is now immense. For example, more than 57 million people arrived at UK ports in 1993 (National Audit Office, 1995, p. 10). Some 11.5 million passengers used Schipol Airport in the Netherlands in the first six months of 1995 (Air UK, *Approach for the Business Traveller*, Winter 95/6). The preconditions of this expanding international migration include large-scale investment in technologies of transportation (the jet aircraft, high-speed trains) which reduce travel times and increase passenger loads, the expansion of capital invested in passenger transportation and a reduction in travel costs, and the expansion of the infrastructure for passenger transportation (airports, sea ports, railway stations), etc. Concerning the latter, BAA plc reported a £1.4 billion investment in the improvement of airport facilities, and annual pre-tax profits of £366 million, in its Annual Report for 1995. In other words, the scale and velocity of the international migration of people has a symbiotic relationship with the expansion and concentration of capital in the means of transportation within the world economy.

Given that the twentieth century is distinguished by the fact that the states at the centre of the world capitalist economy have very actively sought to control and restrict migration into the territories that they dominate, one might anticipate that this increasing migration across international borders is paralleled by a major state investment in both labour power and new technologies in order to ensure what successive UK governments have defined as 'strict immigration control'. Yet, there is a counter-tendency. The project of 'rolling back the state' means a continuous review of state expenditure in order to reduce taxation: deregulation, privatization and the abolition of certain state functions are all now familiar processes. Here we find an interesting focus for a political economy of migration control: as the scale of international migration increases, will there be more, or less, expenditure on state migration control?

In order to investigate this, it is necessary to explore the organization and practice of state migration control. Monitoring and controlling the very large numbers of people who cross international borders requires the employment of people as agents of control and the maintenance of a system of negotiated procedures. What does this cost? Moreover, such is the scale of international migration that one can go on to pose the interrelated questions: 'Is effective control cost effective?' and indeed 'Is effective control possible at all?' Of course, answers to such questions depend very much upon the precise meaning of 'effective control' and 'cost effective'. I confine my objective here to demonstrating the significance of asking these questions.

THE COST OF STATE MIGRATION CONTROL

Responsibility for controlling migration into and out of the UK is vested in the Immigration Service, which is part of the Home Office

Immigration and Nationality Department. The Immigration Service is divided into two sections: the Ports Directorate is responsible for the operation of passport controls for arriving and departing passengers at the UK's 51 designated air and sea ports (special arrangements apply in the case of the Channel Tunnel, which is formally designated as a landlink rather than a port) while the Enforcement Directorate is responsible for enforcing immigration law and detecting and removing people who contravene the conditions of entry. Hence, an analysis of the operation and cost of the Immigration Service will provide evidence relevant to the questions concerning the cost of state migration controls, and the efficiency of the system of control. However, the work of both Directorates is conducted in collaboration with, or is dependent upon, other state departments. For example, the Immigration Service does not make decisions regarding asylum applications, these being the responsibility of a separate division of the Immigration and Nationality Department, while the issue of visas is administered jointly with the Foreign and Commonwealth Office. Hence, the cost of the Immigration Service does not represent the full cost of the UK's system of migration control.

Between November 1993 and April 1994, the Immigration Service was the subject of an enquiry by the National Audit Office, which focused on the effectiveness and efficiency of controls on entry into the UK. The Office's report on the outcome of the enquiry, published in February 1995, provides information about the cost, staffing and implementation of the UK state's immigration policy and law. The Ports Directorate cost £83 million in financial year 1993/94 and employed 2,425 staff at 31 March 1994. The corresponding figures for the Enforcement Directorate were £28 million and 564 staff (National Audit Office, 1995; pp. 11–14). The total cost of the Service for financial year 1993/94 was therefore £111 million, and a total of 2,989 staff were employed.

Not surprisingly, the work of the Immigration Service is labour-intensive and, less obviously, it is concentrated on arrivals control and related case-work. The National Audit Office enquiry calculated that staff costs account for nearly 80 per cent of the Ports Directorate budget and that approximately 70 per cent of staff time in 1993/94 was devoted to dealing with the 57 million arrivals (1995, p. 35). One is tempted to suggest that, with 2,425 staff seeking to monitor 57 million arrivals, there is considerable scope for 'inefficiency'. But such a calculation is too simple.

Not all arrivals are checked with the same degree of rigour. This is reflected in the way in which international passengers arriving at

British ports are organized into two separate channels, one for EU nationals and the other for non-EU nationals. Nationals of EU member states have the right to enter the UK and so the responsibility of the Immigration Service is 'limited' to establishing that each EU arrival is in possession of a valid passport: the Audit Office describes the exercise of this responsibility as a 'brief check' (1995, p. 35), which takes, on average, 6 seconds (1995, p. 40). Approximately 83 per cent of the 57 million arrivals in 1993/94 were EU nationals so this 'brief check' was carried out on 47.3 million people. In practice, the check is a momentary visual scan of the passport to assess its validity, and a comparison of the photograph with the passenger's face.

More time is spent dealing with non-EU nationals, who require 'leave to enter' and who are asked a series of questions about the purpose and length of their intended stay in the UK. Where possession of a visa is a legal requirement for entry into the UK, these and other questions will have already been posed, highlighting the extent to which part of the organization and cost of control is transferred to the country of departure. Minimally, this process at the port of arrival takes a minute or two (the Audit Office suggests that the average time per passenger is 1 minute and 40 seconds (1995, p. 40)) but, if the answers are not considered to be satisfactory, the passenger is delayed for further questioning and other enquiries may also be carried out. This can take anything from thirty minutes to several days. During 1993/94, some 10 million people were processed through this system, of whom approximately 63,000 were subjected to further examination (National Audit Office, 1995, pp. 35, 55). It seems likely, therefore, that in practice Immigration Service staff are deployed primarily to determine whether or not non-EU nationals should be granted 'leave to enter' the UK.

Moreover, the arrival flow is not evenly distributed throughout the day. In the case of airports, flight arrivals peak at certain points in the 24-hour cycle (intercontinental flight arrivals peak in the early morning, for example), while at busy sea ports such as Dover there are both seasonal and daily peaks even though there is a regular schedule of sailings throughout the day and night. The National Audit Office expressed concern that 'variable arrival patterns can result in "downtime" of up to 50 per cent of control time', although it noted that staff are redeployed to other activities in these periods (1995, p. 43). The corollary is that the task of checking arriving passengers' passports is actually concentrated into specific periods, rather than evenly distributed throughout the 24-hour cycle, thereby reinforcing the pressure to make decisions quickly.

Formally, the Immigration Service is responsible for monitoring not only all arrivals but also all departures. This has meant that the passports of all departing passengers have been checked, a practice that in 1993 absorbed 14 per cent of Immigration Service staff time (National Audit Office, 1995, p. 44). In principle, this has permitted the Immigration Service to check whether all non-UK nationals return to their country of origin and whether, in particular, those non-EU nationals who have been given 'leave to enter' actually abide by the condition that they depart from the UK by a given date. However, in a little-publicized decision, the UK state terminated departure controls for flights and sailings to European Union destinations from all ferry ports and from small airports in February 1994, permitting a redeployment of staff to other activities and/or other ports (National Audit Office, 1995, pp. 14, 44). Consequently, the Immigration Service now only monitors departures to EU destinations from the larger UK airports.

The UK government's refusal to sign the Schengen Treaty is well known, as is its argument that its accession to the Treaty of Rome and to the Single European Act do not necessitate the abolition of controls over passengers arriving in the UK from other EU countries. The retention of controls is legitimated by reference to the need to control illegal entry and to contain drug-smuggling and terrorist activity. Yet, given the many millions of arrivals at UK ports and now through the Channel Tunnel from other EU countries, in relation to the number of Immigration Service staff, the result is a momentary visual scanning of passports: the practice of control at least for EU migrants is therefore primarily symbolic. This conclusion is reinforced by the recent decision to abolish controls over passengers departing to other EU destinations from ports and small airports: this includes the port of Dover, which, having recorded 8.4 million arrivals in 1993 (National Audit Office, 1995, p. 16), presumably recorded a similarly high level of departures.

THE LIMITS OF CONTROL: ILLEGAL AND CLANDESTINE MIGRATION

One of the dominant features of political debate about migration and the need for state control over migration is an emphasis upon numbers. Many advocates of control in the UK have highlighted what they identify as the threat of 'swamping' both numerically and culturally that arises from 'just too many immigrants, whoever they are'. Such people have a vested interest in making the strongest possible case, an interest that ensures that they tend not to err on the side of caution when making claims about current and future migration flows. In this context, there is a particular potency in the argument that 'official statistics' actually hide the 'real truth' about immigration, either because certain categories of immigrant are excluded from the state's criteria and systems of measurement or because so many people actually and successfully seek to evade state controls, thereby confirming their alleged undesirability.

Acutely aware of the need to avoid trespassing on the racists' terrain and compromising their arguments with the logic of the racists' assertions, British academics have tended to avoid being drawn into the 'numbers game'. And with good reason: for the racist, one of the Other is one too many. A corollary of this concern has been a reluctance to show interest in the process of illegal and clandestine migration: research into illegal and clandestine migration carries the potential to produce knowledge about scale and practices which can be exploited by politicians with an interest in advocating stricter controls. Yet, there is no doubt that illegal and clandestine migration takes place: the International Labour Organization has recently suggested that there are some 2.6 million illegal migrants living in the EU (*Observer*, 7 January 1996).

There are at least two reasons for studying illegal and clandestine migration which have little to do with numbers *per se*. First, research exposes not only the poverty of the lives of those who cross international borders without the formal approval of the state, but also the ways in which their illegal status makes them especially vulnerable, and therefore valuable, to those who employ them (e.g., Portes, 1983). Secondly, the process by which migrants become illegal or clandestine is itself commodified and is therefore an integral feature of the world capitalist system, a moment in the ongoing globalization process. Like all migrants, illegal and clandestine migrants purchase knowledge, documentation and a mode of transport, although the knowledge may be misleading, the documentation will be forged and the mode of transport will probably be uncomfortable and even extremely dangerous (*Observer*, 12 January 1997 and 19 January 1997). Illegality ensures a premium price for the service purchased. Journalists who have interviewed such migrants report sums of $9000 per person for migration from Afghanistan to Germany and $30,000 per person from China to Germany via the Czech Republic (*Guardian*, 13 June 1995). Some female migrants are offered 'free' passage but later find themselves forced into prostitution (*Guardian*, 29 November 1995).

No doubt, the organization of these illegal and clandestine flows varies from localized, small-scale petit-bourgeois enterprises to larger, international enterprises which embody the principles of rational efficiency, organization and profitability. Those with some knowledge of this excellent example of capitalist enterprise report tax-free income of $7 billion for a single 'smuggling ring' (*Guardian*, 13 June 1995). Another organization has estimated that 'crime syndicates' earned between $100m and $1 billion from organizing the illegal and clandestine migration into Europe in 1993 (*Observer*, 7 January 1996, 12 January 1997).

In the light of the millions of people who are known to cross the UK's national borders, the National Audit Office enquiry into the Immigration Service made some interesting observations about the effectiveness of current control systems in relation to illegal migration. We have already seen that the main strategy of control is a visual check on passports at points of entry into the UK. This is justified primarily in terms of cost: 'It can cost twelve times as much to identify and remove an illegal immigrant than to refuse a passenger entry' (1995, p. 23). Yet, as we have also seen, there are immense constraints on the time that each immigration official can devote to checking the passport of each passenger arriving at the border of the UK. In the light of the volume of movement, any increase in time devoted to checking both passports and the passengers' rationale for entry will slow down the rate of entry. Without an increase in staffing and space at ports of entry, there would be an increase in queuing and passenger time lost while waiting to be given permission to enter. 'Customer dissatisfaction' would then become a major problem. The contradiction is recognized by the Audit Office (1995, p. 35):

> The Immigration Service face conflicting pressures in managing the arrivals control. They must carry out sufficient checks to ensure that only passengers entitled to enter are admitted; but they have also to clear passengers as quickly as possible.

What information is provided to Immigration Service staff to help them to identify illegal migrants? At the time of the Audit Office enquiry, the Immigration Service provided a book listing the names of approximately 10,000 persons and the recommended action if those persons presented themselves at a UK port of entry. This listing was updated manually on a daily basis, at a cost of approximately £1 million in staff time. The information contained in the book included less than 2 per cent of the available information on potential offenders against UK immigration law: to include all the available information would have created a very large book that would have been difficult to use. Moreover, the book only contained information on non-EU nationals and was therefore of no assistance in checking the validity of passports held by EU nationals (National Audit Office 1995, p. 27). It therefore seems that Immigration Service staff are provided with very limited information about only non-EU nationals, on which to make decisions about to whom 'leave of entry' should be granted and to whom it should not.

The fact that the decision to grant 'leave of entry' has to be taken very quickly and is not well informed by reliable data creates the space for other criteria to influence the outcome. The Audit Office, commenting on the difficulty inherent in mediating the contradiction between the need to process large numbers of arriving passengers quickly and the need to identify those who should be refused entry, observes that 'these decisions are largely instinctive and based on experience' (1995, p. 41). 'Instinct' is socially constructed through an interaction between the individual's evolving belief and value systems and the information and presumptions articulated in the multiple social contexts in which she or he participates: there is good reason to believe that the result of that interaction can be an 'instinctive' racism. The six or one hundred seconds in which the decision on entry is taken constitutes the time when power is exercised: if the exercise of that power is 'instinctive', then this is the socially organized moment within which racism can influence the outcome of that decision. It is a socially organized moment because it is the state which determines not only that the decision has to be made but also the allocation of resources which structure the circumstances in which the decision is made.

An increase in the quantity and quality of surveillance and information has the potential to reduce the 'instinctive' dimension of decision making but it also has the potential to raise costs unless there are at least corresponding savings in other areas of migration-control practice. Let us consider two examples discussed by the Audit Office. First, at a time when information technology is identified as the solution to many problems, it is not surprising that the Immigration Service has sought to replace the manually up-dated index of suspected persons with a computerized database which would also include information on immigration rules and procedures. The Audit Office estimated that the cost of establishing this computerized database would be

£13.7 million, with annual running costs in the region of £4.7 million and annual staffing costs of £1.2 million once it is fully implemented (1995, p. 28). It predicted that computerization would save staff time both by abolishing the manual updating of the existing index and by speeding up the process of checking the passport of each passenger. But it also noted the view of the Immigration Service that these savings could be minimal and, indeed, could be offset by an increased workload prompted by the improved information base for decision making, which would result in a larger number of passengers being refused 'leave to enter' (1995, p. 28). One presumes that such an increase in refusals would be interpreted as increased efficiency, although such success also has cost implications as we shall see shortly. The most generous conclusion is that computerization of this aspect of the work of the Immigration Service will not inevitably reduce costs. It is relevant to recall that one of the reasons for the repeated delays in the implementation of the Schengen Treaty arose from the difficulties of creating and operating the Schengen Information System, a large database containing information on suspected terrorists, drug dealers and other people to whom entry into the EU should be denied, which had to be linked to computer systems in nine countries (Agence Europe, 19 October 1993; Reuters, 15 November 1993; *Computer Weekly*, 24 March 1994; Agence Europe, 5 July 1994). The computer system cost DM10 million (Reuters, 21 November 1994).

Secondly, increased levels of surveillance and investigation in order to make immigration control more 'effective' are likely to increase the costs arising from the detention of those seeking entry. The Immigration Service has the power to detain any person in 'secure accommodation' if it believes that further information is needed in order to reach a decision on admission or if that person has been refused entry to the UK but cannot be removed immediately. In addition, persons found subsequently to have breached the conditions of entry may also be detained in 'secure accommodation'. In 1993, 10,530 people were detained overnight or longer for these reasons. In July 1994, the secure accommodation constituted six detention centres run by the Immigration Service, providing 342 overnight places, a Prison Service institution providing 129 overnight places, and police cells.

There has been widespread concern expressed about the quality of accommodation provided in these facilities, especially for those detained for long periods. 'Customer satisfaction' was not surveyed by the National Audit Office in this aspect of its investigation. However, it did comment that a great deal of existing accommodation is 'of a poor standard' (1995, p. 71) and is 'often full or close to capacity' (1995, p. 67), with the result that persons who should have been detained on arrival at a UK port were often granted temporary 'leave to remain' while further investigations were conducted. Not surprisingly, the perceived solution to this problem is to increase the number of places in 'secure accommodation' and the Immigration Service reported having plans to provide 377 net additional places by the middle of 1996 (1995, p. 70). The Audit Office recommended an improvement in the system for monitoring accommodation use and an extension of co-ordination arrangements to include the whole of the UK. The cost of increasing the number of overnight places in 'secure accommodation' and of monitoring and co-ordinating accommodation usage was not estimated by the Audit Office.

Hence, the Audit Office's investigation of the Immigration Service reveals scope for illegal and clandestine immigration to take place. This is especially the case where entry into the UK is through the EU-national channel, because of the very limited nature of the checks. The more general problem is identified in the following passage in the Office's report (1995, pp. 19–20):

> In common with almost all other countries the United Kingdom does not systematically record the movement of all those subject to immigration control in and out of the country. Given the very large numbers involved this would require a heavy investment in information technology, with associated data recording costs; and it is doubtful whether this would be an effective means of tracing offenders, many of whom change address on entering the United Kingdom.

There is further evidence in the Audit Office's report to sustain scepticism about the possibility of 'effective control'. The Immigration Service created the Enforcement Directorate in 1991 in an attempt to intensify activity to prevent illegal entry and to detect immigration offenders. The creation of the Directorate doubled the number of Immigration Service staff involved in enforcement work but 'the number of people detected increased by only around 50 per cent' (1995, p. 20). This does not seem to constitute an adequate 'rate of return', especially as the Audit Office claims elsewhere in its report that detecting illegal entrants at the point of entry is more cost-effective than after they have entered the UK.

Moreover, the Audit Office demonstrates that most immigration offenders are identified by 'chance' action rather than by systematic investigation by Immigration Service staff. An analysis of the sources of information leading to the detection of immigration offenders in 1993 revealed that 34 per cent of offenders were identified as a result of police investigation of an unrelated offence and 25 per cent as a result of information volunteered by the public. A further 19 per cent were identified from the examination of Home Office files and just 10 per cent were identified by targeted operations or research into offence patterns (National Audit Office, 1995, p. 22).

While the possibility of illegal migration is revealed by the 'loopholes' in the current systems of migration control, the scale of such migration is not and cannot be easily known. And this discussion has been limited to those people seeking entry through the legally constituted procedures by means of some form of deception. It does not take account of those seeking entry to the UK by means that seek to evade the systems of control (for example, by hiding in the wheel hatch of a Boeing 747 aircraft). The only statistics available are those of the number of apprehended immigration offenders, which include persons who enter the UK without legal entitlement and persons who enter legally but who subsequently breach their conditions of 'leave to enter' or to remain. There were 10,300 such offenders in 1993 (1995, p. 20), an infinitesimally small proportion of the total of more than 57 million people who arrived at UK ports that year. Yet, undaunted, the Audit Office concluded that 'there is little doubt that the numbers involved and the associated costs are significant' (1995, p. 20).

One interpretation of this unsubstantiated guess is to construe it as a further example of deliberate exaggeration in order to legitimate and sustain the practice of 'strict immigration control'. But it can also be interpreted as an understandable, if not entirely accurate, conclusion in the light of the difficulties in enforcing control given the very large numbers of people who seek to enter the UK and the limited resources devoted to control. Put another way, it could be concluded that the Audit Office is implicitly acknowledging that the state's objective of 'strict immigration control' has not been achieved and perhaps cannot be achieved.

THE PRIVATIZATION OF MIGRATION CONTROL

In the case of the UK, and in accordance with the general strategy of seeking to reduce the cost of state functions (if not to eliminate them completely), part of the responsibility and cost of migration control has been passed from the state to private companies who provide the means of travel. The Immigration (Carriers' Liability) Act of 1987 made airline and ferry companies liable to a 'fine' for each person they transport into the UK without proper documentation or with documentation that is forged, as well as for the costs of deportation. It should be noted that there is nothing new about such an arrangement: under the terms of the 1905 Aliens Act, ship's captains were under a formal obligation on arrival in a UK port to provide a list of alien passengers to state officials (Bevan, 1986, p. 70). Moreover, the UK is not alone in partially privatizing the practice of migration control: many other states have introduced similar legislation. The International Air Transport Association (IATA) claimed in 1991 that nearly 20 states, including half of the EU member states, fined airlines for carrying passengers who breached migration laws. IATA estimated that such fines totalled $46 million in 1991 (Reuters, 19 November 1991).

For capital invested in air and sea passenger transportation, this has meant an additional triple cost: company staff have additional responsibilities for which specialist training is required, check-in and boarding times are increased to allow passport checks to take place (perhaps to the extent of requiring the appointment of additional staff), and a fine is levied where it is proved that a passenger has deceived the airline or ferry company. Seen from the perspective of the state, not only is responsibility for (and therefore the financial cost of) control now shared with private companies, but the financial incentive for companies to put effective systems of control into place has the effect of realizing an income for the state. As of 31 December 1993, more than £62 million of charges had been levied on transport companies (National Audit Office, 1995, p. 31). Not only has responsibility for what the state has been unable to deliver been passed on to private capital but, in addition, private capital is then 'taxed' in proportion to its failure to put into effect a system of 'strict immigration control'.

But collecting fines also costs money. A section of the Immigration Service (the Ports Directorate) is responsible for recovering fines not paid by transport companies and it seems not to have been very efficient in carrying out this responsibility: of the £62 million in fines levied by the end of 1993, only approximately £40 million had actually been paid to the state by that date. The Audit Office explained: 'Debt recovery had been hampered by inadequate information systems and insufficient staffing' (National Audit Office, 1995, p. 32). The

Immigration Service has come under considerable pressure to recoup outstanding debts, although the process is hampered by the fact that the rules allow the Immigration Service to waive the fine in certain circumstances, and transport companies have at least two opportunities to seek the application of the waiver clause. Their use of this provision has resulted in a significant reduction in (but not the elimination of) the amount owed by private companies to the state. Moreover, money is lost to the state if the transport company goes into liquidation before the fines are paid. Of the £12 million outstanding in 1993, it was anticipated that, at best, £6.8 million would be collected by the state (National Audit Office, 1995, p. 33).

And there are other costs to the state arising from this privatization of migration control. For example, the Immigration Service has the responsibility for 'providing guidance on document requirements, making training visits to overseas ports and providing intensive training in all aspects of legislation and forgery detection' (National Audit Office, 1995, p. 34). Significantly, the Audit Office did not attempt to calculate or even estimate the costs of debt recovering and training for the Immigration Service so that we have no way of knowing whether the fines recovered by the Service exceed the costs of partially privatizing migration control.

Private capital has not been slow to complain about the imposition of responsibilities for migration control. Airline companies (including British Airways) lodged appeals to the Home Office about the legislation and refused to pay fines (*The Times*, 23 September 1989). Following the announcement that the Immigration (Carriers' Liability) Act of 1987 would not apply to either Eurotunnel or Eurostar, Hoverspeed lodged a formal complaint with the European Commission on two grounds. First, it argued that the UK government should abandon immigration controls on all those arriving in the UK from another EU country in order to comply with the Treaty of Rome. Second,ly it claimed that the arrangements put in place for Eurotunnel and Eurostar (whereby immigration controls are effected at the point of departure or during travel rather than on arrival as is the case with ferry and air passengers) should also be introduced for ferry companies in order to ensure parity. During 1993, Hoverspeed had been fined £171,000 under the terms of the Act and its managing director claimed 'We are in the business of serving our customers, not the immigration business' (*Daily Telegraph*, 3 August 1994; Lloyd's List, 4 August 1994). 'Rolling back the state' is not always without negative consequences for capital.

THE MIGRATION OF CAPITAL AND THE MIGRATION OF PEOPLE

The vociferous and highly contested political and public debate within the EU about realizing the objective of freedom of movement for EU nationals within the EU contrasts sharply with the relative silence about the freedom of movement for capital and commodities within the EU: the latter is assumed to be a 'good thing'. The contrast is even sharper in the case of the migration of people, capital and commodities into the EU: supporters of the Schengen Treaty are generally strongly committed to reinforcing controls over the migration of people into the EU (and hence the importance of the Schengen Information System) but there is widespread agreement that everything possible should be done to ensure the free movement of capital and commodities into the EU.

   This contrasting treatment of people in relation to capital and commodities is rarely remarked on and has only been intermittently addressed within the academic literature. One recent exception included an essay by the political philosopher Brian Barry, who argued that 'immigrants are people and societies are made up of people. Adding new people, especially if they are culturally distinctive, will inevitably change the society.... By contrast, foreign capital has far less effect on the everyday life of a country ...' (1992, p. 286). Asserted as if this were self-evidently true, this claim is likely to receive widespread assent: right-wing discourse concerning the supposed threat posed to Our culture and way of life by the migration of 'culturally distinct' people is so widely diffused in common sense that the first part of Barry's claim would not be questioned, leaving the second half to stand as proof of the validity of the first.

   The claim is worthy of further consideration in order to provide an opportunity not only to challenge common sense but also to extend the boundary of the political economy of migration to include the migration of capital and commodities alongside the migration of people. The essence of the critique that arises from such a comparative analysis is that the migration of capital and commodities constitutes not only the spatial movement of value but also the spatial movement of cultural practices and cultural meanings. Indeed, it is because commodities are simultaneously exchange-values and use-values that they necessarily carry with them as they move through space a potential cultural impact, as therefore does the capital that migrates to produce commodities in another spatial location: the commodity's use-value may result in its owner adopting new practices and new beliefs. As I have shown elsewhere, if spatially mobile capital and commodities were not having a substantial effect upon the everyday life of a country, the French state would not have played such an active role in resisting the demand of the US government during the recent renegotiation of GATT to permit free trade in audiovisual products (see Frank, Mess and Miles, 1996).

Representatives of the French state and of the French 'cultural industries' claimed that free trade in audiovisual products would threaten simultaneously the French 'mode de vie' and the French film industry. Concerning the former, it was argued that the French cinema was an integral part of national identity and culture and an expression of the national language: films, whatever their medium of viewing, contained images and meanings which embodied their national origin, with the result that the free import of films from the USA entailed the import of commodities which could change the French way of life. This argument was often reinforced by the drawing of a distinction between US cinema as entertainment and French cinema as high art. Concerning the latter, the French film industry has for a long time been supported by state subsidies, a fact that goes some way to explain why, with 156 film releases in 1991, it is the strongest and most successful in the EU. In the same year, 129 films were produced in Italy, 72 in Germany, 54 in Spain and 51 in the UK. But, with 435 films produced in the USA in 1991, the French film industry is engaged in a very unequal competition with Hollywood, dominated as it is by a small number of transnational corporations.

The French state could not function as an autonomous force in opposing free trade because the EU, represented by the European Commission, constituted the negotiating partner in the GATT negotiations. The French state was therefore faced with a struggle on two fronts, one against the USA and another to persuade other EU member states to support its concerns about the threat of free trade to national culture and identity. This was attempted by representing the French film industry and its products as a component part of a wider European film industry, a representation that was not without validity because the European Commission had been seeking a strengthening and a rationalization of the European film industry, partly through the provision of various kinds of subsidy, since 1988. This action was in anticipation of the implementation of the European Single Market in 1992 but it took on a new significance in the light of the potential inclusion of the audiovisual sector in the GATT negotiations.

In the immediate aftermath of the ending of these negotiations, the Commission published in April 1994 a Green Paper on the strategy options for the audiovisual industry, the objective of which was to identify how the EU could 'contribute to the development of a European film and television programme industry which is competitive on the world market, forward-looking and capable of radiating the influence of European culture and of creating jobs in Europe' (COM (94), 96 final, 6 April 1994, p. 2). Clearly, the European Commission also believed that the commodities produced by the reorganization of European capital invested in the film industry contained a cultural content with the capacity to have effects within and beyond Europe.

CONCLUSIONS

Within western Europe, the state's struggle to erect and sustain systems of 'strict immigration control' is very much a twentieth-century phenomenon. Uneven capitalist development within the world system, along with massive capital investment in the means of international transportation, has produced within the past thirty years international movements of people on such a scale that, in the absence of the commitment of substantial additional resources, the capacity of the state (relatively if not absolutely) to effectively monitor and control those movements has steadily declined. The collapse of communism in central and eastern Europe has only reinforced this development because it eliminated a model of 'strict immigration control' that both obviated the need for western European states to sustain effective systems of control viz-à-viz eastern and central Europe and permitted them simultaneously to assert claims to possession of a superior political morality.

The Schengen Treaty is an understandable response to these developments. Despite the many delays in implementation and despite the ongoing disputes between the signatory states (most notably over the Dutch state's drugs policy), the Treaty is being institutionalized in airport organization. As part of the expansion of Schipol Airport, the expanded lounge area has now been divided by a glass wall into Schengen and non-Schengen areas: passengers entering or leaving the Netherlands through Schipol who are arriving from or departing for the other countries who have signed the Schengen Treaty no longer pass through immigration control. Viewed from the perspective of nineteenth-century nationalist theory, and therefore also from the perspective of the UK state, this spatial and administrative transformation of Schipol Airport symbolizes a structural transformation of the political and economic organization of the world capitalist economy and delivers to some human beings rights already accorded to capital and commodities. Passengers arriving at Schipol from the UK, including UK nationals, can observe through that glass wall the consequences of what has been denied to them a state that sustains a rhetoric of 'strict immigration control' that privileges capital and commodities over human beings, alongside a reality of control which, while producing racist and sexist outcomes, is in part symbolic and for the rest is perhaps only partially effective.

Of course, the Schengen Treaty has exclusionary and control consequences too: the justification for the elimination of 'internal controls' within the EU means more rigorous controls at the exterior frontiers of the EU, at least for the nationals of the peripheries of the world capitalist economy (but not necessarily for the products of their labour power). But while highlighting the nature and consequences of that exclusion, we should not minimize the historical significance of the effective abolition of an aspect of state control that refracted the nationalist political and economic agenda created within Europe during the nineteenth century. This constitutes a significant change to the terrain within which social identities are constructed. Moreover, when we consider the determinants of that change, we should consider the limits to effective state control created by mass movements of people across national borders, movements that are created and sustained by the huge quantities of capital invested in international transportation and which can only be effectively controlled by a major increase in state power and expenditure. Perhaps there is still a moment at which the 'economic' will be a decisive factor.

ACKNOWLEDGEMENTS

I am very grateful to Janie Ferguson who provided invaluable assistance in identifying data sources and to Suzanne Audrey who read and commented on an earlier draft of this chapter.

NOTE

1. There has been a parallel increase in the number of passengers passing through sea ports, from 24.9 million in 1988 to 37.0 million in 1994. About half of passenger movements through sea ports occur through the port of Dover (*Transport Statistics Great Britain 1995*, p. 142).

REFERENCES

Barry, B. (1992), 'The Quest for Consistency: a Sceptical View', in B. Barry and G. Goodwin (eds), *Free Movement: Ethical Issues in the Transnational Migration of People and Money* (London: Harvester Wheatsheaf).

Bevan, V. (1986) *The Development of British Immigration Law* (London: Croom Helm).

BAA (British Airports Authority) (1988), *Annual Report and Accounts*.

BAA (British Airports Authority plc) (1993), *Annual Report and Accounts*.

BAA (British Airports Authority plc) (1995), *Annual Report and Accounts*.

Brubaker, W. R. (1990), 'Immigration, Citizenship and the Nation-State in France and Germany: a Comparative Historical Analysis', *International Sociology*, 5, pp. 379–407.

Carter, B., Harris, C., and Joshi, S. (1987), 'The 1951–55 Conservative Government and the Racialization of Black Immigration', *Immigrants and Minorities*, 6, pp. 335–47

Dummett, A., and Nicol, A. (1990), *Subjects, Citizens, Aliens and Others: Nationality and Immigration Law* (London: Weidenfeld and Nicolson).

Frank, S., Mess, A., and Miles R. (1996), 'Free Movement of Capital and its Cultural Consequences for the European Union: The Case of the Audiovisual Industry', in H. Schwengel (ed.), *Globalizierung und europäische Kultur: Freiburger Arbeitspapiere zum Prozess der Globalizierung*, vol. 1 (Freiburg: Albert-Ludwigs-Universität).

Harris, C. (1987), 'British Capitalism, Migration and Relative Surplus Population', *Migration*, 1, pp. 47–90.

Joshi, S., and Carter, B. (1984), 'The Role of Labour in Creating a Racist Britain', *Race and Class*, 25, pp. 53–70.

MacDonald, I. (1991), *Immigration Law and Practice in the United Kingdom*, 3rd edn (London: Butterworths).

Miles, R. (1993a), *Racism After 'Race Relations'* (London: Routledge).

Miles, R. (1993b), 'Racisme institutionel et rapports de classe: une relation problématique', in M. Wieviorka (ed.), *Racisme et modernité* (Paris: Editions la découverte).

Miles, R., and Phizacklea, A. (1984), *White Man's Country: Racism in British Politics* (London: Pluto Press).

Miles, R., and Thränhardt, D. (ed.) (1995), *Migration and European Integration: The Dynamics of Inclusion and Exclusion* (London: Pinter Publishers).

National Audit Office (1995), *Entry into the United Kingdom* (London: HMSO).

Portes, A. (1983), 'Modes of Structural Incorporation and Present Theories of Labor Immigration', in M. M. Kritz, C. B. Keely and S. M. Tomasi (ed.), *Global Trends in Migration: Theory and Research on International Population Movements* (New York: Center for Migration Studies).

WING (Women Immigration and Nationality Group) (1985), *Worlds Apart: Women under Immigration and Nationality Law* (London: Pluto Press).

10 Crossing Borders: Mobility of Goods, Capital and People in the Central European Region

CLAIRE WALLACE

Globalization is often discussed in rather general terms as the world-wide transmission of media symbols and consumer lifestyles (see Sklair, 1991) or capital and markets (Wallerstein, 1983; Harvey, 1989; Jameson, 1991). Such flows of communication can result in new social relations as people become 'disembedded' from their normal contexts and are connected in other ways with those from other contexts at a transnational level (Giddens, 1990). Sassen (1996) has described the role of 'global cities' as poles of attraction for these international flows of people and capital, emphasizing in particular the creation of an immigrant underclass often working in the informal economy, which is juxtaposed with a 'post-industrial' class of professionals. However, these discussions are pitched at a very general level rather than looking in detail at particular instances. They tend to consider globalization in terms of universal principles and the economic imperative is seen either implicitly or explicitly as the inevitable driving force towards globalization. In this respect Marxists, post-Marxists and neo-liberal economists converge in agreement: seeing the market as

> that concrete, time-bounded, space-bounded integrated locale of productive activities within which the endless accumulation of capital has been the economic objective or 'law' that has governed or prevailed. (Wallerstein, 1983, p. 18)

Our argument in this chapter is that in the Central European region we should understand investment, trade and migration rather in terms of cultural, historical and social factors. Ethnic and linguistic ties play an important part in this patterning of economic relations. Such factors ensure that economic imperatives are socially embedded (see Wallace et al., 1997). However, such embeddedness is very complex and here we shall try to unravel some of the ways in which this embeddedness is important in economic relations across borders.

These general perspectives on globalization also assume that borders can be crossed relatively freely, and often underestimate the impact of closed borders and selective control of trade and migration. Indeed these perspectives often imply that national borders are increasingly irrelevant (Jameson, 1991). We argue, by contrast, that opening and closing borders *creates* various kinds of economic and social interchange. Therefore we need to understand this political control of flows of people and goods at a local level in order to understand economic relations across borders. In this chapter we explore what happened to the Central European Region (i.e., Germany and Austria to the west; Hungary, Poland, the Czech and Slovak Republics in the middle; and Ukraine and Belarus, and Russia to the east) when borders were closed, opened, selectively restricted or moved altogether. We consider the implications of the opening of this area towards liberal capitalist market relations along with political democracy and therefore more open access to global capitalism. We concentrate particularly on the post-1989 period and especially upon the circulation of goods, capital and people within the central European area.

THE BUFFER ZONE

A new region of Europe has been created which we have elsewhere termed the 'buffer zone' (see Wallace, Sidorenko and Chmouliar, 1996). The buffer zone includes the countries which border the European Union: Poland, Hungary, the Czech and Slovak Republics. They are now sandwiched between an affluent West (Germany and Austria) and an increasingly less affluent East (Ukraine, Russia, Belarus). Whereas to the south, Yugoslavia used to be a buffer zone between the Communist and non-Communist countries, the war there helped to seal borders and limit communications. This role may be changing once more with the official cessation of the war.

The creation of the buffer zone is partly the consequence of European Union policies. The EU countries, keen to ensure social and political stability in the 'new world order' as well as to develop new markets for their products, have created a range of association agreements with the privileged rim countries: Poland, the Czech and Slovak Republics, and Hungary. These countries have enjoyed development aid programmes such as PHARE, TEMPUS and other EU schemes in the early round of reforms (although such programmes were later extended elsewhere). These countries were themselves very keen to join the European Union and have patterned their institutional reforms to harmonize with EU standards and norms. They fully expect to join the European Union in the near future and are westward looking in their orientation. These buffer-zone countries have attracted more investment per capita than countries further east and this has been both a cause and a consequence of their political and economic stability and their successful transition towards becoming liberal, market democracies. New forms of prosperity are visible in the increasing numbers of Western cars on the roads (although very often bought second hand), extensive private and business use of computers, fashionable clothes, mobile telephones and a private house-building boom. Although incomes are still low, consumption is high (Wallace 1997a). The buffer-zone countries are becoming the most prosperous of the post-Communist world (Haerpfer and Zeilhofer, 1995). They are examples of the 'successful' transition from Communism.

One aspect of the integration of the buffer-zone countries into western Europe is a range of agreements to regulate migration (Niessen, 1992; Kussbach, 1992). Whereas they were previously only *emigration* countries, the buffer-zone countries are increasingly targets of *immigration* and have had to formulate policies accordingly. These policies have tended to be modelled upon visa, work-permit and asylum policies adopted in western Europe and have become more restrictive with every month that passes. The countries in western Europe, such as Germany and Austria, most threatened by the new migrations from the east have developed their own co-ordinated policies and bi-lateral agreements for the return of illegal 'third country nationals' between states – that is, they prefer to turn back illegal migrants to the last country they crossed legally: in most cases the buffer zone.

In describing a 'buffer zone' consisting of four countries, we are claiming that they have a number of features in common with one another. However, there are also internal differences between each of these countries. Whereas Poland and the Czech Republic have been marching ahead on the road to economic reform, Slovakia has lagged behind somewhat and Hungary, after an early head start, has fallen back. In terms of migration policies, each country evolved its own rather than making collective arrangements, but during the period 1991 to 1995 they have all introduced similar policies, albeit with different timings. There is also some mobility within the buffer zone itself.

With the fall of Communism, activities which had previously been illegal – such as trading, currency speculation, starting business ventures and making profits – were no longer so. Indeed these very same activities, which had previously been frowned upon, were now encouraged. Street stalls satisfied the demand for groceries and consumer goods which the general stores were unable to fulfil. Many people moved around or found jobs, uninhibited by any regulations, since these had not yet been developed to deal with them. The second economy, which had always existed as a necessary adjunct to the socialist economy, became now part of the formal capitalist economy as businesses were legalized and underground activities emerged into the open. Yesterday's crook became today's capitalist (Sik, 1993). However, many activities remain underground as laws have not yet been enacted to regulate them or, where they have been enacted, are not always fully implemented. At first a whole range of activities were therefore neither legal nor illegal although now we are seeing a gradual formalization, regulation and institutionalization of such activities.

MOVEMENT ACROSS BORDERS IN THE BUFFER ZONE

Here we shall concentrate upon specific aspects of the circulation of *goods*, *capital* and *people* in the Central European Region. In the words of Appadurai (1990) this represents the 'ethnoscape' and the 'technoscape' aspects of globalization.

1 The Circulation of Goods

During the Cold War period, the Communist-bloc countries were members of a trading arrangement between themselves known as Comecon. Goods produced in one country were exported to other countries in return for goods or raw materials, and a deliberate system of interdependence was constructed between these countries. Exports and imports to the West were very limited and had even declined since the 1970s (Wallace, 1997a). On the other side of the former border, the creation of a free-trade zone within the European Union helped to create a trading bloc within which much exchange takes place. Austria, for example, trades more than 90 per cent of her goods within the European Union. For the Cold War period these two trading blocs were standing back to back, as it were.

The collapse of Communism brought the disintegration of the former Comecon trading relations. However, in a very rapid space of time the buffer-zone countries reoriented their trade towards western Europe. Thus, whilst in 1990 Hungary was taking only 31 per cent of its imports from the EU, by 1995 this was 61.5 per cent. On the other hand, exports to EU countries rose from 32.2 per cent to 62.7 per cent in the same period (Wallace, 1997a). For each Central European country, it is the countries on the immediate western borders which play the most important role, as we can see in the fact that for the Czech Republic 55 per cent of its trade is with its neighbouring countries (Wallace, 1997a).

The Central European countries mainly export energy, raw materials and semi-finished products whereas from the EU they import high-technology goods, foodstuffs and consumer goods. Export to the European Union would be even higher if it were not for the protectionist measures erected by the EU, afraid of their goods being undercut by cheap Eastern European imports. Despite this rapid reorientation of trade, there is little trade *within* the buffer-zone countries even though a free-trade zone known as CEFTA (Central European Free Trade Area) was set up in 1993. The direction of trade is generally from East to West and from West to East. Thus, it is possible to buy Czech wine in British supermarkets but not in Polish ones. The pole of attraction is increasingly towards the EU rather than towards the East and this makes the buffer-zone countries even more keen to join the European Union.

One way in which goods circulate is through shopping. In the period after 1988 when the borders were first opened, consumer-starved buffer-zone citizens flocked over the border to undertake a shopping frenzy in Austria, and Austrian shops boomed at this time. Mariahilferstrasse, the main shopping centre in Vienna, was nicknamed 'Magyarhilferstrasse' in honour of the many Hungarians who shopped there. Economic indicators show that Hungarians were spending far more in Austria than Austrians were in Hungary (Wallace, 1997a). After 1990 this was reversed as there was a flow of Austrians to Hungary to buy cheap goods and even food. Now this shopping has balanced out more, but still with Austrians spending more money in Hungary than vice versa. A similar pattern happened between Poland and Germany. New, large supermarkets and shopping centres have opened up along the borders offering goods to cater for this trade and there are also many small stalls selling baskets, gherkins and garden gnomes. In the buffer-zone countries, the spirit of free enterprise has brought in flexible opening hours with shops and shopping centres often open on Sundays, Saturday afternoons and evenings. In Germany and Austria strict control of opening hours means that shoppers have to go to the buffer zone if they wish to shop after midday on Saturday. Now they have started to introduce more flexible opening hours, but this does still not include Sundays. From being economically deprived, depopulated and desolate places, the border areas (especially those to the west) have become thriving economic regions which attract internal migration.

There was an influx of traders from Ukraine, Russia and Belarus selling goods in Poland (Chmouliar, 1996). So-called 'Russian markets' appeared like mushrooms after the rain in every street and even in quite remote villages. They sold products which could be obtained cheaply in those countries (often through theft from factories), such as tools, toys, glassware, underwear, pins, clocks, watches. Traders stayed for just a few days, arriving on buses, trains or in organized groups before returning to their normal jobs. In the words of one respondent:

> After 1989 people opened to the world. They started literally flowing into Europe like a spring river. Everybody cherished some hope that now a miracle would happen and they would become rich … just like that, overnight. People then were travelling without any immediate destination … [they thought that] just by going somewhere they would make piles of money.   (Bulgarian doctor describing his travels between Bulgaria and the former DDR)

Trading of this kind was neither legal nor illegal. It was seen as a sign of the growing opportunities of capitalism by both consumers and vendors. The artificially low price of items such as electrical goods, cameras, vodka and food in the former Soviet Union meant that these could be sold at a profit in Central Europe, and traders brought back goods which were unavailable at home (for example, ladies' tights, condoms, cosmetics).

From 1992 onwards the situation changed quite radically. From this time, the introduction of taxation systems in the Central European countries of Poland, Hungary, Slovakia and the Czech Republic, along with their attempts to join the European Union (and associated partner status), resulted in a crackdown on small-scale trading in the buffer zone. The Eastern borders were increasingly controlled and smuggling was limited (although bribery could still find a way around this). Finally migration into the buffer zone was controlled following fears about an influx of Eastern Europeans trying to storm the walls of fortress Europe. This made it more and more difficult for people from beyond the buffer zone to get in or to stay, and foreigners were likely to be stopped and asked to show their documents on the streets or in the markets. Those without the right documents could be fined and deported or have their passport stamped so that they could not return.

After 1992, hyper-inflation in Russia and Ukraine and changes in the exchange rate meant that prices for many goods were now much higher than in the buffer-zone countries. Instead of coming to sell, the Ukrainians, Russians and Belarusians were increasingly coming to buy. The stock piles of goods had run out and the factories had ceased to produce. Many workers were laid off or their factories closed down leaving them without work. Real wages fell. During 1996, at the time the research was carried out, many were simply not paid for months on end. Everybody was forced to resort to other forms of income-generation, such as trading. This increased the competition and made it less profitable. People risked fines and deportation to make a few dollars from smuggling cigarettes or vodka from Ukraine to Slovakia and then buy food and second-hand clothes to take home, because otherwise they had no income or insufficient on which to live. Now it was not so much profit as survival which was the important incentive.

Whilst in Hungary, the Czech Republic and Slovakia the clamp-down on foreigners and upon illegal trading helped to clear the streets of traders, or at any rate, drive them underground, in Poland the markets continued to flourish on a grand scale, creating an estimated 5 billion US dollars turnover, making it one of the biggest industries (in terms of turnover) in Poland. According to official statistics in Poland, foreigners bought 4.8 per cent of all retail goods in Poland, most of the purchasing being done by citizens of neighbouring states. The biggest trade was on the western borders in 1995, but the eastern and southern borders showed the largest rate of growth since 1994 with a 66 per cent and 45 per cent growth in the value of goods being taken out respectively. Thus, this border trade can be seen to be big business for Poland and is reckoned as an important element of Polish exports to neighbouring countries. It is also an important element in developing the prosperity of the border regions. Poland was producing once more for export to Eastern Europe, not on a nationally planned basis, after the fashion of Comecon, but in the form of a myriad small, private ventures. The goods (especially clothes, cosmetics, toiletries) produced in Poland were thought to be of better quality than the Chinese or Turkish and they were in great demand east of the buffer zone. Although at an individual level this kind of shuttle trading was very small scale ('we are like ants', in the words of one respondent, 'we go everywhere with our goods on our backs'), in aggregate it is quite significant. As a result, Poland was described in one economic report as the 'tiger' economy of Eastern Europe (*Kurier*, 14 February 1997, p. 21).

Why was Poland fulfilling this role more than other countries? According to Polish contributors to a volume by Wedel (1992), the activity known as 'handel' was a tradition of continuous small-scale trading which was associated with Jewish communities. After the large Jewish population in Poland was exterminated, the tradition of 'handel' continued, but now carried out by Poles. It was further encouraged by the shortages in the Polish economy after Communism and by the relative freedom of Poles to travel. In addition, there exists a large Polish diaspora stretching from Central Asia and Siberia (as a result of deportations over the last few centuries) to the USA and Australia. There are strong Polish communities in Austria and Germany, which maintain their national cohesiveness, often around the Polish Catholic Church. Poles therefore had a pre-existing network of contacts with whom to operate and it is such networks which explain the way in which migration and the flow of goods takes place. The same advantage was enjoyed by Gypsies, some of whom also prospered from the opening of the borders (IOM, 1994).

Hungarian trading has some special features. In Hungary there is a large Chinese population (estimated to be about 6,000–7,000 although nobody knows for sure), which has increased since the 1980s when it was first established (Nyiri, 1995). These Chinese operate a wholesale trade selling incredibly cheap clothes, shoes, toys in bulk from the Far East, which are then bought by other traders for resale in Hungary or elsewhere. Although Budapest was the main centre of their operation, the Chinese have also opened wholesale warehouses in Slovakia and the Czech Republic.

Another distinctive feature of Hungary is that it borders Serbia, which was until last year under an international trade embargo and where prices for ordinary commodities continued to be very high.

Hence, there were always queues of Serbian 'Excursion' buses waiting at the Chinese market for their passengers to finish their shopping, but people also came from Romania and Bulgaria to trade or to shop in Hungary, mainly in the so-called 'Chinese market' in Budapest. Meanwhile, the border regions also developed their own markets. Places such as Pecs, Uzhgorod and Przemysl became important nodes of communication in this cross-border flow of goods. For example, Bulgarians generally sold pirated CDs and went back to Bulgaria with medical products, vitamins, computer parts or things which they had purchased in the Chinese market.

Finally, it is worth noting that consumption styles, fashion and taste started to become an important source of differentiation. In some cases ethnic groups differentiated themselves by their consumption styles. Those who identified with relatives or co-nationals in Germany or Hungary (in the case of Germans and Hungarians in Romania for example) tried to differentiate themselves through their superior 'western' taste and possessions. Citizens of the buffer zone often felt superior to their Eastern neighbours on the grounds that the latter had primitive tastes in clothes, fashion accessories and domestic interior architecture and equipment. They were regarded as backward and under-developed people on these grounds. Consumption sector cleavages – particularly in terms of house ownership in countries where people very often built their own houses – could be very important in distinguishing social groups, especially since there was traditionally not much distinction based upon employment.

2   The Circulation of Capital

Another form of circulation is that of capital and investment. It was believed by many people in the buffer zone that foreign investment would help to restructure domestic industry away from the large industrial plants and towards more high-technology and service industries. There has been significant foreign investment in the buffer-zone countries, but much of it has come from the neighbouring countries of Austria and Germany. In each country, Austria or Germany (or both) are the main sources of foreign investment (Wallace, 1997a). The main exception is Poland, where the USA plays the greatest role. Figure 10.1 indicates the way in which Austrian investment has moved away from western Europe and is increasingly directed towards the neighbouring countries of the East. The buffer-zone countries have therefore come under the economic influence of Germany and, to

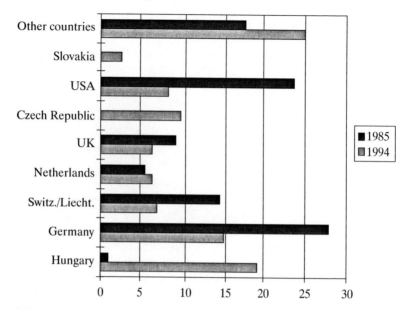

Figure 10.1 *The shift of investment from West to East: Austrian direct investment by destination countries*

Source: Invested nominal capital in millards of schillings (*Statistisches Montasheft der österreichsichen Nationalbank*, No. 6/1996).

some extent, Austria. Given the displacement of people described in the first part of this chapter, it is evident that there are many personal and historical connections between people from Germany and Austria and those countries to the east. Many German and Austrian citizens originated in the buffer-zone countries and are able to speak or understand the relevant languages there, and this can be an advantage in developing trade and investment links.

However, rather than helping to restructure local industries, much of the investment has been into the older and more traditional areas of the economy – into large industrial plants, car manufacture and so on (Wallace, 1997a). Rather than making these plants more modern, the foreign investment has tended to preserve their large-scale monopolistic structure. For foreign firms, the buffer-zone countries present a cheap but skilled workforce. Figure 10.2 illustrates the difference in average wages between the different countries under consideration. From their perspective, the industrial plants already

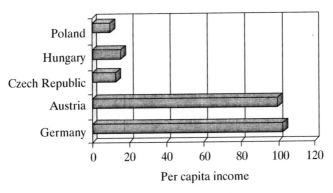

Figure 10.2 *Comparative per capita income (exchange-rate measures) in 1995 (Austria = 100)*

Source: *Czech Report to the Trends Project* (Wallace, 1997a).

exist and there are few environmental controls of the kind existing in Germany and Austria or elsewhere in the European Union. Even where plants are built *de novo*, they are still cheaper than opening a similar plant in Germany or Austria. Parts of the production process in many industries have therefore been transferred to the buffer zone. The automobile industry is one example. Thus, many of the heavy industries have been closed or scaled down in Austria and Germany but these are the very sectors which are targets of foreign investment in the buffer zone. There is therefore perhaps a connection between the de-industrialization of the western European neighbouring countries and the perpetuation of old-fashioned industries in the buffer zone (Wallace, 1997a).

For Austrian firms, the main reason given for this investment was to secure future markets because the buffer zone is seen as a potential future source of expansion (see Wallace, 1997a). Indeed some companies actually moved entirely out of Germany and Austria and simply relocated over the border – the Austrian car-tyre manufacturer Semperit is an example of this, as it relocated in the Czech Republic.

However, Austrian and German capital can also be seen in the range of banks which opened branches in the buffer zone in order to further help trade and investment. One of the main ones, the Raiffeisenkasse, claims that it makes more money from its eastern European subsidiaries than it does from its many thousands of branches in Austria and Bavaria, where it is the main rural bank. In addition, supermarket chains have moved in, many of them being also Austrian and German. Billa, the Austrian supermarket chain, was attractive for take-over by a Germany company precisely because of its foothold in the East European market. Increasingly for Austrian and German business the neighbouring countries to the east are the most attractive prospects for expansion.

Many German and Austrian firms have developed flexible production strategies whereby some of their work is sub-contracted eastwards and then re-imported as finished products. In their desire to attract foreign investment, the buffer-zone countries have offered attractive tax breaks and lifted restrictions on the flow of capital. However, some such ventures are still handicapped by the corruption and legal uncertainty which plagues the privatization process.

It seems therefore that investment has turned eastwards – but not very far eastwards – only just across the borders. Although globalization is often talked about as a world-wide process, in this region it is a local process. Steel and chemical production shifts not to Bombay but to Brno, which is only 70 kilometres away across the border. The relatively higher costs of production there (compared with locations in the developing world) is compensated by the convenience of location. This results in a regional division of labour with heavy industrial jobs going to the buffer zone in unmodernized plants, forcing business in Germany and Austria to become more flexible.

We are arguing that for this region, globalization in the sense of the circulation of capital, displacement of jobs and industries and movement of people, does not take place at a world-wide level but is rather regionalized. Furthermore, the patterns of investment, trade and mobility follow established cultural and social patterns. Much of the Austrian investment, for example, and mobility to and from Austria, can be seen as re-creating former cultural links along the Danube basin and within the Austro-Hungarian empire. German patterns of investment also tend to follow the earlier patterns of settlement and influence, with Germans being a larger trading partner for Poland than for Hungary, whilst Austrians are more important in the latter country. This is partly associated with established linguistic, ethnic and family links across the borders, which act as conduits for other kinds of economic exchange. This phenomenon could also be seen as a distinguishing characteristic of economies such as those of Germany and Austria, for whom neighbouring countries, rather than countries outside of Europe, have always been important for trade and for cultural exchange. This is in contrast to countries such as the USA and

UK, which have had a different pattern of industrial development and for whom world-wide links are more important (Lash and Urry, 1994; Traxler and Unger, 1994). It could be that this regionalization is therefore continuing more established traditions in Germany and Austria.

3 Circulation of People

It was not only jobs which moved from Germany and Austria towards workers in the buffer zone countries, but also workers who moved towards jobs in Germany and Austria; these two countries having absorbed the majority of East European guest workers. Buffer-zone citizens working in Germany and Austria fill the typical role of guest workers in foreign countries (Stalker, 1994). They undertake jobs on the bottom layers of the labour market, especially in agriculture, personal services (domestic cleaning, for example) or construction. Some half a million Czechs are working in Germany and most of these are just across the border in prosperous Bavaria – this represents some 1.5 per cent of the Czech workforce (Horakova, 1993). Germany and Austria have agreed annual quotas of seasonal workers with their Eastern neighbours, who have increasingly replaced Turks, Yugoslavs, Portuguese and Italians as 'guest workers' (Morakvasic and Rudolph, 1994). They are preferred as guest workers since they are often highly skilled and well educated, do not make demands upon the health and social security system (since they go home at the end of the week or even the end of the day) and are, of course, cheaper to employ. Although officially they should be given the same money as native workers, in practice this has seldom been the case (Horakova, 1993). They may also work longer hours. As well as these official guest workers, there are a large number who enter on their 'tourist' visas and work unofficially, although control of such illegal workers by the authorities is increasingly stringent.

However, people travelling to western Europe *from* the buffer zone is only part of the story. The other part is people travelling from further east *into* the buffer zone in order to undertake similar kinds of activities. They are resident in the buffer-zone countries as migrant workers and have the same status as 'guest workers' in Germany and Austria. They are even called 'Gastarbeitery' in a slavic appropriation of the German word.

In the post-Communist countries, the majority of native workers were traditionally manual workers in large enterprises – the labour market was heavily weighted towards its bottom end. Recent research indicates that despite the liberalization and modernization of the labour market through opening it to foreign investment and privatization, the majority of the jobs of the local population continue to be manual ones, and foreign investment may even have reinforced this tendency as foreign investors have invested mainly in heavy traditional industries (Wallace, 1997a). What is lacking is a large or thriving service sector of the kind in western Europe and although this is expanding in the buffer-zone countries, it is expanding only by a small amount relative to the manual sector. Therefore there is space for foreigners to come in and develop the service sector, and indeed, this is where new skills are required. Much of this development has been concentrated in the main cities, where in fact most of the foreigners are working. The opening and reconstruction of the economy created many service industries associated with tourism and communications – language schools, cafés, video sales, marketing and so on – which were more or less new and were rapidly expanding sectors. Furthermore, many foreign experts were brought in with international companies, as 'advisers' or just to try their luck in a newly expanding region. The better educated migrants were able to find places in these sectors or to start businesses and we found that this group often earned *more* than the native population. Many of these migrants came from the West.

Some migrants managed to establish businesses successfully in the destination country. They may have moved there originally in order to escape economic collapse (in the case of the Armenians and some Ukrainians), to avoid anti-Semitism or to avoid being a national minority (in the case of the Hungarian-Romanians), or to escape from wars and the consequences of international embargo (the case of Serbs, Croats and Bosnians). However, once they arrived, they were able to establish businesses, which may actually take advantage of their migrant status – for example, using import/export trading or acting as middlemen and go-betweens for their compatriots.

Another category we have termed 'post-modern migrants'. Post-modern migrants differ from other migrants in that the purpose of their trip is most often fun, adventure or self-fulfilment rather than earning a living. Post-modern migrants often have lower salaries in their destination country than they would have had back home and often live on money which is sent from home (rather than vice versa, as in the case of the 'classic' modern migrant). The main example of this was the 12,000–20,000 Americans living in the Czech Republic (mainly Prague) who founded their own English-language newspapers, radios, book stores and even restaurants. Post-modern migrants are generally young and without any family responsibilities, which is why they are able to prioritize their own goals and aspirations. Migration for them is part of a life-strategy to gain experience before going on to careers at home or elsewhere.

The majority of migrant workers coming from the East into the buffer zone are low-paid manual workers, similar to the 'Gastarbeiter' in Germany and Austria. The main target for these guest workers is the Czech Republic where a very low unemployment rate and a boom in construction helps to attract guest workers from Ukraine and elsewhere. The numbers of work permits granted has increased everywhere. The largest increases in work permits are for Ukrainian workers, who officially number about 40,000. However, the unofficial numbers are estimated to be at least twice that high (Drbohlav, 1997). In the Czech Republic there were about 67,000 work permits granted in 1995, in Slovakia this was 2,700, 20,000 in Hungary and 11,000–12,000 in Poland in 1995. However, our research and that of others (see Drbohlav, 1997) indicates that the majority are working without any permission, although they may have residence rights as students or 'tourists'. Thus unofficial working figures range from twice the legal number (usually cited in the Czech Republic) to ten times the legal number (usually cited in Poland). This is despite the fact that Poland has an unemployment rate of 14.9 per cent, Slovakia 12.8 per cent and Hungary 10.3 per cent (WIIW, 1996a). Guest workers are still thought preferable to native workers, especially in seasonal work, because they work longer hours for only half the wages of the locals and will work weekends and holidays as well.

As with shopping, trading and investment, lines of communication for migrant workers have tended to follow ethnic and family ties or other social networks. In Hungary, the majority of migrant workers were ethnic Hungarians from Romania and according to Hars (1995) many of them also did the sort of construction jobs which Ukrainians were doing elsewhere. However, in our sample, ethnic Hungarians were mostly young, male and middle-class with some Higher Education – and very ambitious. Their strategy was often to undertake another Higher Education course in Hungary and to remain in Hungary to become Hungarian citizens. This group were able to speak the language fluently already and saw many advantages to being in a place which they regarded as having a higher cultural level (at least for Hungarians) than Romania. Furthermore, they were no longer in the position of a national minority. Within a few years they lost their regional accents and were more or less assimilated as Hungarians. This group usually had many friends in Hungary, had visited often and found jobs through the labour exchange or the newspaper. They took advantage of scholarships which were available to them. Many of them were therefore students and working at the same time. Usually, whatever their specialisms were previously in Romania, they moved towards computing and communications studies in Hungary and were able to find good jobs as a result. They had little interest in going back to Romania, especially since many of their friends had also emigrated.

Migrant workers enter different sections of the labour market depending both on their own skills and upon the needs of that market. Since the majority of our respondents were illegal migrant workers, they were automatically consigned to particular areas of the labour market. Migrant manual workers were found mainly in the construction industry, usually constructing private houses. However, some were also found in agriculture and in factory work. Whereas men were construction workers, it was often women who were working in factories such as textiles or shoe manufacture. It was sometimes the case that these enterprises where eastern European women were working, either legally or illegally, were ones owned by foreign or western companies who had subcontracted services to a local middleman, who in turn hired foreign workers to cut costs and increase his share. Another niche for women was as personal service workers. Just as a growing number of private households in Germany and Austria are able to take advantage of casual migrant labour to have a domestic cleaner or someone to look after children and elderly parents, so this is increasingly the case in the buffer-zone countries, where these tasks are undertaken by women from further east.

For those workers who are working illegally, it is particularly important to be sheltered by social, family or ethnic networks through which information can flow and which can help with providing accommodation, transport and so on. Increasingly the requirements for a work permit must be fulfilled *before* the migrant comes into the country, so migrants need to have information about working opportunities before they set off. There has been a long tradition of people from Transcarpathia and parts of Western Ukraine working seasonally. Since there were few industries, but people were anchored by their houses, their small plots of land and their families, they traditionally went elsewhere to seek work. However, it is an indication of the economic crisis in the Ukraine that these traditional migrant workers are joined by people from other parts of Ukraine who were not traditionally migrant. Previously they went to Russia or Siberia, often working in logging camps, and they were able to earn very good incomes. However, this has become more difficult now owing to the break-up in relations between the two countries and because of the unreliable nature of payment in Russia. Now most migrants go to the Czech Republic where there is still a strong demand for workers and low unemployment and where wages can be higher. Others go to the other 'buffer-zone' countries which we have considered here, typically as construction workers.

Many others have used ethnic, family and friendship networks to their advantage. As in the case of trading, information often flowed through loose networks of ties. Often families found jobs for each other or even worked together at the same place (there were a number of examples of this), with one member of the family being replaced by another when they went home for a period. This tended to reinforce the pattern of traditional ethnic connections –Belarusians and Western Ukrainians to Poland, Romanians and ethnic Hungarians to Hungary, and Transcarpathians to the Czech and Slovak Republics. However, new ties were being forged as travellers were concerned to develop strategic links with the most relevant and useful people in the country to which they travelled – with middlemen for example.

> At first I came across the border to do business, I concentrated on my studies, especially since I did not have the right connections. Without connections you cannot make a profit... . I came back to Hungary because I could not get a job in the Czech Republic last summer, I do not know the language and without connections I had no chance. You know: in order to find a job you should know somebody. Maybe somebody from the University you went to, or from the town you came from or some countryman of yours abroad. So that's why I am here now [in Hungary].   (Romanian student who works during his vacations in Hungary)

The migrants themselves represented only one part of a family situation which spanned the two countries (Sidorenko, 1995). In most cases it was the man who was the migrant labourer and the woman who was the trader. Often this was a husband-and-wife strategy since he would bring goods home for her to sell. In addition she might do some additional trading herself. This was the basic survival strategy of many Ukrainian households. As previously mentioned, this might be combined with house-building and peasant small-holding to supplement living standards.

The former Communist regime had encouraged a sense of intense family solidarity and mutual help between generations (Mozny, 1994). It seems that under the new circumstances family solidarity was also a means of survival (Wallace, 1995). Indeed, we might argue that a sort of 'amoral familism' was emerging where the collapsing state, which was seen with bitterness by many respondents in Ukraine for not taking care of them better, was not seen as deserving loyalty or obligation. The main loyalty was first and foremost to the family, which demanded the strongest support and sacrifice. Next in priority was the loose network of friends and connections, which needed to be attended to for instrumental, but sometimes also for other reasons (Wallace et al., 1997).

Sassen (1996) claims that migrant workers are usually an informalized sub-group at the bottom of the labour market. This was certainly the case with the buffer-zone citizens working as guest workers in Germany and Austria. It was also the case with many of the Eastern European guest workers working in the buffer zone. However, the situation of the buffer zone as a newly opened capitalist region resulted also in the need for a layer of foreign experts and people with special skills in newly forming parts of the economy, ones in which indigenous workers were not so well equipped to work, and here we had the importation of highly skilled foreign workers. One source of these was émigrés who had fled the previous regimes, or the children of émigrés who returned with skills, capital and ambition and who were sometimes able to reclaim property. In general the flow of skilled workers was from West to East, whilst the flow of unskilled workers was from East to West.

Another influx of people into the region was in the form of refugees. The war in Yugoslavia led to 4–5 million refugees, the majority of whom were displaced within the territory of the former Yugoslavia. One million found their way into Europe. Whereas to begin with Germany was the main target country with three-quarters of asylum seekers in 1991 applying there, the tightening of the legislation after 1992 led to a sharp drop, and to asylum seekers being pushed towards other countries (Munz, 1995). The countries of western Europe responded by closing their borders to the victims of ethnic cleansing in Croatia, Bosnia, Voyvodina and Kosovo, which pushed many people into the buffer zone. The main recipient of refugees in the buffer zone was Hungary. They arrived in two waves.

Between 1988 and 1991, 51,533 arrived from Romania escaping from the still-repressive regime there. Their aim was to settle in Hungary (Nagy, 1995). In the second wave, 68,262 arrived from the former Yugoslavia, but their main aim was to return to their homes as soon as possible and many of them refused to leave the southern border strip which was nearest to their countries. Many of them have in fact returned already. Although the Czech Republic, Poland and Slovakia have also received refugees, these number only 1,000–3,000 in each country – most of them were also from the former Yugoslavia. However, the majority of people fleeing from the former Yugoslavia are not registered as refugees and instead fall into one of the other main categories of migrants described here: traders, students or workers. In 1993 the numbers of refugees from the former Yugoslavia dropped.

THE IMPORTANCE OF ETHNIC, CULTURAL AND HISTORICAL CONNECTIONS

We can see that although economic imperatives play an important part in the circulation of peoples, cultural and social factors are also important. Economic changes can tell us part of the story about *why* mobility of people, capital or goods takes place, but social and cultural explanations can tell us *who* actually moves and *how* (Portes, 1995). Political decisions in terms of visa requirements for different national groups, customs, residence and working permission policies also affect how economic relations take place.

The patterns of migration in Central Europe tend to follow cultural and historical patterns. People move to places where they can speak the language or where they have friends and relatives. Furthermore, they do not in general move very far – they go mainly to the neighbouring countries. Refugees from former Yugoslavia often went to Germany and Austria because many of their friends and relatives were living there as guest workers. People from Poland and Hungary and from the Czech Republic joined communities of their compatriots who were already living in Germany and Austria. In Poland, migrants were either Poles whose families had been deported to Central Asia and Siberia under Stalin, or people with Polish connections from neighbouring Ukraine and Belarus. Otherwise there were Russians, Ukrainians and people from Belarus, the neighbouring countries, who did not find it too difficult to learn the language. In Hungary we find mainly migrants from Romania, ethnic Hungarians either from Transylvania or from neighbouring Serbia and Croatia. In Slovakia we find migrants mainly from Transcarpathia, formerly part of Czechoslovakia. In the Czech Republic we find mainly migrants from Ukraine and Slovakia or Poland. However, there are also some longer-distance migrants, including the Chinese and Vietnamese and the Armenians and Georgians who have occupied a particular place in the social structure. These new circulations of people have helped to create some new ethnic groups – Chinese and Vietnamese traders, workers and business people are new to the region. The western English teachers and advisers, or employees of international companies, can also be seen in this context.

In Germany and Austria it was often believed that a large number of migrants would settle permanently there from the East if they only had half a chance. In fact very few of our respondents (from 350 interviews collected) mentioned any ambition of this kind. Their main aim was to go only a short way from home and then to return with money to support their families. Those with ambitions to emigrate often wanted to emigrate not to western Europe, but to the buffer-zone countries (although their ambitions may well have been shaped by the fact that they knew that emigration to western Europe was very restricted). A significant minority (about 20 per cent) of our respondents did have ambitions to settle in the buffer zone. They said that in the buffer-zone countries they felt more at home, and were more familiar with the language, culture and lifestyle. Furthermore, they pointed out that with a Polish, Czech or Hungarian passport, they could visit the European Union in any case if they wanted to. Since these buffer-zone countries are expected to join the European Union in due course, it was a viable medium-term strategy. Rather than crossing the border, they were waiting for the border to cross them.

However, these new forms of circulation also revive older ethnic relations, sometimes antagonistically. In a paper by Hann (n.d.) he analyses the increasing tensions in the town of Przemysl on the Polish/Ukrainian border, from which Ukrainians were purged and which has lingering memories of Ukrainian brutality during the Second World War. The return of Ukrainians in the form of cross-border traders and shopping tourists has helped to waken some of these tensions and encourage Polish nationalist rhetoric. Elsewhere in Poland, the mobility of people has made it possible for the German minority, suppressed for many years, to become more militant and even to form their own political party. In all the buffer-zone countries, foreigners were initially welcomed as signs of a new 'opening' but attitudes against foreigners have gradually hardened (Csepeli and Sik, 1995).

Indeed it is often the very foreigners who visit most often who may be most disliked. With increasing communication can also come friction and the revival of other antagonisms too. If your neighbour is more often in your garden (to use Bauman's metaphor), he or she is also more likely to get on your nerves. Thus, the ancient antagonisms between Czechs and Germans have resurfaced in a string of complaints about the behaviour of German tourists in the Czech Republic, and their mistreatment by Czechs. For example, there were complaints by the Germans about being harassed and even shot at for traffic violations in the Czech Republic, and by the Czechs, most recently, that Germans are coming across the border at Cheb to dump their rubbish and avoid high disposal charges in Germany (*Prague Post*, 12–18 February 1997). A continually weeping sore in the Czech relations with Germany is the question of the Sudetendeutsch, 2.9 million of whom were expelled between 1945 and 1948 and who formed societies of expatriates in their countries of exile (mostly Germany and Austria). These expatriate societies are now demanding compensation (although in fact they were already compensated) and the right to resettle or reclaim their former properties. They have been active in the local politics of their former towns and homelands (Muller and Uherek, 1996). This point is frequently raised in negotiations between the two countries.

The circulation of people also results in the transfer of consumer aspirations, life-styles and tastes. The small suitcase traders discover new consumer trends in the Polish street-markets, which they then take back to Ukraine. This kind of small-scale production is able to be very flexible and responsive to consumer tastes and needs. Styles of living seen on TV or in shops are transmitted from Austria and Germany to the buffer zone and then from the buffer zone eastwards leading to certain regional fashions. This can be seen most clearly in house-building, since buffer-zone building workers work on private houses in Germany and Austria whilst Ukrainian building workers work in the buffer zone. Certain fashionable features for houses are transferred or spread within the region at a rapid rate (for example, flights of steps up to the front door, arched windows, turrets, arcades and swimming pools or small lakes in the garden).

So far we have discussed the issue of people moving across borders. But it is also the case that the border itself moves. Many people in this region have become migrants without ever moving. Poland was moved some 500 kilometres westward at the end of the Second World War, and the eastern borders have likewise changed many times. An elderly person living in Uzhgorod, for example, could have been Hungarian, Czechoslovakian, Russian and Ukrainian without ever leaving home. These changes of border have nevertheless left many people with family and cultural links which straddle the border and these family and cultural links are being revived once more now the borders are opened. The rapidly changing contours of the European Union open up this possibility once more.

CONCLUSIONS

From this research it is evident that whilst a buffer zone has developed between western Europe and eastern Europe, parts of the buffer zone are significant for different kinds of mobility. People go to Poland to trade, to the Czech Republic to work, whilst refugees and settlers go mainly to Hungary. This reflects the different situation of each country with respect to East and West Europe. The dominant direction in the flows of workers is from east to west as the European Union rather than the Soviet Union becomes the dominant source of economic and political power. Thus, the building workers in Germany and Austria are mainly from the buffer zone, whilst in the buffer zone, the building workers are drawn from further east in a sort of migration-linked chain effect. The same holds for prostitutes and domestic cleaners. Meanwhile the flow of goods at present operates mainly in the opposite direction, although this can change very quickly.

However, another finding from the research is that the opening of the borders, allowing for free communication between countries, resulted not so much in globalization as in *regionalization*. In this region it seems that when people go abroad, they move mainly only over the next border. The same is true for investment and trade. It is the neighbouring relations which are the most important. We can explain this in terms of the traditional historical, cultural and social ties, which act as conduits for economic activities. This means that new kinds of relationships develop between the neighbouring countries, as the buffer zone becomes the site of heavy industries and partial production which is moving out of the West.

The limits of migration are determined by the limits of the resources of the migrants in terms of language, family and social networks and these are bounded by the cultural, historical and ethnic factors described at the beginning of this chapter. In the case of some migrants this can stretch over very large distances (as in the case of the Chinese for example) but in most cases it stretches rather shorter distances and takes advantage of social and historical configurations of linkages. This has encouraged a certain amount of ethnic revivalism which can help both to close and to open borders.

Although the subject of this chapter has been crossing borders, it is evident that borders are not fixed. They can be more or less permeable and more or less fluid. They can allow no-one to pass or only selected people to pass. They can allow people to pass in one direction but not another. They can be constructed in different ways and extend in different directions. In this region, the construction of borders has always been somewhat arbitrary and subject to external political interference, often by powers who understand little about the region. The effect is that borders and populations have been moved and are not necessarily fixed and permanent. For some of our respondents, the strategy was not so much to cross the borders themselves, as to wait for the borders to change, which is likely to happen when the buffer-zone countries finally join the European Union. Then there will be a new configuration of interests and mobility and perhaps a new buffer zone further east.

ACKNOWLEDGEMENTS

I would like to acknowledge the following sponsors for this research: the Austrian Ministry for Science; the Austrian National Bank; the International Organization for Migration; the research board of the Central European University. I would also like to thank the following people who helped on the project: Oxana Chmouliar, Elena Sidorenko, Natalia Pohorila, Svetla Baloutzova, Andrii Palyanitsya, Vasil Bedzir, Agota Scharle, Jaroslava Stastna and Bohdan Jung. I am also grateful for comments from Josef Langer and Mary Hickman. Finally I am grateful for the intellectual support of Christian Haerpfer. My perspective owes much inspiration to conversations with Jiri Musil and Jirina Smejkalova.

REFERENCES

Appadurai, A. (1990) 'Disjuncture and Difference in the Global Cultural Economy', in M. Featherstone (ed.), *Global Culture* (London: Sage).

Chmouliar, O. (1996), 'Cross Border Trading in the Czech Republic', *Migracijske teme* 12 (3), pp. 159–204.

Csepeli, G., and Sik, E. (1995), 'Changing Content of Political Xenophobia in Hungary – Is the Growth of Xenophobia Inevitable?', in Fullerton, Sik and Toth (eds), *Refugees and Migrants: Hungary at the Crossroads* (Budapest: Hungarian Academy of Sciences).

Drbohlav, D. (1997), 'Labour Migration in Central Europe (with special reference to Poland, the Czech Republic, Slovakia and Hungary). Contemporary Trends', paper presented to the European Science Foundation Network Meeting, *Social Transformations in Eastern Central and Eastern Europe*, Prague, February 1997.

Giddens, A. (1990), *The Consequences of Modernity* (Cambridge: Polity Press).

Haerpfer, C., and Zeilhofer, H. (1995), 'Household Portfolios of Micro-Economic Behaviour in Post-Communist Societies: A Seven Nation Study', in ESOMAR (ed.), *Towards a Market Society: Beyond the Point of No Return* (Amsterdam: ESOMAR).

Hann, C. (n.d.), 'Ethnic Cleansing: Poles and Ukrainians beside the Curzon Line', University of Kent, UK.

Hars, A. (1995), 'Migration and the Labour Market', in M. Fullerton, E. Sik and J. Toth (eds), *Refugees and Migrants: Hungary at the Crossroads* (Budapest: Hungarian Academy of Sciences).

Harvey, D. (1989), *The Condition of Post-Modernity* (Oxford: Basil Blackwell).

Horakova, M. (1993), Pilot study on the short-term labour migration from the Czech Republic to the Federal Republic of Germany, Berlin (mimeo).

IOM (1994a), *Transit Migration in the Czech Republic* (Budapest: International Organization for Migration).

IOM (1994b), *Transit Migration in Poland* (Budapest: International Organization for Migration).

Jameson, F. (1991), *Postmodernism and the Cultural Logic of Late Capitalism* (London: Verso Press).

Kussbach, E. (1992), 'European Challenge: East–West Migration', *International Migration Review*, vol. XXVI (2), pp. 646–67.

Lash, S., and Urry, J. (1994), *Economies of Signs and Space* (London, California, New Delhi: Sage).

Morokvasic, M., and Rudolph, H. (eds) (1994), *Wanderungsraum Europa, Menschen und Grenzen in Bewegung* (Sigma, Berlin: Wissenschaftszentrum für Sozialforschung).

Mozny, I. (1994), 'The Czech Family between Social and Economic Capital', in S. Ringen and C. Wallace (eds), *Social Reform in the Czech Republic: Prague Papers on Social Responses to Transformation*, volume 2 (Prague: Central European University).

Muller, B., and Uherek, Z. (1996), *Alltag in Jablonec* (Vienna: IFK Materialen).

Munz, R. (1995), 'Where Did They All Come From? Typology and Geography of European Mass Migration in the Twentieth Century', *Demografie Aktuell* (Berlin: Humboldt University).

Nagy, B. (1995), 'Changing Trends, Enduring Questions Regarding Refugee Law in Central Europe', in M. Fullerton, E. Sik and J. Toth (eds), *Refugees and Migrants: Hungary at the Crossroads* (Budapest: Hungarian Academy of Sciences).

Niessen, J. (1992), 'European Community Legislation and Inter-Governmental Co-operation on Migration', *International Migration Review*, XXVI (2), pp. 676–84.

Nyiri, P. D. (1995), 'From Settlement to Community: Five Years of the Chinese in Hungary ', in M. Fullerton, E. Sik and J. Toth (eds), *Refugees and Migrants: Hungary at the Crossroads* (Budapest: Hungarian Academy of Sciences).

Portes, A. (ed.) (1995), *The Economic Sociology of Immigration* (New York: Russell Sage Foundation).

Sassen, S. (1996), 'New Employment Regimes in Cities: The Impact on Immigrant Workers', *New Community*, 22 (4), pp. 579–94.

Sidorenko, E. (1995), 'Gender, Migration and the Formation of Ethnic Niches in the Labour Market: The Case of Ukrainian Workers in the Czech Republic', *Migracijske teme*, 11 (2), pp. 127–50.

Sik, E. (1993), 'From the Second Economy to the Informal Economy', *Journal of Public Policy*, 12 (2), pp. 153–75.

Sklair, L. (1991), *Sociology of the Global System* (Brighton: Harvester Wheatsheaf).

Stalker, P. (1994), *The Work of Strangers* (Geneva: International Labour Organization).

Traxler, F., and Unger, B. (1994), 'Governance, Economic Restructuring and Competitiveness', *Journal of Economic Issues*, XXVIII (1), pp. 1–23.

Wallace, C. (1995), 'Young People and Families in Poland: Changing Times, Changing Dependencies', *Journal of European Social Policy*, 5 (2), pp. 97–109.

Wallace, C., Sidorenko, E., and Chmouliar, O. (1996), 'The Eastern Frontier of Western Europe', *New Community*, 22 (2), pp. 259–86.

Wallace, C. (1997a), *Trends towards 2000: From Modern to Postmodern?*, Research Report to the Ministry for Science, Culture and Traffic, Austria.

Wallace, C. (1997b), *Economic Mobility in the Buffer Zone*, Final Report to the Jubliaumsfonds der Oesterreichische Nationalbank.

Wallace, C., Bedzir, V., and Chmouliar, O. (1997), *Spending, Saving or Investing Social Capital: The Case of Shuttle Traders in Post-Communist Central Europe* (Stumpergasse 56, 1060, Vienna, Austria: IHS Materialien).

Wallerstein, I. (1983), *Historical Capitalism* (London: Verso).

Wedel, J. R. (1992), *The Unplanned Society* (New York: Columbia University Press).

WIIW (Wiener Institut für Internationale Wirtschaftsvergleiche) (1996a), No. 225: Transition Countries: Economic Developments in 1995 and 1996.

WIIW (Wiener Institut für Internationale Wirtschaftsvergleiche) (1996b) No. 228.

Wodz, J., and Wodz, J. (1997), 'Transborder Regions in Central Europe as a Political and Social Problem: The Example of Upper Silesia in Poland', paper presented to the European Science Foundation Network meeting, *Social Transformations in Eastern Central and Eastern Europe*, Prague, February 1997.

11 Migration and Globalization in Intellectual Life: a Case Study of the Post-1956 Exodus from Hungary

JENNIFER PLATT and PHOEBE ISARD

INTRODUCTION

The general literature on migration has been largely concerned with mass movements, and in recent times is closely connected with the literature on race and ethnic relations. These concerns, very appropriate to the study of the mass movements, are of less relevance in relation to the migration of intellectuals, especially when the intellectuals in question do not come from a group seen as racially/ethnically distinct in the receiving society. Sociological or historical work directly on the migration of intellectuals is rarer, and has concentrated on a limited range of possible situations; commonly it has been concerned with 'brain drain' – the loss to the country of emigration – rather than the effects on the country of immigration. The major exception to that generalization is the many studies which have been made of the refugees from Hitler who went to the USA in the 1930s and 1940s. Implicitly, at least, it has often been assumed that such a well-studied case can be treated as a general model. This chapter reports work on the migration of Hungarians after the 1956 uprising, and its impact in Britain; this work was undertaken to extend the range of work in this field beyond the refugees from Hitler. The Hungarian exodus was similar in that it involved flight from an oppressive political regime, rather than a normal pattern of academic interchange or economically motivated individual movements. The assumption of similarity was supported by the fact that some organizations in Britain, such as the Society for the Protection of Science and Learning (SPSL), which had originally been set up to assist refugees from Hitler, were reactivated to cope with the Hungarians. It will, none the less, be argued here that there were important differences, and that these extend our knowledge of the circumstances under which migration leads to intellectual change, and of the ways in which it may or may not promote globalization in the life of the mind.

In the work which has been done on the possible contribution of migrants to intellectual innovation, there are two broad perspectives or theses, of opposite implication:

The selection thesis

This perspective is one which sees immigrants as self-selected, or selected by the system in the receiving country, in such a way that those who come (and choose to stay) bear ideas so compatible with what is already dominant that they make little important difference intellectually. One special version of this which has had some prominence is Perry Anderson's (1968) attack on the 'white migration' to Britain. The alternative to 'white' here is 'red', not 'black'; this version adds an imputed political or ideological basis of selection to the intellectual one. (It is unlikely that Anderson would have viewed the Hungarian emigrants in this light, since he was part of a movement created by the impulse to dissociate Marxism or socialism from Stalinism). His ideas are used here as a potentially general model, not as an account intended to deal with our particular case.

The export/interaction thesis

This alternative thesis is highlighted in the many studies (e.g. Fleming and Bailyn, 1969; Jackman and Borden, 1983; Mosse et al., 1991) of the immense contributions made, in a variety of cultural areas, by the migrants who left Europe to escape Hitler: it stresses the importance in the new setting of what they brought with them, introducing valued approaches and skills to new countries. A particularly significant variant of this version (e.g., Hoch, 1991) identifies cases where they did not merely bring with them what were novelties in the new setting, but created fresh novelties as a result of the interaction of what they brought with the ideas and emphases dominant in the new setting.

It cannot be claimed that our data are appropriate to test these alternatives as general hypotheses (and neither has been explicitly stated as such). However, we evaluate how far either type of account has an adequate fit to our data on the relationship of the Hungarian emigrants to intellectual life in this country, and so raise questions about their general value.

We also discuss some implications for the role of migration in intellectual globalization. Albrow's account (1990, pp. 6–7) identifies a sequence of stages (for him, in the growth of sociology): universalism, national sociologies, internationalism, indigenization, globalization. He does not discuss the possible role of factors external to sociology in bringing about movement from one stage to another in this sequence, except to say that globalization 'results from the freedom individual sociologists have to work with other individuals anywhere on the globe'. But of course not all individuals in practice have such freedom to the same extent, and, if they have it, the likelihood that they will exercise it is strongly affected by circumstances. There has long been a tradition of academic mobility, often associated with relations between centre and periphery. In established systems of that kind, the dominance of the centre means that intellectual innovation is less likely to follow from the migratory movements. But migration on less established patterns may, for instance, create local enclaves of different ideas, even if those do not find a place in the mainstream or become dominant. Thus there could be a version of the concept of globalization where the emphasis is on the local diversity of the ideas represented rather than on their world-wide uniformity. For migration to promote such an outcome, migrants must bear ideas different from those already present in the receiving country; they are more likely to do so if their migration does not follow the well-trodden routes between periphery and centre.[1] From Hungary to Britain was certainly not one of those routes, so an analysis of some of the consequences of our case bears on these questions.

METHODS

More than 150,000 Hungarian refugees reached Austria; around 21,000 came to Britain, of whom it is estimated that about 14,000 stayed. There is no central list of the Hungarians who came to Britain, so it is too hard to establish a satisfactory sampling frame for the intellectuals among them, for any formal claim to representation of the whole group to be plausible. The broad strategy of the project was, therefore, to compile basic factual data about as many cases as possible, and against this background to look at selected case studies. The data-collection has drawn on a range of sources. The general picture of the historical background used a combination of existing academic work and the reports of informants. A data-base with schematic basic information on relatively large numbers of migrants has been created using mainly the 1991 edition of *Prominent Hungarians: Home and Abroad*[2] and the SPSL records, supplemented by several more scattered sources. This data-base includes all those identified who went to the UK, USA or Canada and ended up as academics, researchers in the public or private sector, or engineers. A small number of unstructured interviews was carried out with the migrants themselves, to learn both about their personal careers and the situations they had experienced and about other migrants they knew of; for those who were willing and could provide one we collected copies of formal CVs. The early experience of this group was one which made 'social science' suspect, especially when collecting personal data or asking politically relevant questions, so it was necessary to proceed rather cautiously in such areas, and this has limited our data. For the individuals on whom we have focused for case studies, interviews have sometimes also been conducted with others from the same field who can give a view on their impact, or, when the person in question is now dead, can provide career information about them. Such sources as obituaries and festschrifts have been drawn on when available. The analysis here mobilizes the parts of these data relevant to the immediate question in hand.

A key problem of any method is that we cannot know how complete our coverage of the group in question is. Part of the problem is one of information, and part is one of definition. The problem of information is simply that whatever the definition, we can never know that we have identified all those who fit it. Arguably, however, the obvious bias towards more successful people matters less for our topic than it would for some, in that one may assume that those who are likely to have an impact and produce innovations are more likely to be represented. Another possible bias is that towards networks of acquaintances, produced by the supplementary technique of snowball sampling to track down subjects. Again this may matter less than it often does, in that there were special reasons why this group of Hungarians should know each other. Many had been students together and involved in revolutionary activity together; they left the country over a very short period of time, they were sent to a small number of refugee camps in Austria and then Britain, and many were then given special treatment as members of a group for whom English classes and other forms of collective support were arranged.

On the problem of definition, what is an intellectual? If any university teacher can be deemed to be one *ex officio*, what about, say, poets whose job is working in the Hungarian section of the BBC, librarians, museum workers, or engineers in industrial research labs? In so far as we are concerned in particular with those who came to Britain, how long did they need to stay there to qualify? Clearly there is no right answer to such questions, and we have not dealt with them altogether consistently, in that for the quantifiable data-base we have used fixed definitions, while for individual studies we have permitted ourselves more flexibility. This does not create difficulties as long as the interpretation bears in mind the limitations of the type of data.

THE SELECTION THESIS

What would the selection thesis mean in our case? It would imply that intellectual compatibility operated to select the émigrés who came to Britain and stayed, who would be only those whose contribution would make little real difference. The mechanisms of selection could, presumably, lie in either the choices made by the émigrés, their reception in the UK, or both. What we should look at, therefore, is not just what they actually did contribute, but also how it came about that they reached Britain, what decisions they made at later choice points, and how they were received intellectually. The Anderson argument was that those émigrés who came to Britain, stayed, and became intellectually prominent, were a group selected for their elective affinity with a dominant right-wing culture, who fled the violence and instability of their own societies for the tradition and continuity of Britain.[3] Here, they had become part of an intellectual culture which Anderson characterized as one of an insular 'slovenly empiricism', without a centre of the kind that would have been provided by a classical sociology or a national Marxism. The same sorts of data are relevant to this version of the selection thesis, but in relation to political factors in the selection process. (It is not practical with such a diverse group to attempt to look also at the content of their intellectual work.) Below, we review our data on the processes by which migrants came, first for the more general selection thesis and then in relation to the 'Anderson' version.[4]

Opportunities to leave Hungary after the failure of the revolt were very limited; there was only a short period of time during which the borders were not closed. There was no time for support from outside

Hungary to affect who was able to leave, and certainly no system by which some were formally allowed to leave while others were not. These were 'acute' rather than 'anticipatory' refugees (Holmes, 1988, p. 280), taken by surprise by the course of events as everyone else was. Those who lived near borders, or near the major transport arteries such as those from Budapest, had a considerable advantage. Many more might have left if they had been able to do so.

It is not evident that, as one might suspect, those who actually did leave were simply the most strongly motivated to do so, the most hostile to the regime, or the most dissident intellectually. (Although of course those who were known to have been prominent in the revolt – who could come from right or left – had good reason to put themselves out of the way of retaliation.) However, a major factor contributing to some people's decision to take the opportunity, whether or not they had been active in the revolt, appears to have been the Communist policy of denying educational and occupational opportunities to those of bourgeois or aristocratic class origin. For young people from such backgrounds, even if they might have supported the regime's general aims, personal career chances were limited. Known Catholics or orthodox Jews were also disadvantaged in career terms, as well as having some difficulty in pursuing their religious lives, so the devout would have had that motive also for leaving.[5]

Another important impetus to take the opportunity to leave, among those we have seen, was simply the recognition that the regime's policy meant that this might be the only opportunity they would ever have to go abroad. Going abroad was attractive for its intellectual opportunities (e.g., access to more advanced scientific equipment, ability to publish literary works without political censorship), for its more general political freedom, for its economic opportunities to achieve a higher standard of living – and simply because it's good to see the world. Some were in effect forced to choose emigration who, in another situation, might only have made relatively short visits abroad.

The history of Hungary had created a strong sense of threatened but valued national identity, especially reflected in literature, that needed to be preserved. (The official Marxist approach, which was the alternative had they stayed in Hungary, was not particularly sympathetic to specifically Hungarian tradition and its national(ist) literature.) The 1956 revolt was one for, not against, indigenous Hungarian concerns, so emigration by those involved in it did not imply the rejection of their national origins which some of the German and Austrian refugees from Hitler made. Individuals could well have multiple motives. Some of those who left had initially expected to be able to return quite soon, and were taken by surprise when they found that was not possible.

The net effect of these considerations is that there is every reason to believe that those who left Hungary were a very mixed bag in their motives and attitudes, if not a cross-section of Hungarian culture.[6] Those who did leave seem, however, to have been mainly in the age range 20–40; this no doubt reflects both the high number of students who had been involved in the uprising, and the kind of people it was that had few enough investments and ties to feel able to leave at such short notice.[7]

Leaving was one process, ending up in Britain was another. Where decisions were made, these were not always well-informed ones. The barriers the emigrants were escaping from, which the Hungarian regime had placed between them and the outside world, meant that they had had little opportunity to learn much of what that world was like. Perhaps more importantly, the accounts of some of those we interviewed show accident playing a key role. Many emigrants were held initially in refugee camps in Austria. There, trains would suddenly be announced leaving for one destination or another, and who took which could depend on very little:

> When we arrived in Austria and were put into a camp ... we just simply settled for the first group willing to take us out and allow us to continue our studies... . We actually registered with three countries, Sweden, France and England, and the British were the first ... in fact I wanted to go to Switzerland initially, because I knew some German.[8]

Many of those who left did not at that stage expect it to be permanent, and so they were not thinking of long-term career decisions. Cold War politics, combined with sympathy for the victims of the extensively reported brutal repression of the revolt, meant that the emigrants were seen as deserving, and full employment meant that they were not seen as a threat to jobs. One of the most striking features of this migration, as compared with others before or since, was the extremely warm welcome which was given to the Hungarians collectively, and the efforts that were made to accommodate them.

That reception was after the migrants had arrived. Deliberate selection of those who were to come was, however, sometimes made by the receiving country. For instance, Britain was much more encouraging in the formal admissions process to students in scientific and technical fields than to those with backgrounds in the humanities, because the former were seen as more likely to be able to find employment which made use of their skills[9] – as well, of course, as more likely to be economically useful to Britain. (As our cases show, however, not all of those from types which received less encouragement were prevented from coming.) Communist policy had emphasized scientific and technical training, so a high proportion of students were in those fields, which made such a criterion less selective than it might otherwise have been. The SPSL, which helped some academics to find their feet, had a policy of only concerning itself with relatively high-qualified people who had a good chance of university employment in Britain. At a period of high industrial employment, but before the major expansion of the universities which started in the late 1960s, engineers and others prepared to go into industrial research had excellent opportunities, but the opportunities were more limited for people committed to academic work, for whom chances were much better in the larger university systems of the US and Canada (to which many of them sooner or later went).[10]

The students, recent graduates and educated young people among the emigrants were not at a career stage where it was to be expected that they would already have made significant new contributions to knowledge; they were still at intellectually formative stages, and likely to be at least in part moulded by the influences of their new country. They benefited from special help; there was a scheme to place them in British universities (with prior courses in English) so that they could complete their degrees, or gain a British qualification, and many took advantage of this. If successful, as most were, this meant that they were in the mainstream of normal British career routes, which many took. Arguably, thus, such institutional good treatment made it less likely that Hungarian origins would lead to any distinctive influences in Britain. For this group too there was some selection favouring scientific and technical backgrounds (Cushing, 1994), though some humanists were accepted. Some of these found themselves under pressure, once in British universities, to take courses seen as suitable; this meant that, for instance, one young man found himself again studying the hated Russian language, which had been imposed in Hungary – though he managed to change university and course to avoid this. Such pressures may have done something further to move those who had started in the humanities away from what was distinctively Hungarian, as there were few opportunities for Hungarian teaching in Britain, or obvious vocational outlets for those with such qualifications.

Once the emigrants had reached Britain, the question still arose of whether they should stay. For those who had arrived first from a refugee camp, there was in the short run a practical reason to stay, which was that once they had reached another country they ceased to be classified as refugees and so receive special treatment, and became formally ordinary migrants. However, that was probably not very important. People who came to Britain and could not find a job, or could not find a job which they regarded as satisfactory, were likely to leave if a satisfactory one emerged elsewhere, and a number of scientists are known to have left for America, Canada or other countries for this reason. The move across the Atlantic was actively assisted by the established role of the Rockefeller and other US foundations in promoting trans-Atlantic scientific mobility for the benefit of US intellectual standards. In Vienna there were representatives of the Ford and Rockefeller Foundations, and the National Academy of Sciences, encouraging scientists and engineers to go to the US and, in some cases, providing funds for researchers at institutions in Canada. The interest this showed continued to be relevant after the earliest stages of the emigration, and some of those who came initially to the UK left shortly for more attractive job offers there.

Several of our cases did take jobs elsewhere for a period, and then returned either from choice or because the job came to an end:

> in '65 I came back, we came back from the States ... without knowing what job I shall have because my wife had a *Sehnsucht* for Europe, for Vienna, of course, and Europe and in general for England. I had a terrible longing for Europe. I liked Berkeley in a way, it was beautiful weather, but it's totally rootless. ... New England I liked much better because it is more like England and I was quite happy there but at Harvard I couldn't stay more than a year.

Others rejected opportunities:

> I was there once in '61 and I had an offer from Bell Telephone Laboratories and it seemed to be too rigid, too much concentrated on getting results and too little leisure, too little culture ... their annual holidays were two weeks.
>
> ... several times we had jobs offered from various parts of the United States, and there were several ideas that we might go, but

we preferred Europe and we preferred Britain ... our children were already born, and ... I did not take to the culture and I didn't fancy that I would particularly like to bring the children up. ... This was a deliberate choice, and I think I regret it professionally.

There are clear patterns of choice here, but not ones primarily based on intellectual compatibility in the professional field.[11] The only comment on that came from a literary scholar:

Britain made a big impact on me; there are certain things I really like here as compared with, say, Germany. ... Hungary was a very long time overrun by Germany, and the Germans love theories. In this country it is down to earth, pragmatic, you have to examine it in detail and then make up your mind. I find this quite useful in literary analysis. ... [In teaching] I found the non-Hungarian students quite interesting in the sense that even after living in this country for quite some time they could still come up with angles I didn't think of and thought were quite British.

Thus the only systematic selection we have found was that in favour of scientific subjects; this can certainly not be seen as selection for politico-intellectual compatibility, since its basis was a practical, economic one. Those with experience in areas directly related to work in progress were eagerly received, but especially so if they could add something to what was already going on. The natural scientists we have talked to who had started their post-graduation careers in Hungary appear to see themselves as having continued to do essentially the same type of research as before, without any relevance of national style. The greater the extent to which a field is already internationalized, as much natural science has been, the less the opportunity for new syntheses of different national traditions. Hungary had not been behind the Iron Curtain for long, and its higher-education system was strongly influenced by German traditions; moreover, some of the potentially relevant syntheses had already been made by earlier generations. There was certainly no intentional selection in favour of increasing the number of academics working on Hungarian history or literature, though this happened, if with very small numbers; to the extent that it did, this was not definable as even unintentional selection of particular styles of work. At earlier stages of the process, the high levels of accident in who was able to leave and who finished up where[12] make it seem unlikely that intellectual compatibility typically played much role.

SELECTION: THE 'ANDERSON' VERSION

The selection processes which did operate may have had political consequences, in the sense that there is some evidence that young people
not sympathetic to the politicization of intellectual life in Hungary
chose science and engineering fields in part because those were relatively immune from that.[13] Thus discrimination in favour of those
fields may have had the unintended consequence of also selecting
those who found such politicization less congenial. One respondent,
himself from the left, suggested that in general in the refugee camps,
when there was a choice, left-wing people chose France and right-wing
ones Britain. However, he and his wife were left-wing but chose
Britain because his wife had a relative who was a successful business-
man in India with British contacts; thus even those for whom political
considerations were salient did not necessarily make practical choices
in accordance with them.

There could have been some non-intellectual political selection
operated by the immigration authorities but, at least in the short term,
this does not seem to have happened. Things were being done so
swiftly that there was hardly time for checks. Clearly Marxists were
allowed in. The migrants report that it was accepted that even those
who had been Communist Party members were not treated as suspect,
though when they came to apply for British citizenship they were
liable to be interrogated about their background. It is, of course, not
obvious how to classify in our terms the politics which made people
take an active part in the uprising. Participation in it could have followed from what in more general terms would be seen as left, right or
local ad hoc positions. Some of those involved certainly remained
faithful to their ideals of socialism, and acted in its name to try to
reform the regime (Hoensch, 1988, pp. 208–20; Lomax, 1976,
pp. 22–9, 40–5). From the official British point of view, however, the
assumption seems to have been in effect that hostility to the regime
sufficient to have led people to leave was sufficient indication that
they were not spies (though a few probably were, if only on the other
refugees). Perhaps such *sang froid* is one of the unsung advantages of
a stable conservative regime.

If we classify our cases politically, which can only be done somewhat impressionistically, into three categories – declared continuing
Marxists, active participants in the revolt who do not identify themselves as Marxists, and the rest – there is perhaps a pattern there: the
active participants, especially those with positions in the reformist

Nagy government, have been active in Britain too, and come across as particularly lively and entrepreneurial in their diverse fields, while 'the rest' have been more conventional in style. This seems to tell us more about their individual characteristics than about the social situation. Sufficient of those who were broadly left-wing, as well as liberal or right-wing, have been successful in the UK to suggest that politics has not been important in their reception. We have no evidence that those on the left were less likely to have come intentionally, or more likely to leave the country at an early stage if they had the opportunity.

The political content of the migrants' intellectual work is also relevant – but Anderson was largely concerned with people whose normal work could be seen as having a socio-political content, which is hardly the case for the natural scientists. However, such innovations as those identified among our sample are not clearly innovative enough to be counted as self-evidently inconsistent with his version. In so far as politics was relevant to their work, the humanists probably often oriented their politics towards Hungary, which has had little relevance for the internal British situation. Those we know of who have been really politically/intellectually active are the Marxists, who have of course contributed to the left, not the right. It is not known why those of them who did stay in Britain, but they did. The small number of known Marxists in our sample have had rather mixed worldly success, but lack of success in that sense has been to some extent a choice made from principle. They have probably been more influential politically than the rest, simply because they have been more active in that sphere in this country. We may note, as Anderson did in later work, that very shortly after he published his original article major changes in British intellectual life became evident, with 'the emergence of a substantial culture of the Left' (Anderson, 1990, p. 48); some of the migrants took part in the movements which led to this. Mészáros and Krassó (on whom see below) have been quite influential intellectually, as part of the larger movement. Thus the 'Anderson' version does not look convincing for the Hungarian group.

INNOVATION AND SYNTHESIS? THE EXPORT/INTERACTION THESIS

The selection thesis has been rejected, so we turn now to consider the evidence for innovation and synthesis as a result of the migration. We need to try to distinguish between Hungarian contributions, which are in some sense national, and contributions of individual Hungarians which are personal rather than national (cf. Hoch and Platt, 1993). Below are presented case studies from our sample described in terms of these themes, chosen to demonstrate the range of types of possible contribution, and their relationship to the Hungarian background and to the fact of migration. The use of pairs of similar cases is useful in suggesting the possible interactions between background and situation, some pairs available in the data are therefore treated jointly. No claim is made that the set of cases presented is representative of the group of migrants as a whole, although other examples of the same type could be found for most.

1	An electrical engineer in his middle twenties, who had just graduated with only a few months of work experience in Hungary, almost at once obtained a job in an industrial research laboratory, where he made major contributions to several projects, including the invention very shortly after arrival in Britain of a device which won a patent, as well as publishing several papers in the first years in this country. Later he joined a consultancy firm and became head of a large engineering department in higher education. He obtained jobs with little trouble because Hungary was at the time the Comecon country which specialized in electronics, and was at the forefront internationally in that field; moreover, his diploma work had been on an area of telecommunication technology directly relevant to what leading English firms were trying to develop. (Being outstandingly able and already knowing some English naturally also helped). Although Hungary was backward on the practical side, and had very poor equipment in the universities, so that his laboratory education was relatively weak, theoretical training there was very strong. He found that a good grasp of the theoretical side enabled him to see the practical applications. In this case, therefore, the initial contribution to innovation in Britain can be directly attributed to Hungarian training and experience, against a background of larger economic and political decisions made in Hungary, though later this must have ceased to be relevant.

2	Imre Lakatos[14] left Hungary at the age of 35, after a politically dramatic and controversial career there which included periods both in jail and as an official in the ministry of education. He had studied mathematics and physics. He was a Communist, if with revisionist tendencies; some people suggest that he may have been a KGB agent in Britain, though he was not active in left-wing politics in this country, and was on the 'right' in relation to the student revolt at the LSE. Be that as it may, in Britain he took a doctorate in the philosophy of science and became generally recognized as a leading thinker in the field. An obituary said of him that he 'had been a star member of the most important Marxist school of thought of this century, and subsequently also a major contributor to the finest intellectual liberal movement of the day. The particular quality of his brilliance reflected the blending of these two traditions' (Gellner, 1974). It is not clear how far his specific technical work drew on the Hungarian background, though his compatriot Polya, another leading thinker in the area, is reported to have drawn his attention to the problem on which he wrote his British doctoral thesis. His views on the philosophy of mathematics, to which he made a major contribution, are however said to have departed from those of Polya (Worrall, 1976; Agassi, 1976, p. 14).

3   Two men have played roles at the intersection of politics and academic Marxism.[15] Istvan Mészáros, who in 1956 was 26, reached Britain after a short time in Turin, held lectureships at St Andrews and Sussex and eventually, after an interlude in Canada, became a professor of philosophy at Sussex. Miklós[16] Krassó went to Oxford as a doctoral student, but did not complete his degree and appears not to have held any long-term full-time job in England, though he did some part-time teaching at less prestigious institutions around London. From 1967 to 1985 he was a member of the editorial committee of the important left-wing journal *New Left Review* (*NLR*); his first article there is regarded as a key one in defining the journal's distinctive political position. Both men remained Marxists. They published work which came to form part of the large intellectual movement towards versions of Marxism of the late 1960s and 1970s in Britain. They were important in introducing unfamiliar continental thinkers from the Marxist tradition and its context to English speakers[17] as well as in developing their own contributions to the literature. Mészáros became a conventional academic; Krassó had a Bohemian lifestyle, but was enormously well read in continental philosophy and exercised much influence through café life and conversation rather than through his sparse publications (Blackburn, 1995). Mészáros has probably not been politically active in other senses;[18] Krassó took part in demonstrations and occupations, though he was not a disciplined party activist.

Although both reacted against the version of Communism which became dominant in Hungary in the 1950s, their initial Marxist culture and broader frames of reference obviously owed something to the Communist Party's practical political dominance, as well as to central European intellectual traditions more generally. Mészáros had been a student and colleague of Lukàcs,[19] which gave him a reflected glory additional to his personal claims. Krassó was also a disciple of Lukàcs; he had been a Communist since the age of 14, active in the opposition to Rakosi's Stalinism, and deeply involved in the movement of workers' councils in 1956 (Krassó, 1985). Their political role in Britain was made possible by a climate on the left in which there was a reaction against the Stalinist Communist Party catalysed by the repression of the Hungarian revolt, but a reluctance to go along with a revisionist Labour Party. Out of this emerged the 'New Left', with two journals which in 1960 merged to form the *NLR* (in whose formation Oxford students such as Perry Anderson and Stuart Hall were prominent); this became largely a theoretical organ, strongly influenced by contemporary French trends and by the thought of Gramsci (Blackburn, 1992). *NLR* played a key role in the reorientation of social theory in Britain to look across the Channel rather than across the Atlantic.

4   A student of literature and history, who already had some publications in Hungary, was placed in a leading British university and eventually completed a doctorate on the reception of Hungarian literature in Britain. In her subsequent career in this country she has worked at a national library, published a major work of reference on Hungarian literature, and done much freelance work for newspapers and the BBC external service as well as some university teaching. She has continued to publish on literary topics, mainly Hungarian ones and often in Hungarian, sometimes in émigré journals. She was also active in organizing a Hungarian literary society in the UK which has provided a forum, for both émigrés and visiting Hungarians, in which discussion was possible of a kind that could not take place in Hungary. Although one cannot identify a single innovation in this career, as one can for some of the scientists, it is clear that she has made a difference by advancing knowledge of Hungarian literature in the anglophone world, and acting as an intermediary between Hungarian literature in the anglophone world, and acting as an intermediary between Hungarian and British culture.

Perhaps more interestingly, she has also had a role as part of a larger phenomenon, the development of a distinctively émigré literary culture separate from that in Hungary. This, she says, does not merely explore themes which have been forbidden under the Communist regime in Hungary itself, but has its own emphases and a critical perspective of a kind which could not have been developed inside the country; it reflects wider experiences and different frames of reference. With the opening up of the Hungarian situation, it is now feeding back into the main Hungarian culture, though not always greeted enthusiastically there.

In this case, specifically Hungarian identity and traditions are essential to the contribution made. Without emigration her publications in English would have been very unlikely, she would probably not have done the same comparative work or studied the British reception of Hungarian work, and many of her publications in Hungarian might have been impossible. Less tangibly, ideas among the larger group of literary exiles, of which she is one representative, would not have moved in the same directions.

Several other émigrés have made careers in Britain which they would not have had without the emigration – though they might have had close equivalents in Hungary – which draw specifically on their Hungarian background. These careers have been either in academic work on Hungarian language, literature, history or politics, or working in the BBC's Hungarian section. They have often published in both languages, and have sometimes written on comparative topics, introduced Hungarian themes to British audiences or vice versa, or made translations of literary work. All of these would, presumably, have been much less likely without the emigration.[20] Most have not created markedly novel developments, though it is likely that without the migration such positions would have been filled, and such activities undertaken, less satisfactorily or not at all.

What do these cases show about the intellectual effects of the migration? We have an interesting range of innovations in one sense or another due to the migration, although not all can be characterized as new stylistic and substantive syntheses. Without closer and more detailed work than is practical in investigating a wide range of fields we cannot make strong statements about the precise intellectual difference made by our cases, but we can examine and classify the broad types of contribution made. We find:

- The application in Britain of what was at the time distinctively Hungarian training and experience in research, leading to industrially valuable new developments.

- The creation in Britain of important new ideas which drew on, but went beyond, influences from both Hungary and Britain.
- The transmission in Britain of ideas originating in Hungary and its wider intellectual context, contributing to a reorientation of thought and influences in that field.
- The application while in Britain of Hungarian language and literary skills, also informed by the British experience, to create new critical approaches and creative styles in work in Hungarian.
- The application in Britain of skills not distinctively Hungarian to tasks where such skills were less common, in jobs which the holders would not have taken in circumstances of more choice, leading to the development of commercially important innovations.
- The application in Britain of Hungarian language, and literary and historical knowledge, to increase knowledge of Hungarian culture here among those not of Hungarian background.
- Migrants who have not made what can clearly be labelled as innovations, but have had successful and valuable careers which do not draw in any identifiable way on their Hungarian origins and are barely distinguishable from those of their equivalents of British origin. Interestingly, however, for a number of these people Hungarian identity and background has again become a valued resource, as distinct from a private identity, with the recent opening up of Eastern Europe on the collapse of the Communist system: they have become active in arranging TEMPUS schemes (for academic exchanges), in representing the Hungarian government abroad, and in assisting commercial contacts. This draws attention to the extent to which individuals may or may not use their national identities, and to the ways in which these uses can be affected by circumstances.

Migration has led to these developments by bringing to the United Kingdom people who already had different intellectual traditions, higher training standards, or experience of more advanced levels of work, and, once they were here, giving them new experience – which led to new perspectives – or positions not commonly taken by people with those characteristics. Although some of these developments fit the model of a synthesis between previously different intellectual traditions, others do not. The range of possibilities of innovation following from migration is seen to be more varied than that model allows for.[21]

CONCLUSIONS

Important differences from the migration of those who fled from Hitler have become salient in the Hungarian case. This was another partially forced emigration, but it happened under different circumstances and involved different groups. Distinguished intellectual leaders were not picked out for invitation, and there was no time for negotiations over jobs. Of special significance is that, because the Hungarian revolt was student-led, many of those who left the country were still students, which meant that they did not have established positions as intellectuals and were not known abroad. The prior restrictions on leaving the country meant that even among those who were older few had been able to establish the foreign intellectual contacts which played an important role in the flight from Hitler; cross-national post-doctoral placements and visiting professorships had not been part of their world. The youth of many, and the warmth of their reception, meant, however, that they had exceptionally good opportunities to assimilate to the new society, which many took. Older refugees were to a greater extent than the young at the mercy of luck, but many did well, largely in science and engineering. This migration may not have been unique, but it was sufficiently different from others for general accounts based on those which are better known, not to describe it adequately.

The Hungarian emigrants as a whole have certainly made their mark, and those we have identified are indeed an impressive group. However, they have only done this *as Hungarians* to the extent that for some their intellectual field has become Hungarian culture. In so far as there were inconsistencies between the British and the Hungarian occupational structures, this seems even to have led to easy placements, because Hungarians could fill urgent vacancies; the theory of comparative advantage (in fields such as electrical engineering and Marxist philosophy) has obvious application. There were not many of the difficulties in finding positions for people in their original scientific subfields which led to innovation-generating placements outside those areas for some of the German-language migrants to America.[22]

We conclude that neither of the theses with which we have compared our data has a good fit to this migration. Assimilation was too early and successful for strikingly novel syntheses to emerge, though valuable contributions of other kinds were made, including some which drew on the Hungarian background in other ways. The impressive early contributions made in scientific and technical fields by some of the émigrés seem due to similarity between the countries' concerns as much as to the differences. (It follows that some of their contributions could better be seen as additive to the total of what has been done here, rather than interacting with it to produce contributions of new kinds.) The processes by which migrants came to this country were not such that there was a high degree of selection by any criteria, though there was a skew in the direction of science – which did not make it politically more selective. The nature of the differences made by intellectual migration needs more careful and various specification before theorizing can be fully convincing. Among the factors which such theorization clearly needs to take into account are the characteristics of particular groups of migrants, the similarities and differences between the sending and receiving countries, and the particular historical conjunctures of socio-economic features at the time of arrival. Other cases which would merit investigation are the movement of Italians to Latin America, and the recent exodus from the former USSR.

What does our material show about the role of migration in globalization? If that means global intellectual homogeneity, this migration made at most a modest contribution. Where those in more universalistic fields such as natural science were responsible for innovations, those seem to have been due to personal as much as national characteristics; in less universalistic fields, their contribution has rested on the maintenance of some distinctive national identity. If, however, globalization means the local representation of a wide range of ideas of different national origins, they certainly contributed to that, though a greater contribution might be made by a less assimilated group. But some unassimilated groups stay in intellectual ghettos of fellow migrants from the same background; that mode of local representation makes little impact. Probably neither easy assimilation nor the maintenance of ghettoized identities does much to promote globalization; somewhere in between lies the greatest potentiality. Circumstances which permit interchange across national boundaries, while at the same time encouraging some preservation of original identities, maximize the likelihood.

NOTES

1. For further general discussion of such issues, see Hoch and Platt (1993).
2. This is a *Who's Who* type of publication, written in English. It does not set very high standards of 'prominence' to qualify for inclusion, and includes a high proportion of academics, writers and artists. Its completeness of coverage of the groups aimed at is not known, but it is widely referred to in the Hungarian community.
3. In so far as this is a comparative argument, suggesting that those who went elsewhere were politically preferable, it is deeply implausible. His favoured examples are few in number, and most of them ended up in America; he gives no attention to the fact that very large numbers of others also went to America. His examples include the Frankfurt School of Marxists, who could not be said to have been altogether at ease there intellectually or politically.
4. This account draws on Dare and Hollander (1959) as well as on the reports of our interviewees; although very useful, Dare and Hollander's work is limited by being only about those in Britain who were students.
5. It is possible that there are differences connected with religion/ethnicity between these migrants and the largely Jewish groups studied previously, but we do not have the material to discuss this.
6. They also included many non-intellectuals, among them groups of miners, but we are not concerned with those here.
7. Hungary's turbulent history meant that there had been several previous surges of intellectual migration. This might imply that those left among older generations were people who in one way or another had chosen, or been able, to accommodate to the regime, whatever their views about it.
8. This quotation, and subsequent ones not otherwise attributed, come from interviews with or letters from our respondents. All our interviewees appear here anonymously, as most of them wished. Minor details such as field or gender have sometimes been changed to help preserve anonymity, and names are used only for those people on whom the data come from public sources.
9. It does not seem surprising that a man with experience in rocket research was easily placed. The migrants also included some 2,000 coal miners selected by the National Coal Board (Carlin, 1989, p. 53).
10. Cf. Niederland (1991) on the German-Jewish emigration on the 1930s; he shows how a key determinant of the direction of migration flows was the specific occupational and financial opportunities known to be available in alternative destinations. He also shows that at that stage a high proportion of the academics and professionals emigrating came to Britain, and that many academics were successfully placed by the SPSL.
11. America appears as the alternative in these instances, and that is probably not accidental. European countries other than Britain would have been equally European, as opposed to American, but jobs were probably scarcer there. Those who have ended up in other countries will not have been interviewed by us, so we have only minimal information

about them; this does, however, show that there were a number who moved on after a few years in Britain. It is not clear that any particular meaning can be attached to this; nothing could be more normal than for some of a group of youngish people largely in scientific fields to go to work elsewhere.

12.   It would, obviously, be desirable to carry out a comparative study of those who ended up in other countries, to pursue this issue further.

13.   The language factor mentioned in some of the cases in the previous section sometimes operated to Britain's advantage, when there was any choice of destination, because English was seen as the language of science. However, its status as such may have been due as much to American as to British scientific leadership, so this can hardly be treated as associated with a choice of anything distinctive to *British* society in the processes by which people came to have learned some English.

14.   He has died, and so could not be interviewed.

15.   Neither of these men has been interviewed; much material about them therefore comes from published sources, which is why their names are given. Krassó is dead; his close colleague and friend Robin Blackburn was interviewed about him, and comments on him were also volunteered by other respondents.

16.   His first name became anglicized to Nicolas or Nicholas.

17.   In his obituary of Krassó, Blackburn quotes Isaac Deutscher as saying that he had never met anyone else so well read in the Marxist classics. For Mészáros, public sources are drawn on.

18.   Mészáros was initially denied a visa to take up a professorship in Canada in 1972 on the grounds that he was a security risk. Representations and protests were organized in the UK, supported by leading members of the academic left (Tom Bottomore, Eric Hobsbawm, Ralph Miliband); it was pointed out that in 13 years in Britain he had given no indication of being a security risk. One of our interviewees suggested that behind the Canadian stance was the objection to him of some Hungarian émigrés – presumably relatively right-wing – in Canada.

19.   Lukàcs was a Hungarian philosopher and literary theorist who was a longstanding intellectual Marxist and Communist, though he had not been enthusiastic about every turn of the situation under Stalin. At the time of the revolt, he had sided with the opposition sufficiently to be Minister of Education in the Nagy government. At the period in question his work was treated among leftist intellectuals in Britain as of central importance.

20.   It is interesting that at least one person has played such a role while holding a job (as a senior librarian) to which it has no formal relation. Possibly he would not have become a librarian if he had not emigrated, in which case the librarianship and any innovations made there might also be regarded as a result of the emigration.

21.   In addition, we may note that, although it is outside the remit of this chapter, the migration has also had some consequences for Hungary, in that Hungarian history and literature have developed in ways in which

they otherwise would not have done, and works have been written that introduce English-language thought to a Hungarian audience to a greater extent than would otherwise have been likely.

22. Or if there were, those people may have gone on to other countries with wider opportunities. The size of the British university sector at the time meant that even placements outside a specialist field were likely not to be available there.

REFERENCES

Agassi, Joseph (1976), 'The Lakatosian Revolution', in R. S. Cohen et al. (eds), *Essays in Memory of Imre Lakatos* (Dordrecht: Reidel), pp. 9–15.

Albrow, Martin (1990), 'Introduction', in M. Albrow and E. King (eds), *Globalization, Knowledge and Society* (London: Sage), pp. 3–16.

Anderson, Perry (1968), 'Components of the National Culture', *New Left Review*, **50**, pp. 3–57.

Anderson, Perry (1990), 'A Culture in Contraflow – I', *New Left Review*, **180**, pp. 41–78.

Blackburn, Robin (1986), 'Nicolas Krassó, 1930–1986', *New Left Review*, **155**, pp. 125–8.

Blackburn, Robin (1992), 'A Brief History of *New Left Review*, 1960–1990', in *Thirty Years of New Left Review: Index, nos. 1–184 (1960–1990)* (London: New Left Review), pp. v–xi.

Blackburn, Robin (1995), interview with Platt.

Carlin, James L. (1989), *The Refugee Connection* (London: Macmillan).

Cohen, Robert S., Paul K. Feyerabend, and M. W. Wartofsky (eds) (1976), *Essays in Memory of Imre Lakatos* (Dordrecht: Reidel).

Cushing, George (1994), interview with Phoebe Isard, June.

Dare, Alan, and Paul J. Hollander (1959), 'Hungarian Students in Great Britain', unpublished manuscript in the library of the School of Slavonic and East European Studies of the University of London.

Fleming, D., and B. Bailyn (eds) (1969), *The Intellectual Migration* (Cambridge, MA: Harvard University Press).

Gellner, Ernest (1974), 'Imre Lakatos', *The Times*, 8 February, p. 18.

Hoch, Paul K. (1991), 'Some Contributions to Physics by German-Jewish Émigrés in Britain and Elsewhere', in W. E. Mosse et al. (eds), *Second Chance: Two Centuries of German-speaking Jews in the United Kingdom* (Tübingen: J. C. B. Mohr), pp. 229–241.

Hock, Paul K., and Jennifer Platt (1993), 'Migration and the Denationalization of Science', in Elizabeth Crawford, Terry Shinn and Sverker Sörlin (eds), *Denationalizing Science* (Dordrecht: Kluwer), pp. 133–52.

Hoensch, J. K. (1988), *A History of Modern Hungary 1867–1986* (London: Longman).

Holmes, Colin (1988), *John Bull's Island* (Basingstoke: Macmillan).

Jackman, J. C., and C. M. Borden (eds) (1983), *The Muses Flee Hitler* (Washington, DC: Smithsonian Museum).

Krassó, Nicholas (1985), 'Hungary 1956: A Participant's Account', in T. Ali (ed.), *The Stalinist Legacy* (Boulder, Colorado: Lynne Rienner).

Lomax, Bill (1976), *Hungary 1956* (New York: St Martin's Press).

Mosse, Werner E., et al. (eds) (1991), *Second Chance: Two Centuries of German-speaking Jews in the United Kingdom* (Tübingen: J. C. B. Mohr).

Niederland, Doron (1991), 'Areas of Departure from Nazi Germany and the Social Structure of the Emigrants', in Mosse et al. (eds), *Second Chance: Two Centuries of German-speaking Jews in the United Kingdom* (Tübingen J. C. B. Mohr), pp. 57–68.

Worrall, John (1976), 'Imre Lakatos: Philosopher of Mathematics and Philosopher of Science', in Cohen et al. (eds), *Essays in Memory of Imre Lakatos* (Dordrecht: Reidel), pp. 1–7.

Index

233